21世纪高等学校国际经济与贸易系列规划教材

International
Economics

国际经济学

（汉英对照）

主　编　谢孟军
副主编　姜爱英　王冰心　李德震　徐晔嘉

ZHEJIANG UNIVERSITY PRESS
浙江大学出版社

前言

Preface

为了适应当前经济全球化的发展趋势，满足广大高等院校培养高素质国际经济人才的需求，我们在研究、梳理、总结当前国际经济领域出现的新形势、新问题和新做法的基础上，借鉴国内外学者相关研究成果，组织编写了这本教材。

本教材的主要特色是汉英对照。与国外原版英文教材相比，本教材保持了英文表述的原汁原味，同时为了更好地满足国内读者的需求，教材的章节标题、关键词和知识点等都配有中文注释，以便读者能够更快地理解教材内容并掌握重点知识；与国内中文教材相比，本教材基于当前世界政治、经济、文化的国际背景，用英文表述国际经济学的课程内容，尽量保持国内外知识的同步，教材空白处的设计可以留给学生做笔记或翻译之用。本教材共13章，包括国际贸易理论、国际贸易政策和国际金融三部分内容。其中第1章为引言，主要介绍当前的国际经济背景及教材的总体内容和框架体系；第2章至第5章为国际贸易理论部分，主要介绍经典的国际贸易理论及当代具有代表性的国际贸易理论，从多角度、多层面来解释商品和生产要素国际流动的原因；第6章至第10章为国际贸易政策部分，主要介绍国际贸易中的两类工具（关税和非关税贸易壁垒）、两类国家（发展中国家和发达国家）的贸易政策，以及国际社会中的一类组织（区域性贸易合作组织）；第11章至13章为国际金融部分，主要介绍货币国际流动的现状、原因及应对策略。

本教材由谢孟军博士负责总体框架设计并担任主编，姜爱英博士、王冰心博士和李德震博士参与了教材的编写。徐晔嘉博士负责教材英文内容的审校，谢孟军博士负责教材的审核及统稿。在教材的编写过程中，编者参考了中华人民共和国商务部、中国人民共和国海关总署、中国人民银行、中国国际贸易促进委员会及各专业公司网站上的相关信息。同时浙江大学出版社的领导和编辑为教材的策划、编辑、出版付出了辛勤的劳动。在此，特向上述单位和相关人员表示衷心的感谢！

限于编者水平，教材中的缺点和不足之处，欢迎广大读者批评指正。

编者

2020年6月

Contents 目录

Chapter 1
Introduction

第一章
绪　论

You could say that the study of international trade and finance is where the discipline of economics as we know began. Historians of economic thought often describe the essay "Of the Balance of Trade" by the Scottish philosopher David Hume as the first real exposition of an economic model. Hume published his essay in 1758, almost 20 years before his friend Adam Smith published *The Wealth of Nations*. And the debates over British trade policy in the early 19th-century did much to convert economics from a discursive, informal field to the model-oriented subject it has been ever since.

Yet the study of international economics has never been as important as it is now. **In the early 21st-century, nations are more closely linked through trade in goods and services, flows of money, and investment in each other's economies than ever before.** And the global economy created by these linkages is a turbulent place: Both policy-makers and business leaders in every country, including the United States, must now pay attention to what are sometimes rapidly changing economic fortunes halfway around the world.

21世纪以来，国与国之间通过货物贸易和服务贸易、资本流动、对外投资等形式变得越来越紧密。

A look at some basic trade statistics gives us a sense of the unprecedented importance of international economic relations. The levels of U.S. exports and imports as shares of gross domestic product from 1960 to 2009 shows that the most obvious feature of the figure is the long-term upward trend in both shares: International trade has roughly tripled in importance compared with the economy as a whole.

Almost as obvious is that, while both imports and exports have increased, imports have grown more, leading to a large excess of imports over exports. How is the United States able to pay for all those imported goods? The answer is that the money is supplied by large inflows of capital, money invested by foreigners willing to take a stake in the U.S. economy. Inflows of capital on that scale was once inconceivable; now they are taken for granted. So the gap between imports and exports is an indicator of another aspect of growing international linkages, in this case the growing linkages between national capital markets.

Finally, notice that both imports and exports took a plunge in 2009. This decline reflected the global economic crisis that began in 2008, and is a reminder of the close links between world trade and the overall state of the world economy.

This book introduces the main concepts and methods of international economics and illustrates them with applications drawn from the real world. Much of the book is devoted to old ideas that are still as valid as ever: The 19th-century trade theory of David Ricardo and even the 18th-century monetary analysis of David Hume remain highly relevant to the 21st-century world economy. At the same time, we have made a special effort to bring the analysis up to date. Over the past decade the global economy threw up many new challenges, from the backlash against globalization to an unprecedented series of financial crises. Economists were able to apply existing analyses to some of these challenges, but they were also forced to rethink some important concepts. Furthermore, new approaches have emerged to old questions, such as the impacts of changes in monetary and fiscal policy. We have attempted to convey the key ideas that have emerged in recent research while stressing the continuing usefulness of old ideas.

1.1 What Is International Economics About?

1.1 国际经济学研究什么？

国际经济学使用和经济学的其他分支学科相同的研究方法，因为国际贸易中的个体行为动机和国内交易中的个体行为动机相同。

International economics uses the same fundamental methods of analysis as other branches of economics, because the motives and behavior of individuals are the same in international trade as they are in domestic transactions. Gourmet food shops in Florida sell coffee beans from both Mexico and Hawaii; the sequence of events that brought those beans to the shop is not very different, and the imported beans traveled a much shorter distance than the beans shipped within the United States! Yet international economics involves new and different concerns, because international trade and investment occur between independent nations. The United States and Mexico are sovereign states; Florida and Hawaii are not. Mexico's coffee shipments to Florida could be disrupted if the U.S. government imposed a quota that limits imports; Mexican coffee could suddenly become cheaper to U.S. buyers if the peso were to fall in value against the dollar. By contrast, neither of those events can happen in commerce within the United States because the Constitution forbids restraints on interstate trade and all U. S. states use the same currency.

The subject matter of international economics, then, consists of issues raised by the special problems of economic interaction between sovereign states. **Seven themes recur throughout the study of international economics: (1) the gains from trade, (2) the pattern of trade, (3) protectionism, (4) the balance of payments, (5) exchange rate determination, (6) international policy coordination, and (7) the international capital market.**

国际经济学主要从以下七个方面进行研究：(1)贸易所得；(2)贸易模式；(3)贸易保护；(4)国际收支平衡；(5)汇率决定因素；(6)国际政策协调；(7)国际资本市场。

1.2 The Gains from Trade

1.2 贸易所得

Everybody knows that some international trade is beneficial—for example, nobody thinks that Norway should grow its own oranges. Many people are skeptical, however, about the benefits of trading for goods that a country could produce for itself. Shouldn't Americans buy American goods whenever possible, to help create jobs in the United States?

Probably the most important single insight in all of international economics is that there are gains from trade—that is, when countries sell goods and services to each other, this exchange is almost always to their mutual benefit. The range of circumstances under which international trade is beneficial is much wider than most people imagine. It is a common misconception that trade is harmful if there are large disparities between countries in productivity or wages. On one side, businesspeople in less technologically advanced countries, such as

国际经济学中最重要的一个观点可能是，贸易总能带来收益，即国与国之间互相销售自己的产品和劳务总是对双方都有利的。

India, often worry that opening their economies to international trade will lead to disaster because their industries won't be able to compete. On the other side, people in technologically advanced nations where workers earn high wages often fear that trading with less advanced, lower-wage countries will drag their standard of living down—one presidential candidate memorably warned of a "giant sucking sound" if the United States were to conclude a free trade agreement with Mexico.

Yet the first model this book presents of the causes of trade demonstrates that two countries can trade to their mutual benefit even when one of them is more efficient than the other at producing everything, and when producers in the less efficient country can compete only by paying lower wages. We'll also see that trade provides benefits by allowing countries to export goods whose production makes relatively heavy use of resources that are locally abundant while importing goods whose production makes heavy use of resources that are locally scarce. International trade also allows countries to specialize in producing narrower ranges of goods, giving them greater efficiencies of large-scale production.

Nor are the benefits of international trade limited to trade in tangible goods. International migration and international borrowing and lending are also forms of mutually beneficial trade—the first a trade of labor for goods and services, the second a trade of current goods for the promise of future goods. Finally, international exchanges of risky assets such as stocks and bonds can benefit all countries by allowing each country to diversify its wealth and reduce the variability of its income. These invisible forms of trade yield gains as real as the trade that puts fresh fruit from Latin America in Toronto markets in February.

Although nations generally gain from international trade, it is quite possible that international trade may hurt particular groups within nations—in other words, international trade will have strong effects on the distribution of income. The effects of trade on income distribution have long been a concern of international trade theorists, who have pointed out that:

总的来说，国家作为一个整体可以从国际贸易中获益。但是，国际贸易也极有可能使得国家内部的某些团体受损。换句话说，国际贸易会显著影响收入分配。

International trade can adversely affect the owners of resources that are "specific" to industries that compete with imports. In other words, they can not find alternative employment in other industries. Examples would include specialized machinery, such as power looms made less valuable by textile imports, and workers with specialized skills, like fishermen who find the value of their catch reduced by imported seafood. Trade can also alter the distribution of income between broad groups, such as workers and the owners of capital.

These concerns have moved from the classroom into the center of real-world policy debate, as it has become increasingly clear that the real wages of less-skilled workers in the United States have been declining even though the country as a whole is continuing to grow richer. Many commentators attribute this development to growing international trade, especially the rapidly growing exports of manufactured goods from low-wage countries.

1.3 The Pattern of Trade

1.3 贸易模式

Economists can not discuss the effects of international trade or recommend changes in government policies toward trade with any confidence unless they know their theory is good enough to explain the international trade that is actually observed. **As a result, attempts to explain the pattern of international trade—who sells what to whom—have been a major preoccupation of international economists.**

解释国际贸易的模式，即谁把什么卖给了谁，是国际经济学家的重要任务。

Some aspects of the pattern of trade are easy to understand. Climate and resources clearly explain why Brazil exports coffee and Saudi Arabia exports oil. Much of the pattern of trade is more subtle, however. Why does Japan export automobiles, while the United States exports aircraft? In the early 19th-century, English economist David Ricardo offered an explanation of trade in terms of international differences in labor productivity, an explanation that remains a powerful insight. In the 20th-century, however, alternative explanations were also proposed. One of the most influential, but still controversial, explanations links trade patterns to an interaction between the relative supplies of national resources such as capital, labor, and land on one side and the relative use of these factors in the production of different goods on the other. Recent efforts to test the implications of this theory, however, appear to show that it is less valid than many had previously thought. More recently still, some international economists have proposed theories that suggest a substantial random component in the pattern of international trade.

1.4 Protectionism

1.4 贸易保护

If the idea of gains from trade is the most important theoretical concept in international economics, the seemingly eternal debate over how much trade to allow is its most important policy theme. **Since the emergence of modern nation-states in the 16th-century, governments have worried about the effect of international competition on the prosperity of domestic industries and have tried either to shield industries from foreign competition by placing limits on imports or to help them in world competition by subsidizing exports.** The single most consistent mission of international economics has been to analyze the effects of these so-called protectionist policies—and usually, though not always, to criticize protectionism and show the advantages of freer international trade.

自16世纪出现现代意义上的国家以来，各国政府就一直非常担心国际竞争会影响国内产业的繁荣。它们或是对进口施加限制来保护本国产业，避免与外国竞争；或是补贴出口来帮助本国产业参与国际竞争。

The debate over how much trade to allow took a new direction in the 1990s. After World War Ⅱ, the advanced countries, led by the United States, pursued a broad policy of removing barriers to international trade; this policy reflected the view that free trade was a force not only for prosperity but also for promoting world peace. In the first half of the 1990s, several major free trade agreements were negotiated. The most notable were the North American Free Trade Agreement (NAFTA) between the United States, Canada, and Mexico, approved in 1993, and the so-called Uruguay Round agreement, which established the World Trade Organization in 1994.

Since that time, however, an international political movement opposing "globalization" has gained many adherents. The movement achieved notoriety in 1999, when demonstrators representing a mix of traditional protectionists and new ideologies disrupted a major international trade meeting in Seattle. If nothing else, the anti-globalization movement has forced advocates of free trade to seek new ways to explain their views.

As befitting both the historical importance and the current relevance of the protectionist issue, roughly a quarter of this book is devoted to this subject. Over the years, international economists have developed a simple yet powerful analytical framework for determining the effects of government policies that affect international trade. This framework helps predict the effects of trade policies, while allowing for cost-benefit analysis and defining criteria for determining when government intervention is good for the economy.

In the real world, however, governments do not necessarily do what the cost-benefit analysis of economists tells them they should do. This does not mean that analysis is useless. Economic analysis can help make sense of the politics of international trade policy, by showing who benefits and who loses from such government actions as quotas on imports and subsidies to exports. The key insight of this analysis is that conflicts of interest within nations are usually more important in determining trade policy than conflicts of interest between nations.

1.5 Balance of Payments

1.5 国际收支平衡

In 1998, both China and the Republic of Korea ran large trade surpluses of about $40 billion each. In China's case, the trade surplus was not out of the ordinary—the country had been running large surpluses for several years, prompting complaints from other countries, including the United States, that China was not playing by the rules. **So is it good to run a trade surplus and bad to run a trade deficit? Not according to people of the ROK: Their trade surplus was forced on them by an economic and financial crisis, and they bitterly resented the necessity of running that surplus.**

那么，贸易顺差一定就好，贸易逆差一定就不好吗？韩国的情况就是一个反例。韩国因为先前的经济危机和金融危机而被迫保持贸易顺差，虽然保持顺差并非韩国所愿。

This comparison highlights the fact that a country's balance of payments must be placed in the context of an economic analysis to understand what it means. It emerges in a variety of specific contexts: in discussing foreign direct investment by multinational corporations, in relating international transactions to national income accounting, and in discussing virtually every aspect of international monetary policy. Like the problem of protectionism, the balance of payments has become a central issue for the United States because the nation has run huge trade deficits in every year since 1982.

1.6 Exchange Rate Determination

1.6 汇率决定因素

The euro, a common currency for most of the nations of Western Europe, was introduced on January 1, 1999. On that day the euro was worth about $1.17. By early 2002, the euro was worth only about $0.85, denting Europe's pride (although helping its exporters). By late 2007, the euro was worth more than $1.40; by the middle of 2010, it slid back to $1.29.

A key difference between international economics and other areas of economics is that countries usually have their own currencies—the euro being the exception that proves the rule. And as the example of the euro/dollar exchange rate illustrates, the relative values of currencies can change over time, sometimes drastically.

国际经济学和经济学其他分支的一个重要区别是，不同国家往往欧元拥有不同货币——欧元。正像上述欧元对美元汇率变动的例子所反映的那样，货币的相对价值会随时间的推移发生变化，而且这种变化有时是非常剧烈的。

For historical reasons, the study of exchange rate determination is a relatively new part of international economics. For much of modern economic history, exchange rates were fixed by government action rather than determined in the marketplace. Before World War I the values of the world's major currencies were fixed in terms of gold; for a generation after World War II, the values of most currencies were fixed in terms of the U.S. dollar. The analysis of international monetary systems that fix exchange rates remains an important subject.

1.7 International Policy Coordination

1.7 国际政策协调

The international economy comprises sovereign nations, each free to choose its own economic policies. Unfortunately, in an

主权国家构成国际经济活动的主体，

integrated world economy, one country's economic policies usually affect other countries as well. For example, when Germany's Bundesbank raised interest rates in 1990—a step it took to control the possible inflationary impact of the reunification of West and East Germany—it helped precipitate a recession in the rest of Western Europe. Differences in goals among countries often lead to conflicts of interest. Even when countries have similar goals, they may suffer losses if they fail to coordinate their policies. A fundamental problem in international economics is determining how to produce an acceptable degree of harmony among the international trade and monetary policies of different countries in the absence of a world government that tells countries what to do.

各国可以自由选择自己的经济政策。不幸的是，在融为一体的世界经济中，任何一国的经济政策通常都会影响到其他国家的政策。

For almost 70 years, international trade policies have been governed by an international treaty known as the General Agreement on Tariffs and Trade (GATT). Since 1994, trade rules have been enforced by an international organization, the World Trade Organization, which can tell countries, including the United States, that their policies violate prior agreements. We discuss the rationale for this system in Chapter 10 and look at whether the current rules of the game for international trade in the world economy can or should survive.

While cooperation on international trade policies is a well-established tradition, coordination of international macroeconomic policies is a newer and more uncertain topic. Only in the past few years have economists formulated precisely the case for macroeconomic policy coordination. Nonetheless, attempts at international macroeconomic coordination are occurring with growing frequency in the real world.

1.8 The International Capital Market

1.8 国际资本市场

During the 1970s, banks in advanced countries lent large sums to firms and governments in poorer nations, especially in Latin America. In 1982, however, first Mexico, then a number of other countries, found themselves unable to pay back the money they owed. The resulting "debt crisis" persisted until 1990. In the

1990s, investors once again became willing to put hundreds of billions of dollars into "emerging markets", both in Latin America and in the rapidly growing economies of Asia. All too soon, however, this investment boom came to grief as well; Mexico experienced another financial crisis at the end of 1994, much of Asia was caught up in a massive crisis beginning in the summer of 1997, and Argentina had a severe crisis in 2002. This roller coaster history contains many lessons, the most undisputed of which is the growing importance of the international capital market.

In any sophisticated economy there is an extensive capital market: a set of arrangements by which individuals and firms exchange money now for promises to pay in the future. The growing importance of international trade since the 1960s has been accompanied by a growth in the international capital market, which links the capital markets of individual countries. Thus in the 1970s, oil-rich Middle Eastern nations placed their oil revenues in banks in London or New York, and these banks in turn lent money to governments and corporations in Asia and Latin America. During the 1980s, Japan converted much of the money it earned from its booming exports into investments in the United States, including the establishment of a growing number of U. S. subsidiaries of Japanese corporations.

在任何成熟的经济体中都存在着一个广阔的资本市场：通过一整套协定，个人和公司在当期进行资金交换并保证在将来偿还。

Nowadays, China is funneling its own export earnings into a range of foreign assets, including dollars that its government holds as international reserves.

International capital markets differ in important ways from domestic capital markets. They must cope with special regulations that many countries impose on foreign investment; they also sometimes offer opportunities to evade regulations placed on domestic markets. Since the 1960s, huge international capital markets have arisen, most notably the remarkable London Eurodollar market, in which billions of dollars are exchanged each day without ever touching the United States.

国际资本市场和国内资本市场有着显著差别。国际资本市场必须应对各国针对外来投资制定的特别法规；有时候，国际资本市场也为资本规避国内市场的法规提供了机会。

Some special risks are associated with international capital markets. One risk is that of currency fluctuations: If the euro falls against the dollar, U.S. investors who bought euro bonds suffer a capital loss—as the many investors who had assumed that Europe's new currency would be strong discovered to their horror. Another risk is that of national default: A nation may simply refuse to pay its debts (perhaps because it cannot), and there may be no effective way for its creditors to bring it to court. International financial linkages helped turn the downturn in the U.S. housing market that had begun in 2006 into a global economic crisis.

The growing importance of international capital markets and their new problems demand greater attention than ever before.

1.9 International Economics: Trade and Finance

The international economics can be divided into two broad subfields: the international trade and the international finance. International trade analysis focuses primarily on the real transactions in the international economy, that is, on those transactions that involve a physical movement of goods or a tangible commitment of economic resources. International finance analysis focuses on the monetary side of the international economy, that is, on financial transactions such as foreign purchases of U.S. dollars.

An example of an international trade issue is the conflict between the United States and Europe over Europe's subsidized exports of agricultural products; an example of an international monetary issue is the dispute over whether the foreign exchange value of the dollar should be allowed to float freely or be stabilized by government action.

In the real world there is no simple dividing line between trade and monetary issues. Most international trade involves monetary transactions, while, as the examples in this chapter already suggest, many monetary events have important consequences for trade. Nonetheless, the distinction between international trade and international finance is useful. The first half of this book covers international trade issues while the second half is devoted to international finance issues.

1.9 国际经济学：贸易与金融

国际经济学可以分为两个次一级的领域：国际贸易和国际金融。国际贸易主要分析国际经济中的实际交易，即经济资源实体的流动。国际金融主要分析国际经济的货币方面，也就是金融行为，如美元的购买。

1.10 Has the World Gotten Smaller?

1.10 世界越来越小了吗？

World trade is a moving target. The direction and composition of world trade is quite different today from what it was a generation ago, and even more different from what it was a century ago. Let's look at some of the main trends.

In popular discussions of the world economy, one often encounters statements that modern transportation and communications have abolished distance, so that the world has become a smaller place. There's clearly some truth to these statements: The Internet makes instant and almost free communications possible between people thousands of miles apart, while jet transport allows quick physical access to all parts of the globe. On the other hand, gravity models continue to show a strong negative relationship between distance and international trade. But have such effects grown weaker over time? Has the progress of transportation and communications made the world smaller?

The answer is yes—but history also shows that political forces can outweigh the effects of technology. The world got smaller between 1840 and 1914, but it got bigger again for much of the 20th-century.

答案是肯定的。但是历史表明政治因素比技术的影响要大。1840—1914年世界变得相对较小，但20世纪大部分时间里世界又重新变大了一些。

However, Keynes stated that the age "came to an end" in 1914. In fact, two subsequent world wars, the Great Depression of the 1930s, and widespread protectionism did a great deal to depress world trade. World trade grew rapidly between 1870 and 1913, but suffered a sharp setback in the decades that followed, and did not recover to pre-World War I levels until around 1970. Since 1970, world trade as a share of world GDP has risen to unprecedented heights. Much of this rise in the value of world trade reflects the so-called "vertical disintegration" of production: Before a product reaches the hands of consumers, it often goes through many production stages in different countries. For example, consumer electronic products—cell-phones, iPods, and so on—are often assembled in lower-wage nations such as China from components produced in higher-wage nations like Japan. Because of the extensive cross-shipping of components, a \$100 product can give rise to \$200 or \$300 worth of international trade flows.

1.11 Do Old Rules Still Apply?

We begin our discussion of the causes of world trade with an analysis of a model originally put forth by the British economist David Ricardo in 1819. **Given all the changes in world trade since Ricardo's time, can old ideas still be relevant? The answer is a resounding yes. Although much about international trade has changed, the fundamental principles discovered by economists at the dawn of a global economy still apply.**

It's true that world trade has become harder to characterize in simple terms. A century ago, each country's exports were obviously shaped in large part by its climate and natural resources. Tropical countries exported tropical products such as coffee and cotton; land-rich countries such as the United States and Australia exported food to densely populated European nations. Disputes over trade were also easy to explain: The classic political battles over free trade versus protectionism were waged between English landowners who wanted protection from cheap food imports and English manufacturers who exported much of their output.

The sources of modern trade are more subtle. Human resources and human-created resources (in the form of machinery and other types of capital) are more important than natural resources. Political battles over trade typically involve workers whose skills are less valuable by imports—clothing workers who face competition from imported apparel, and tech workers who now face competition from Bangalore.

As we'll see in later chapters, however, the underlying logic of international trade remains the same. Economic models developed long before the invention of jet planes or the Internet remain key to understanding the essentials of 21st-century international trade.

1.11 旧规则依然适用吗?

自从李嘉图时代以来,国际贸易发生了很多变化,以前的理论还适用吗?答案依然是肯定的,虽然国际贸易发生了很多变化,但是经济学家发现的关于国际经济的基本的、规律性的内容依然有用。

☞ Key Terms

international economics, international trade, international finance, gains from trade, pattern of trade, protectionism, balance of payments, exchange rate determination, international policy coordination, international capital market

☞ 关键术语

国际经济学、国际贸易、国际金融、贸易所得、贸易模式、贸易保护主义、国际收支平衡、汇率决定因素、国际政策协调、国际资本市场

☞ Questions

☞ 本章习题

1. What is international economics about?
2. How to explain the gains from trade?
3. What is the exchange rate? What is the exchange rate determination?
4. Has the world gotten smaller nowadays?
5. Do the old rules still apply in the modern international economics?

Chapter 2

Classical Theories of International Trade

第二章 古典贸易理论

This chapter develops models that provide different explanations or reasons why trade takes place between countries. **The five fundamental reasons underlining why trade may take place are differences in technology, differences in resource endowments, differences in demand, the presence of economies of scale, and the presence of government policies.** The purpose of each model is to establish a basis for trade and then to use that model to identify the expected effects of trade on prices, profits, incomes, and individual welfare.

贸易产生的五个基本因素：技术差异、禀赋差异、需求差异、规模经济及政府政策。

There are very few models of trade that include all five reasons for trade simultaneously. The reason is that such a model is too complicated to work with. Economists simplify the world by choosing a model that generally contains just one reason. This does not mean that economists believe that one reason, or one model, is sufficient to explain all outcomes. Instead, one must try to understand the world by looking at what a collection of different models tells us about the same phenomenon.

In the real world, trade takes place because of a combination of all these different reasons. Each single model provides only a glimpse of some of the effects that might arise. Consequently, we should expect that a combination of the different outcomes that are presented in different models is the true characterization of the real world. Unfortunately, because of this, understanding the complexities of the real world is still more of an art than a science. In this chapter, we could only explore the Ricardian model of trade, which incorporates differences in technologies between countries, concluding that everyone benefits from trade.

古典贸易理论是思想演进的产物。特别是从重商主义到亚当·斯密的绝对优势理论，再到大卫·李嘉图的比较优势理论，这些建立了贸易理论的框架。

Classical trade theory is the product of an evolution of ideas in economic thoughts. In particular, the writings of the mercantilists,

and later those of Adam Smith and David Ricardo, have been instrumental in establishing the framework of trade theory.

2.1 Mercantilism

2.1 重商主义

Economics as an organized discipline of science was originated from the publication of *The Wealth of Nations* by Adam Smith in 1776. However, writings on international trade preceded this date in such countries as England, Spain, France, Portugal, and the Netherlands as they developed into modern national states. **Specifically, during the 17th and 18th centuries, a group of scholars had already been writing essays and pamphlets on international trade that advocated an economic philosophy known as mercantilism. Briefly, the mercantilists maintained that the way for a nation to become rich and powerful was to export more than it imported.** The resulting export surplus would then be settled by an inflow of bullion, or precious metals, primarily gold and silver. The more gold and silver a nation had, the richer and more powerful it was. Thus, the government had to do all in its power to stimulate the nation's exports and discourage and restrict imports (particularly the import of luxury consumption goods). However, since it's impossible for all nations to have an export surplus simultaneously, and the amount of gold and silver was fixed at any particular point of time, one nation could gain only at the expense of the others. The mercantilists thus preached **economic nationalism**, believing as they did that national interests were basically in conflict. To promote a favorable trade balance, the mercantilists **advocated government regulation of trade**. Tariffs, quotas, and other commercial policies were proposed by the mercantilists to minimize imports and protect a nation's trade position. At a more sophisticated level of analysis, there were more rational reasons for the mercantilists' desire for the accumulation of precious metals. With more gold, rulers could maintain larger and better armies and navies, and in turn acquire more colonies. Furthermore, by encouraging exports and restricting imports, the government would stimulate national output and employment.

17—18世纪，一大批主张重商主义的著作问世。该学派的学者主张，一个国家的富有、强盛之道在于贸易盈余。

经济国家主义

主张政府限制贸易

Criticisms of Mercantilism

对重商主义的批判

David Hume developed the **price-specie flow mechanism, which illustrates that a favorable trade balance was possible only in the short run.** Suppose that England were to achieve a trade surplus that resulted in an inflow of gold and silver. Because these precious metals would constitute part of England's money supply, their inflow would increase the amount of money in circulation. This would lead to a rise in England's price level relative to that of its trading partners. English residents would therefore be encouraged to purchase foreign-produced goods, while England's exports would decline. As a result, the country's export surplus would eventually be eliminated.

价格流转学说：一个国家的贸易盈余只能短期存在。

Note that the mercantilists measured the wealth of a nation by the stock of precious metals it possessed. In contrast, Adam Smith proposed that the wealth of a nation should be measured by its stock of human, man-made, and natural resources available for producing goods and services. The greater the stock of useful resources, the richer the nation.

重商主义者认为，衡量一国财富的标准是贵金属的持有量。而亚当·斯密则认为，衡量一国财富的标准是其拥有的用于生产商品和劳务的资源。

2.2 Absolute Advantage: Adam Smith

2.2 绝对优势理论：亚当·斯密

The theory of comparative advantage is perhaps the most important concept in international trade theory, while also one of the most commonly misunderstood principles. There is a popular story told among economists that once when an economics skeptic asked Paul Samuelson (a Nobel laureate in economics) to provide a meaningful and nontrivial result from the economics discipline, Samuelson quickly responded, "comparative advantage".

比较优势理论或许是国际贸易理论中最重要的概念，也是最容易被误解的原则之一。

The sources of misunderstanding are easy to identify. First, the principle of comparative advantage is clearly counterintuitive. Many results from the formal model are contrary to naive logic. Second, it is easy to confuse it with another notion about advantageous trade, known in trade theory as the theory of absolute advantage, which seems more intuitive. The confusion leads many people to think that they understand the former when in fact what they have in mind is the latter. Finally, the theory of comparative advantage is all too often presented only in its mathematical form. Numerical examples or diagrammatic representations are extremely useful in demonstrating the basic results and the deeper implications of the theory. However, it is also easy to see the results mathematically without ever understanding the basic intuition of the theory.

The early thoughts that free trade could be advantageous for countries was, however, based on the concept of absolute advantages in production. Adam Smith wrote in *The Wealth of Nations*, "If a foreign country can supply us with a commodity cheaper than we ourselves can make it, better buy it of them with some part of the produce of our own industry, employed in a way in which we have some advantage."

早期认为自由贸易对国家有利的想法是建立在生产绝对优势的基础上的。亚当·斯密在《国富论》中写道："如果一个国家能为我们提供比我们自己制造的便宜的商品，那么最好进口其具有绝对劣势的商品，出口其具有绝对优势的商品。"

The idea between the lines is simple and intuitive. If our country can produce some set of goods at a lower cost than a foreign country does and the foreign country can produce some other set of goods at a lower cost than we do, then clearly it would be best for us to trade our relatively cheaper goods for their relatively cheaper goods. In this way, both countries may gain from trade.

Smith's concepts of cost differences govern the movement of goods among nations, and he also explored the reasons why costs differ in the first place.

Smith founded his concept of cost upon the labor theory of value, which assumes that within each nation, labor is the only factor of production and is homogeneous, so the cost of a good depends exclusively upon the amount of labor required to produce it. Smith explained further that productivities of factor inputs represent the major determinant of production cost. Smith thus viewed the determination of competitive advantage from the supply side of the market.

In a two-nation, two-product world, according to Smith, each nation benefits by specializing in the production of the good that it produces at a lower cost than the other nation, while importing the good that it produces at a higher cost. Since factors are used more efficiently under specialization, there would be an increase in total output, which is then allocated to the two nations through trade.

2.3 Comparative Advantage: David Ricardo

2.3 比较优势理论：大卫·李嘉图

The original idea of comparative advantage dates back to the early era of the 19-century. Although the model describing the theory is commonly referred to as the "Ricardian model", the original description of the idea can be found in the 1815 *Essay on the External Corn Trade* by Robert Torrens. David Ricardo formalized the idea using a compelling yet simple numerical example in his 1817 book *On the Principles of Political Economy and Taxation*. The idea appeared again in James Mill's 1821 *Elements of Political Economy*. Finally, the concept became a key feature of international political economy upon the 1848 publication of *Principles of Political Economy* by John Stuart Mill.

According to Smith, mutually beneficial trade requires each nation to be the least-cost producer of at least one good that it can export to its trading partner. But what if a nation is more efficient than its trading partner in the production of *all* goods?

Like Smith, Ricardo focused on the supply side of the market.

The immediate basis for trade stemmed from cost differences between nations, which were underlain by their natural and acquired advantages. Unlike Smith, who emphasized the importance of absolute cost differences among nations, Ricardo emphasized comparative cost differences.

2.3.1 Assumptions of Ricardian Model

2.3.1 李嘉图模型假设

The modern version of the Ricardian model assumes that there are two countries producing two goods using one factor of production, usually labor. The model is a general equilibrium model in which all markets (i.e., goods and factors) are perfectly competitive. The goods produced are assumed to be homogeneous across countries and firms within an industry. Goods can be costlessly shipped between countries (i.e., there are no transportation costs). Labor is homogeneous within a country but may have different productivities across countries. This implies that the production technology is assumed to differ across countries. Labor is costlessly mobile across industries within a country but is immobile across countries. Full employment of labor is also assumed. Consumers (the laborers) are assumed to maximize utility subject to an income constraint.

2.3.2 Definition of Comparative Advantage

2.3.2 比较优势的定义

To identify a country's comparative advantage requires a comparison of production costs across countries. However, one does not compare the monetary costs of production or even the resource costs (labor needed per unit of output) of production. Instead, one must compare the opportunity costs of producing goods (say, cloth and wine) across countries.

A country is said to have a comparative advantage in the production of a kind of goods if it can produce the kind of goods at a lower opportunity cost than another country. The opportunity cost of cloth production is defined as the amount of wine that must be given up in order to produce one more unit of cloth. Thus England would have the comparative advantage in cloth production relative to Portugal if it must give up less wine to produce another unit of cloth than the amount of wine that Portugal would have to give up to produce another unit of cloth.

一个国家在某种商品上具有比较优势，是指其生产的机会成本低于另外一个国家。

Another way to define comparative advantage is by comparing productivities across industries and countries. Suppose, as before, that Portugal is more productive than England in the production of both cloth and wine. If Portugal is twice as productive in cloth production relative to England but three times as productive in wine, then Portugal's comparative advantage is in wine, the good in which it has the greatest productivity advantage. Similarly, England's comparative advantage is in cloth, the good in which it has the least productivity disadvantage. **This implies that to benefit from specialization and free trade, Portugal should specialize in and trade the good that it is "most better" at producing, while England should specialize in and trade the good that it is "least worse" at producing.**

另外一种定义方法是比较不同国家不同产品劳动生产率的相对差异。

按照“两利相权取其重，两弊相权取其轻”的原则分工贸易，两国都可以获益。葡萄牙应该专攻并交易其“最擅长”的商品，而英国应该专攻并交易其相对“不是最差”的商品。

2.3.3 An Example of Comparative Advantage

2.3.3 比较优势的例子

Because the idea of comparative advantage is not immediately intuitive, the best way of presenting it seems to be an explicit numerical example provided by Ricardo. Indeed, some variation of Ricardo's example lives on in most international trade textbooks today.

In his example, Ricardo imagined two countries, the United States and France, producing two goods, cloth (which is replaced with cheese in our example) and wine, using labor as the sole input in production. He assumed that the productivity of labor (i.e., the quantity of output produced per worker) varied between industries and across countries.

The example demonstrates that both countries will gain from trade if they specialize in their comparative advantage good and trade some of it for the other good. We set up the example so that one country (the United States) has an absolute advantage in the production of both goods. Ricardo's surprising result was that a country can gain from trade even if it is technologically inferior in producing every good, a case not covered in Adam Smith's *The Wealth of Nations*.

Basis of Trade

贸易的基础

Suppose the exogenous variables in the two countries take the values in Table 2.1.

Table 2.1 Values of Exogenous Variables in the United States and France

United States	$a_{Lc}=1$	$a^*_{LW}=2$	$L=24$
France	$a^*_{Lc}=6$	$a^*_{LW}=3$	$L^*=24$

Where

L = the labor endowment of the United States (the total number of hours the workforce is willing to provide),

a_{LC} = unit labor requirement in cheese production in the United States (hours of labor necessary to produce one unit/pound of cheese),

a_{LW} = unit labor requirement in wine production in the United States (hours of labor necessary to produce one unit/gallon of wine),

* All starred variables are defined in the same way but refer to the process in France.

By assumption, the United States has the absolute advantage

in both cheese production and wine production because $a_{LC}(1) < a^*_{LC}(6)$ and $a_{LW}(2) < a^*_{LW}(3)$.

The United States also has the comparative advantage in cheese production because the cost of producing cheese in the United States is one half gallon of wine per pound of cheese. In France, it is two gallons per pound.

美国在奶酪的生产上享有比较优势，法国在酒的生产上享有比较优势。

France, however, has the comparative advantage in wine production because the cost of producing wine in France is one half pound of cheese per gallon of wine, while in the United States, it is two pounds per gallon, as summarized in Table 2.2.

Table 2.2 Prices of Cheese and Wine in the United States and France (with no international trade)

Prices	In the United States	In France
Price of Cheese(C)	$0.5W/C$	$2W/C$
Price of Wine(W)	$2C/W$	$0.5C/W$

Trade Happens

贸易发生

Now let trade be possible between the United States and France. Merchants will notice the difference between the domestic prices of each good and will try to profit from that difference. The principle is simple and universal: as long as prices differ in two places, there is a way to profit through **arbitrage-buying at the low price in one place and selling at the high price in the other place.**

价格差异导致套利行为的发生。

The International Market Price

国际市场价格

The emerging of profitable international trade will start pushing the two separate domestic relative prices toward a new international equilibrium. As people remove cheese from the United States by exporting it, cheese becomes more expensive relative to wine in the United States. Meanwhile, cheese becomes cheaper in France thanks to the additional supply of cheese imported from the United States. So, cheese tends to get more expensive where it was cheap at first and cheaper where it was more expensive. A similar process occurs for wine. The tendencies continue until the two domestic relative prices become one international equilibrium relative price. Normal trade on an ongoing basis will be conducted at this equilibrium relative price.

What will the equilibrium international prices be? We cannot say for sure without knowing how strongly the two countries demand each of the two products. We do know something—**the equilibrium international relative price must fall within the range of the two domestic relative prices that prevail in each country before trade began:**

国际均衡交换价格应该在两国封闭条件下的均衡价格水平之间。

$0.5W/C \leqslant$ international relative price of cheese $\leqslant 2W/C$.

Or equivalently,

$2C/W \geqslant$ international relative price of wine $\geqslant 0.5\ C/W$.

2.3.4 Gains from Specialization and Trade

2.3.4 国际分工与贸易利得

The initial differences in relative prices of the goods between countries in autarky will stimulate trade between the countries. Since the differences in prices arise directly out of differences in technology between countries, it is the differences in technology that cause trade in the model. Profit-seeking firms in each country's comparative advantage industry would recognize that the price of their good is higher in the other country. Since transportation costs are zero, more profit can be made through export than with sales domestically. Thus each country would export the good in which it has a comparative advantage. Trade flows would increase until the price of each good is equal across countries. In the end, the price of each country's export good (its comparative advantage good) will rise and the price of its import good (its comparative disadvantage good) will fall.

The higher price received for each country's comparative advantage good would lead each country to specialize in that good. To accomplish this, labor would have to move from the comparative disadvantage industry into the comparative advantage industry. This means that one industry goes out of business in each country. However, because the model assumes full employment and costless mobility of labor, all these workers are immediately gainfully employed in the other industry.

The transition to free trade generates an improvement in welfare in both countries individually and nationally. Specialization and trade will increase the set of feasible consumption, compared with autarky, and will make possible an increase in consumption of both

国际贸易提升了国家与个人的福利水平。

goods nationally. These aggregate gains are often described as improvements in production and consumption efficiency. Free trade raises aggregate world production efficiency because more of both goods are likely to be produced with the same number of workers. Free trade also improves aggregate consumption efficiency, which implies that consumers have a more pleasing set of choices and prices available to them.

2.3.5 Comparative Advantage in Monetary Terms

2.3.5 比较优势的货币形式

When both commodities are expressed in terms of the currency of either nation, let us see how the comparative advantage works.

The Ricardian model assumes that the wine and cheese industries are both perfectly competitive. Among the assumptions of perfect competition is free entry and exit of firms in response to economic profit. If positive profit is being made in one industry, then because of perfect information, profit-seeking entrepreneurs will begin to open more firms in that industry. The entry of firms, however, raises industry supply, which forces down the product price and reduces profit for every other firm in the industry. Entry continues until economic profit is driven to zero. The same process occurs in a reversed way when profit is negative for firms in an industry. In this case, firms will close down one by one as they seek more profitable opportunities elsewhere. The reduction in the number of firms reduces industry supply, which raises the product's market price and raises profit for all remaining firms in the industry. Exit continues until economic profit is raised to zero. This implies that if production occurs in an industry, be it in autarky or free trade, economic profit must be zero.

Profit is defined as total revenue minus total cost. Let π_C represent profit in the cheese industry. We can write this as:

$$\pi_C = P_C Q_C - W_C L_C = 0 \tag{2.1}$$

where P_C is the price of cheese in dollars per pound, W_C is the wage paid to workers in dollars per hour, $P_C Q_C$ is total industry revenue, and $W_C L_C$ is total industry cost. By rearranging the zero-profit condition, we can write the wage as a function of everything else to get

$$W_C=\frac{P_C Q_C}{L_C} \tag{2.2}$$

Recall that the production function for cheese is

$$Q_C=\frac{L_C}{a_{Lc}} \tag{2.3}$$

Plugging this in for Q_C above yields:

$$W_C=\frac{P_C}{a_{Lc}} \tag{2.4}$$

If production occurs in the wine industry, then profit will be zero as well. By the same algebra we can get

$$W_W=\frac{P_W}{a_{LW}} \tag{2.5}$$

According to the analysis above, we conclude that even though France is not as efficient as the United States in the production, **its lower wage rate more than compensates for its inefficiency**. At the same time, the fluctuation of the exchange rate between the two currencies will influence the price too.

低工资水平往往可以弥补其低生产效率所形成的不利。

2.4 Comparative Advantage and Opportunity Cost

2.4 比较优势和机会成本

It was left for Haberler in 1936 to explain and base the theory of comparative advantage on opportunity cost theory.

According to the opportunity cost theory, the cost of a commodity is the amounts of a second commodity that must be given up to release just enough resources to produce one additional unit of the first commodity. No such assumption is made here that labor is the only factor of production or that labor is homogeneous. Nor is it assumed that the cost or price of a commodity depends on or can be inferred exclusively from its labor content. Consequently, the nation with the lower opportunity cost in the production of a commodity has a comparative advantage in that commodity.

2.4.1 Gains from Specialization and Trade Opportunity in Terms of Unity Costs

2.4.1 用机会成本表示的分工与贸易利得

As in the example above, in the absence of trade, the United States must give up 1/2 units of wine to release just enough resources to produce one additional unit of cheese domestically, then the opportunity cost of cheese is one half unit of wine. In France, we need to give up 2 units of wine to produce one additional unit of cheese. Therefore, the opportunity of cheese is lower in the United States than that in France, and the United States would have a comparative advantage over France in cheese. In a two-nation, two-commodity world, France would have a comparative advantage in wine. **According to the law of comparative advantage, the United States should specialize in producing cheese and export some of it in exchange for French wine. This is exactly what we concluded earlier with the law of comparative advantage based on the labor theory of value, but now our explanation is based on the opportunity cost theory.**

用机会成本分析方法得出的结论与之前使用劳动生产率相对差异得出的结论是一样的：美国专业化生产奶酪并出口奶酪，进口酒；法国则相反。

2.4.2 Production Possibilities Frontier and Constant Opportunity Costs

2.4.2 生产可能性边界与不变机会成本

Opportunity costs can be illustrated with the production possibility frontier (PPF), or transformation curve. **The production possibilities frontier is a curve that shows the alternative combinations of the two commodities that a nation can produce by fully utilizing all of its resources with the best technology available to it. The production possibilities frontier shows the maximum output possibilities of a nation and maximum consumption possibilities of the nation in autarky. Points inside or below PPF are also possible but are not efficient, in the sense that the nation has some idle resources and /or is not using the best technology available to it. On the other hand, points above the PPF cannot be achieved with the resources and technology currently available to the nation.** Note that we are no longer assuming labor to be the only factor input as Ricardo did.

生产可能性边界：现有技术水平条件下一国全部资源所能生产的两种产品最大产量的不同组合。其不仅反映了该国的最大产出边界，同时也是该国在无国际贸易时的最大消费边界。

生产可能性边界上的点表示资源得到充分利用，内部的点则表示资源有闲置。

How does the production possibilities frontier illustrate the concept of relative cost? The answer lies in the slope of the PPF, which is referred to as **the marginal rate of transformation (MRT)**. **According to the formation of the PPF, the MRT shows the amount of one product a nation must sacrifice to get one additional unit of the other product.**

This rate of sacrifice is sometimes called the opportunity cost of a product. Because the slope of the production possibility frontier is usually negative, the MRT is defined as its absolute value.

根据生产可能性边界的定义，生产可能性边界的斜率等于两种产品之间的边际转化率，表示增加一单位某一产品的生产需要放弃的另外一种产品的数量。

Constant Opportunity Costs

机会成本不变

Turning back to the two production functions and the labor constraint in the previous example, we can describe the PPF quantitatively. First, note that the production functions can be rewritten as $L_C = a_{LC}Q_C$ and $L_W = a_{LW}Q_W$.

Plugging these values for L_C and L_W into the labor constraint yields the equation for the PPF:

$$a_{LC}Q_C + a_{LW}Q_W = L \tag{2.6}$$

This equation has three exogenous variables (a_{LC}, a_{LW}, and L) that we assume have known values and two endogenous variables (Q_C and Q_W) whose values must be solved for. **The PPF equation is a linear equation**—that is, it describes a line. With some algebraic manipulation, we can rewrite the PPF equation into the standard form for an equation of a line, generally written as $y = mx + b$, where y is the variable on the vertical axis, x is the variable on the horizontal axis, m is the slope of the line, and b is the y-intercept, as follows

生产可能性边界公式是一条直线。

$$Q_W = \frac{L}{a_{LW}} - \left(\frac{a_{LC}}{a_{LW}}\right)Q_C \tag{2.7}$$

We plot the PPF on the diagram in Figure 2.1 with Q_C on the horizontal axis and Q_W on the vertical axis. The equation is easily plotted in three steps.

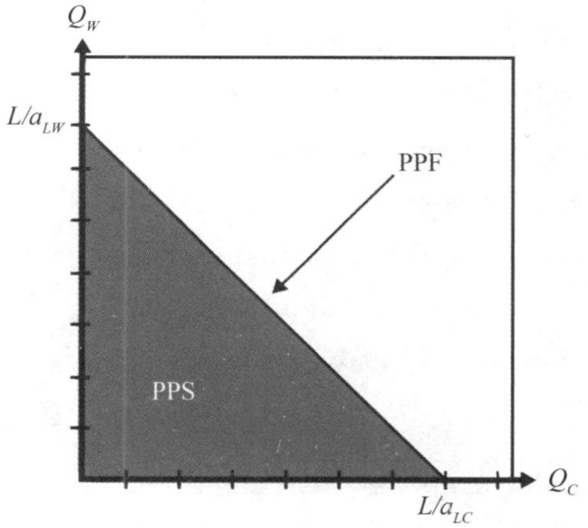

Figure 2.1 Production Possibilities

1. Set $Q_C = 0$ and solve for Q_W. In this case, the solution is $Q_W = \frac{L}{a_{LW}}$. This corresponds to the Q_W-intercept. It tells us the

quantity of wine that the United States could produce if it devotes all of its labor force (L) to the production of wine.

2. Set $Q_W = 0$ and solve for Q_C. In this case, the solution is $Q_C = \frac{L}{a_{LC}}$. This corresponds to the Q_C-intercept. It tells us the quantity of cheese that the United States could produce if it devotes all of its labor force to the production of cheese.

3. Connect the two points with a straight line. The straight downward-sloping line is the production possibility frontier. It describes all possible quantity combinations of wine and cheese that can be achieved in the United States. **A movement along the line represents a transfer of labor resources out of one industry and into another such that all labor remains employed.**

沿着生产可能性边界移动表示劳动力从一个部门转移到另外一个部门,劳动力资源得到充分利用。

Points inside the PPF are production possibilities with underemployment of labor resources. All production possibilities regardless of whether full employment is achieved are referred to as the production possibility set (PPS). The PPS is represented by all the points within and on the border of the triangle in Figure 2.1.

Reasons for Constant Opportunity Costs

机会成本不变的原因

Constant opportunity costs arise when (1) resources or factors of production are either perfect substitutes for each other or used in fixed proportion in the production of both commodities, and (2) all units of the same factor are homogeneous or of exactly the same quality. As a country transfers resources from the production of cheese into the production of wine, or vice versa, the country will not have to resort to resources that are less well suited for the production of the commodity. Therefore, the country must sacrifice exactly the same amount of cheese for each additional wine produced, regardless of how many wine it is already producing.

Basis and Direction of Trade

贸易的基础与方向

Let us now examine trade under constant-cost conditions. Suppose two countries, the United States and France, are initially in autarky. Assume the United States has a comparative advantage in cheese production relative to France. This implies

$$\frac{a_{LC}}{a_{LW}} < \frac{a'_{Lc}}{a'_{LW}} \tag{2.8}$$

which, in turn, implies

$$\left(\frac{Pc}{P_W}\right)^{Aut} < \left(\frac{P'c}{P'_W}\right)^{Aut} \quad (2.9)$$

This means that the autarky price of cheese in France (in terms of wine) is greater than the autarky price of cheese in the United States. In other words, you can buy more wine with a pound of cheese in the French market than you can in the U.S. market.

Similarly, by rearranging the inequality above,

$$\left(\frac{P_W}{Pc}\right)^{Aut} > \left(\frac{P'_W}{P'c}\right)^{Aut} \quad (2.10)$$

The autarky terms of trade (cheese in terms of wine) equals the opportunity cost (of cheese in terms of wine). If the autarky price of wine is higher in the United States (in terms of cheese) than it is in France, then a gallon of wine can be exchanged for more cheese in the United States than it will yield in the French market.

封闭条件下的贸易价格等于机会成本。封闭条件下美国酒的相对价格高于法国，意味着相对于法国市场，在美国市场上酒可以交换到更多的奶酪。

Next, suppose the barriers to trade that induced autarky are suddenly lifted and the United States and France are allowed to trade freely. For simplicity, we assume there are no transportation costs to move the products across borders.

Differences in price ratios between countries and the desire to make more profit are sufficient to generate international trade. To explain why, it is useful to incorporate some friction in the trading process and to tell a dynamic story about how post-trade equilibrium is reached.

相对价格的差异以及对利益最大化的追求促使了国际贸易的发生。

First, note that the higher price of cheese in France means that cheese workers in the United States could get more wine for their cheese in France than in the United States. Suppose one by one over time cheese workers begin to take advantage of the opportunity for trade and sell their cheese in the French market. We assume that some workers are more internationally adroit and thus move first. The motivation here is profit. Workers want to get more for the goods they are selling. As the U.S. cheese workers appear in the French market, the supply of cheese increases. This also represents exports of cheese from the United States to France. The increased supply will reduce the price of cheese in the French market, meaning that over time, the quantity of wine obtained for a pound of cheese will fall. Thus P_C/P_W falls once trade is opened.

Next, consider French wine workers immediately after trade opens. Since the price of wine is higher in the United States, French wine workers will one by one over time begin to sell their wine in the U. S. market. This represents exports of wine from France to the United States. The increased supply of wine to the United States lowers its price on the U.S. market. Thus each gallon of wine will trade for less and less cheese. This means P_W/P_C falls, which also means that P_C/P_W rises.

The International Equilibrium Price

世界均衡价格

两国市场相对价格差异的存在促使两国之间的商品持续流动。

自由贸易的世界价格是世界供给等于世界需求时所形成的价格。

These shifts in supply will continue as long as the prices for the goods continue to differ between the two markets. Once the prices are equalized, there will be no incentive to trade any additional amount. Equalized prices mean that a pound of cheese will trade for the same number of gallons of wine in both markets. **The free trade prices will be those prices that equalize total supply of each good in the world with total demand for each good.**

As a result of trade, the international equilibrium relative price ratio, or terms of trade, will lie in between the two countries' autarky price ratios. In other words, the following inequality will hold:

$$\left(\frac{P_C}{P_W}\right)^{Aut} < \left(\frac{P_C}{P_W}\right)^{FT} < \left(\frac{P_C^*}{P_W^*}\right)^{Aut} \qquad (2.11)$$

Whether the free trade price ratio will be closer to the U.S. or France's autarky price ratio will depend on the relative demands of cheese to wine in the two countries. These demands in turn will depend on the size of the countries. If the United States is a much larger country, in that it has a larger workforce, it will have a larger demand for both wine and cheese. When trade opens, the addition of France's supply and demand will have a relatively small effect on the U. S. price. Thus the free trade price ratio will be closer to the U.S. autarky price ratio.

Complete Specialization with Trade Under Constant-cost Condition: Production

成本不变条件下贸易的完全分工：生产

Once the prices begin to change because of trade, they will also affect the profitability of producing the two goods. In the United States, the price of cheese, its export good, will rise in moving to trade, while the price of wine, its import good, will fall. As shown above, the final price ratio in the United States (cheese to wine) in free trade will be greater than the autarky price ratio.

$$\left(\frac{P_C}{P_W}\right)^{FT} > \left(\frac{P_C}{P_W}\right)^{Aut} \tag{2.12}$$

Because the autarky price ratio equals the opportunity cost of cheese production, it follows that

$$\left(\frac{P_C}{P_W}\right)^{FT} > \frac{\alpha_{LC}}{\alpha_{LW}} \tag{2.13}$$

Note that this inequality will be true as soon as the price deviates from the autarky price and long before the free trade prices are reached. This also means that shortly after trade begins, the price of cheese (measured in terms of wine) exceeds the cost of producing cheese (also measured in terms of wine). Normally, when we measure the price and cost in dollar terms, when the price per unit exceeds the cost per unit, then positive profit is realized. The same is true when we measure the price and cost in terms of wine. **Thus as soon as trade begins to change prices, cheese production becomes more profitable in the United States. And because we assume people are profit seeking, they will therefore seek to expand cheese production.** But where will they find the workers to do so? Wine workers are their best choices. To expand cheese production, the country will have to give up wine production. But why do that?

在美国生产奶酪有利可得，因此生产者会扩大奶酪的生产规模。

Well, when the price of cheese in terms of wine exceeds the opportunity cost of cheese, it is also true, via cross multiplication, that

$$\frac{\alpha_{LW}}{\alpha_{LC}} > \left(\frac{P_W}{P_C}\right)^{FT} \tag{2.14}$$

This means that the cost of producing wine (in terms of cheese) exceeds the price of wine (also in terms of cheese). Because cost is greater than price, profit is negative in the wine industry in the United States and wine producers have an incentive to shut down. And when they do, those workers can be moved into the cheese industry, where profit seekers wish to expand.

Thus, as long as individuals are profit seeking, the price differences that arise in autarky will be sufficient to induce export and specialization in the comparative advantage good completely.

因为利益最大化的逐利行为，封闭条件下的价格差异最终导致完全的专业化分工和出口具有比较优势的商品。

There is no need to use the complicated opportunity cost formula to first identify the comparative advantage good and no need to tell anyone what to do. Instead, the free market mechanism—Adam Smith's invisible hand—is all that it takes.

Welfare Effects of Free Trade: Consumption

自由贸易的福利效应：消费

There are two ways of evaluating the welfare effects of trade in the Ricardian model. The first method evaluates the change of consumption through the real wages of workers as two countries move from autarky to free trade. **It is shown that the purchasing power of all workers' wages in both countries would rise in moving to free trade.**

自由贸易后两国劳动力的购买能力提高。

The focus on real wages allows us to see the effect of free trade on individual consumers in the economy. Nominal wages are not sufficient to tell us if workers gain since, even if wages rise, the price of one of the goods also rises when moving to free trade. If the price rises by a greater percentage than the wage, the ability to purchase that good falls and the worker may be worse off.

For this reason, we must consider real wages. The real wage represents the purchasing power of wages—that is, the quantity of goods the wages could purchase. Real wages are typically measured by dividing nominal wages by a price index. The price index measures the average level of prices relative to a base year. The nominal wage is the amount of dollars the worker receives.

In this model, we need not construct a price index since there are only two goods. Instead, we will look at the real wage of workers in terms of the purchasing power of each good. In other words, we will solve for a real wage in terms of purchases of both wine and cheese (Table 2.3).

Table 2.3 Autarky Real Wages

Real Wages	In Tems of Cheese	In Terms of Wine
Real Wage of Cheese Workers	$\frac{W_C}{P_C}=\frac{1}{\alpha_{LC}}$	$\frac{W_C}{P_W}=\frac{1}{\alpha_{LC}}\frac{\alpha_{LC}}{\alpha_{LW}}=\frac{1}{\alpha_{LW}}$
Real Wage of Wine Workers	$\frac{W_W}{P_C}=\frac{1}{\alpha_{LW}}\frac{\alpha_{LW}}{\alpha_{LC}}=\frac{1}{\alpha_{LC}}$	$\frac{W_W}{P_W}=\frac{1}{\alpha_{LW}}$

Where

P_C = price of cheese;

P_W = price of wine;

W_C = wage paid to cheese workers;

W_W = wage paid to wine workers;

a_{LC} = unit labor requirement in cheese production in the United States (hours of labor necessary to produce one unit of cheese);

a_{LW} = unit labor requirement in wine production in the United States (hours of labor necessary to produce one unit of wine).

The real wage of cheese workers in terms of cheese is the quantity of cheese that a cheese worker can buy with a unit of work. It is calculated by dividing the worker's wage by the price of cheese, written as W_C/P_C. Since zero profit is made in each producing industry, we can simply rewrite the relationship derived above to construct the following formula for the real wage:

$$\frac{W_C}{P_C}=\frac{1}{a_{LC}}. \tag{2.15}$$

The real wage of cheese workers in terms of wine is the quantity of wine that a cheese worker can buy with a unit of work. It is calculated by dividing the cheese worker's wage by the price of wine and is written as W_C/P_W. Using the relationship between wages and prices when zero profit is made in the cheese industry implies that $\frac{W_C}{P_W}=\frac{\left(\frac{P_C}{a_{LC}}\right)}{P_W}=\frac{1}{a_{LC}}\frac{P_C}{P_W}$.

Similarly, we can get the real wage of wine workers.

To calculate autarky real wages, we simply plug the autarky price ratio into the real wage formulae.

Notice that in autarky, the real wage of cheese workers is exactly the same as the real wage of wine workers with respect to purchases of both goods. This occurs because labor is assumed to be homogeneous—that is, all labor is the same—and because there is free mobility between industries. (If workers were paid different wages, the lower-wage workers would move to the higher-wage industry.)

Suppose the United States has an absolute advantage in the production of both goods. In this case, $\frac{1}{a_{LC}}>\frac{1}{a_{LC}^*}$; and $\frac{1}{a_{LW}}>\frac{1}{a_{LW}^*}$. This implies that the real wages of workers in both industries in the United States are higher than the real wages in France. Put another way, workers in France earn lower wages in both industries.

Sometimes cross-country wage comparisons are made and it is suggested that firms in a high-wage country cannot compete with firms in low-wage countries. However, wage comparisons of this kind are not sufficient in this model to determine who will produce what or whether trade can be advantageous. Instead, what matters is relative wage comparisons. In this model, a country will tend to specialize in the good in which it has the greatest real wage advantage. Thus if $\frac{\frac{1}{a_{LC}}}{\frac{1}{a_{LC}^{*}}} > \frac{\frac{1}{a_{LW}}}{\frac{1}{a_{LW}^{*}}}$, then the United States has relatively higher real wages with respect to cheese purchases than it does in wine purchases. When trade opens, the United States will specialize in its comparative advantage good, which, by rearranging the above inequality, can easily be shown to be cheese.

When the two countries move to free trade, the free trade price ratio will lie somewhere between the autarky price ratios (Table 2.4). This means that (P_C/P_W) rises in the United States when moving from autarky to free trade, while P_C^{*}/P_W^{*} falls when moving to free trade.

The other major change that occurs is that the United States specializes in cheese production, while France specializes in wine production. This means that real wages in free trade for wine workers in the United States need not be calculated since the United States will no longer have any wine workers. Similarly, real wages for cheese workers in France need not be calculated.

Table 2.4 Changes in Real Wages (Autarky to Free Trade)

Real Wages	In Tems of Cheese	In Terms of Wine
Real Wage of U.S. Cheese Workers	$\frac{W_C}{P_C}=\frac{1}{a_{LC}}$ (no change)	$\frac{W_C}{P_W}=\frac{1}{a_{LC}}\frac{P_C}{P_W}$ (rises)
Real Wage of French Wine Workers	$\frac{W_W}{P_C}=\frac{1}{a_{LW}}\frac{P_W}{P_C}$ (rises)	$\frac{W_W}{P_W}=\frac{1}{a_{LW}}$ (no change)

Consider the impact on U.S. cheese workers. Since the unit labor requirement for cheese does not change in moving to free trade, there is also no change in the real wage in terms of cheese. However, since the price of cheese in terms of wine rises, U.S. cheese workers can get more wine for each unit of cheese in exchange. Thus the real wage of cheese workers in terms of wine rises. This means cheese workers are at least as well off in free trade as they were in autarky. As for the workers who worked in the wine industry in the United States in autarky, they are now cheese makers earning cheese-maker wages. Since real wages for wine workers were the same as wages for cheese workers in autarky, and since cheese workers are no worse off with free trade, then wine workers must also be no worse off in free trade. Of course, the model assumes that the movement of workers from one industry to another is costless. In the immobile factor model, we address the implications of adjustment costs across industries. Workers in France face the same situation.

The likely welfare effect of free trade, then, is that everyone in both trading countries benefits. At the very worst, some individuals will be just as well off as in autarky. This result occurs for any free trade price ratio that lies between the autarky price ratios.

贸易参与国的所有人都能从贸易中获利。

Aggregate Effects: Production and Consumption

总效应：生产与消费

Figure 2.2 compares autarky and free trade equilibriums for the United States and France. The U.S. PPF is given by the line 1, while France's PPF is given by the line 2. We assume both countries share the same aggregate preferences represented by the indifference curves in the diagram. Note also that if the United States and France had the same size labor force, then the relative positions of the PPFs imply that the United States has the absolute advantage in cheese production, while France has the absolute advantage in wine production. Also, if each country has an absolute advantage in one of the two goods, then each country must also have the comparative advantage in that good.

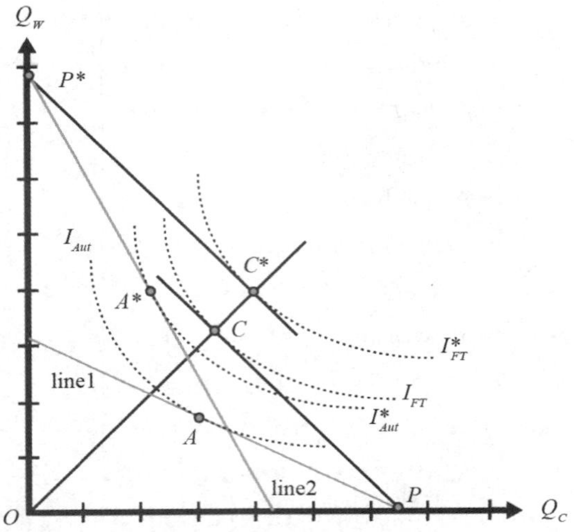

Figure 2.2 Equilibrium in Autarky and Free Trade

The U. S. autarky production and consumption points are determined where the aggregate indifference curve is tangent to the U.S. PPF. This occurs at the point A. The United States realizes a level of aggregate utility that corresponds to the indifference curve I_{Aut}.

The U.S. production and consumption points in free trade are at the points P and C, respectively. The United States specializes in production of its comparative advantage good but trades to achieve its consumption point at C. In free trade, the United States realizes a level of aggregate utility that corresponds to the indifference curve I_{FT}. Since the free trade indifference curve I_{FT} lies to the northeast of the autarky indifference curve I_{Aut}, national welfare rises as the United States moves to free trade.

France's autarky production and consumption points are determined by finding the aggregate indifference curve that is tangent to the French PPF. This occurs at the green point A^*. France realizes a level of aggregate utility that corresponds to the indifference curve $I_{Aut}{}^*$. French production and consumption points in free trade are the points P^* and C^*, respectively. **In free trade, France realizes a level of aggregate utility that corresponds to the indifference curve $I_{FT}{}^*$. Since the free trade indifference curve $I_{FT}{}^*$ lies to the northeast of the autarky indifference curve $I_{Aut}{}^*$, national welfare rises as France moves to free trade. Both countries are better**

自由贸易下法国和美国都可以实现更高的无差异曲线上的消费组合，贸易后两国的福利水平都提高了。

off with free trade.

2.4.3 Trade Under Increasing Opportunity Costs

2.4.3 机会成本递增下的贸易

The previous section illustrated the comparative advantage principle under constant-cost conditions. But in the real world, a good's opportunity cost may increase as more of it is produced.

Increasing Opportunity Cost

机会成本递增

机会成本递增下的生产可能性曲线凹向原点。

Increasing opportunity cost gives rise to a production possibility frontier that appears concave, or bowed outward from the diagram's origin. As is shown in Figure 2.3, with movement along the production possibilities frontier from *A* to *B*, the marginal opportunity cost of producing autos becomes larger and larger in terms of wheat sacrificed. Because the real cost of producing autos rises as more autos are produced, the auto supply schedule is positively sloped. Auto producers will offer more autos on the market only if they are compensated for their rising costs of production. Changes in the quantity supplied and product price are therefore directly related. This is shown in the lower part of Figure 2.4.

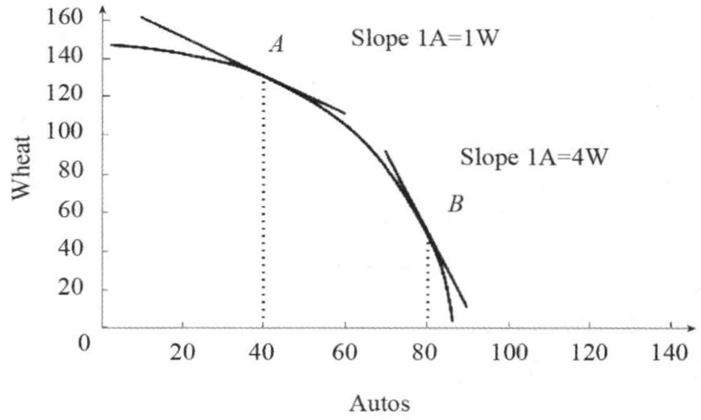

Figure 2.3 Production Possibilities Schedule under Increasing Costs

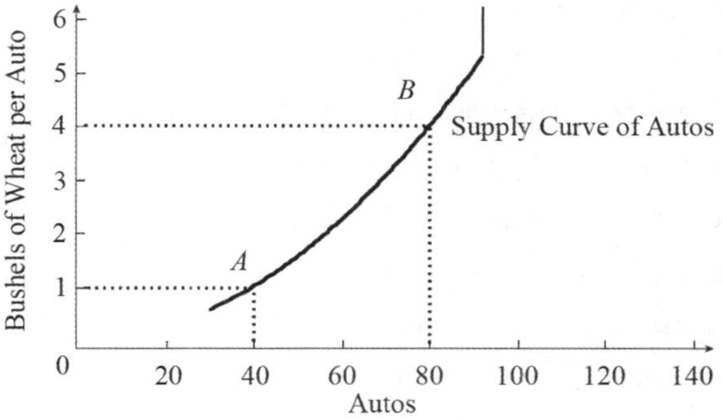

Figure 2.4 Supply Schedule under Increasing Cost

Increasing costs mean that the MRT of wheat into autos rises as more autos are produced. Remember that **the MRT is measured by the absolute slope of the production possibilities frontier at a given point.** With movement from production point A to production point B, the respective tangent lines become steeper—their slopes increase in absolute value. The MRT of wheat into autos rises, indicating that each additional auto produced requires the sacrifice of increasing amounts of wheat.

边际转换率等于生产可能边界的某一点的切线斜率。

Reasons for Increasing Opportunity Cost

机会成本递增的原因

In short, the law of increasing opportunity costs originated from the fact that every additional unit of resources taken away from one industry and used in another would be more efficient at its original use than the new use. With the assumption of technical efficiency, the first few units of resources removed from wheat production and directed toward the autos are those BEST suited to autos and LEAST suited to producing wheat. As such, very little wheat is sacrificed to make the first auto. However, the last few units of resources removed from wheat production are those BEST suited for wheat and LEAST suited for autos. The economy is losing a lot of wheat to make one more auto.

Production in Autarky

封闭条件下的生产均衡

Under increasing costs, the slope of the concave production possibilities frontier varies as a nation locates at different points on the schedule. Because the domestic MRT equals the production possibilities frontier's slope, it will also be different for each point on the schedule. Which point will be a country's production point in autarky to achieve the maximum profit?

Because the production cost should be compensated by price, the opportunity cost will be equal to the relative price of the two commodities when a country realizes equilibrium in autarky. When the price of auto relative to wheat rises, the production of auto will increase subsequently. With the expansion of auto production, the opportunity cost of auto increases correspondingly until the new opportunity is equal to the new price.

因为生产成本应该以价格来补偿，所以封闭条件下的生产均衡点上，产品的相对价格等于其机会成本。

In autarky, the equilibrium production point is the equilibrium consumption point, because the consumption is constrained by the production without trade.

Trade under Increasing-cost Condition

机会成本递增下的贸易

In the absence of trade, the United States achieved equilibrium at point A with equilibrium price ratio t_{US} (Figure 2.5). Similarly, Canada's equilibrium locates at point A′ with equilibrium price ratio t_C (Figure 2.6). Comparing t_{US} with t_C, we find the price difference. Because $t_{US} < t_C$, autos are relatively cheaper in the United States and wheat is relatively cheaper in Canada. According to the law of comparative advantage, the United States will export autos and Canada will export wheat.

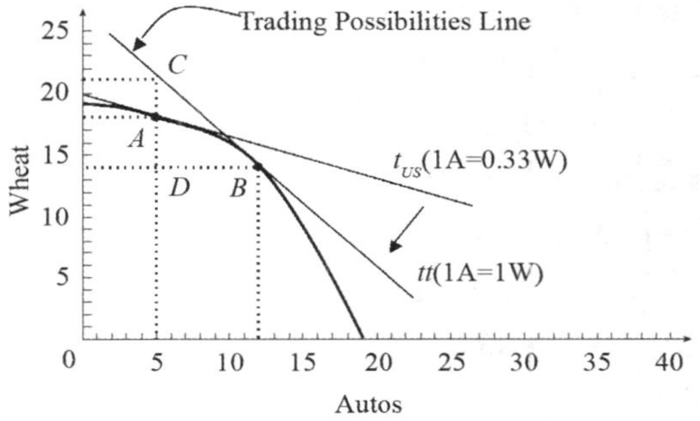

Figure 2.5 Trading Under Increasing Costs: U.S.

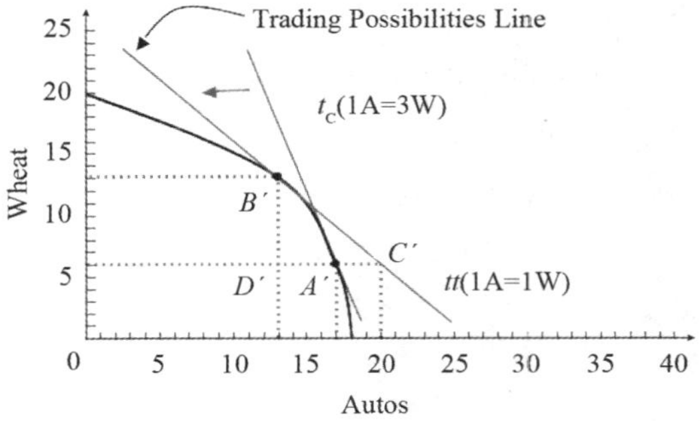

Figure 2.6 Trading Under Increasing Costs: Canada

The World Equilibrium Price

世界均衡价格

世界均衡价格落在两国封闭条件下的均衡价格之间，更靠近哪一个国家的国内价格水平取决于两国的需求力量。

As a result of trade, the world equilibrium price ratio, or terms of trade, will lie in between the two countries' autarky price ratios. Whether the free trade price ratio will be closer to the U. S. or Canada's autarky price ratio will depend on the relative demands of autos to wheat in the two countries. The world price ratio is illustrated as tt, and $t_{US} \leqslant tt \leqslant t_C$.

Partial Specialization

非完全专业化分工

As the United States specialized in auto production with higher auto price, it slides downward along its production possibility frontier from *A* toward *B*. With the expansion of autos, the relative cost of autos rises, as implied by the increase in the absolute slope of the PPF. On point *B*, where the world price ratio is equal to the opportunity cost, the United States achieves the post-trade production equilibrium with more auto and less wheat. At the same time, Canada specialized in wheat and expands the production of wheat. At point *B*', Canada achieves post-trade equilibrium with more wheat and less auto.

One feature of the increasing-cost model analyzed here is that trade generally leads each country to specialize only partially in the production of the good in which it has a comparative advantage. The reason for partial specialization is that increasing costs constitute a mechanism that forces costs in two trading nations to converge. When cost differentials are eliminated, the basis for further specialization ceases to exist.

In our example, the United States has a comparative cost advantage in producing autos, whereas Canada is relatively more efficient at producing wheat. With specialization, each country produces more of the commodity of its comparative and less of the commodity of its comparative disadvantage. Given increasing-cost conditions, unit costs rise as both nations produce more of their export commodities. Eventually, the cost differentials are eliminated, at which point the basis for further specialization ceases to exit.

When the basis for specialization is eliminated, there exists a strong probability that both nations will produce some of each good. This is because costs often rise so rapidly that a country loses its comparative advantage vis-*à*-vis the other country before it reaches the endpoint of its PPF. In the real world of increasing cost conditions, partial specialization is a likely result of free trade.

Consumption Outside of the PPF with Trade

生产可能性边界外的贸易消费

With trade, the domestic consumption can go beyond domestic

production. Take the United States as an example (Figure 2.7). The United States can choose a consumption point along international terms-of-trade line *tt*. In a likewise manner, Canada can choose to consume at some point along international terms-of-trade line *tt*.

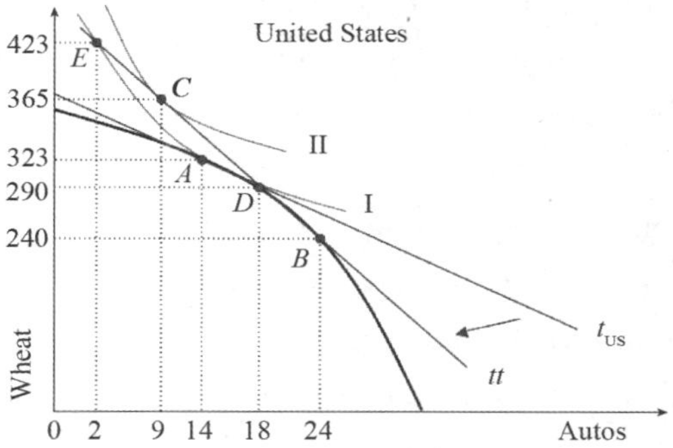

Figure 2.7 Gains from Trade: U.S.

The U. S. autarky production and consumption points are determined where the aggregate indifference curve is tangent to the U.S. PPF. This occurs at the point *A*. The United States realizes a level of aggregate utility that corresponds to the indifference curve Ⅰ.

The U.S. production and consumption points in free trade are at the *B* and *C*, respectively. The United States specializes in production of its comparative advantage good but trades to achieve its consumption point at the *C*. In free trade, the United States realizes a level of aggregate utility that corresponds to the indifference curve Ⅱ. Since the free trade indifference curve Ⅱ lies to the northeast of the autarky indifference curve Ⅰ, national welfare rises as the United States moves to free trade. Same thing happens in Canada.

In the next chapter, we will discuss the H-O theory with increasing-cost PPF.

2.5 Comparative Advantage with More Than Two Commodities and Countries

2.5 多国多产品的比较优势

Many people who learn about the theory of comparative advantage quickly convince themselves that its ability to describe the

很多人认为比较优势理论对现实世界的

real world is extremely limited, if not nonexistent. Although the results follow logically from the assumptions, the assumptions are easily assailed as unrealistic. For example, the model assumes only two countries producing two goods using just one factor of production. The real world, on the other hand, consists of many countries producing many goods using many factors of production. In the model, each market is assumed to be perfectly competitive when in reality there are many industries in which firms have market power. Labor productivity is assumed to be fixed when in reality it changes over time, perhaps based on past production levels. Full employment is assumed when clearly workers cannot immediately and costlessly move to other industries. Also, all workers are assumed to be identical. This means that when a worker is moved from one industry to another, he or she is immediately as productive as every other worker who was previously employed there. Finally, the model assumes that technology differences are the only differences that exist between the countries.

解释能力是有限的。

With so many unrealistic assumptions, it is difficult for some people to accept the conclusions of the model with any confidence, especially when so many of the results are counterintuitive. Indeed, one of the most difficult aspects of economic analysis is how to interpret the conclusions of models. Models are, by their nature, simplifications of the real world and thus all economic models contain unrealistic assumptions. Therefore, to dismiss the results of economic analysis on the basis of unrealistic assumptions means that one must dismiss all insights contained within the entire economics discipline. Surely, this is neither practical nor realistic. Economic models in general and the Ricardian model in particular do contain insights that most likely carry over to the more complex real world. To move in the direction of realism, it is necessary to understand how comparative advantage functions in a world of many products and many countries. As we will see, the conclusions of comparative advantage hold when more realistic situations are encountered.

2.5.1 Comparative Advantage with More Than Two Commodities

2.5.1 多产品的比较优势

When a large number of goods are produced by two countries, operation of comparative advantage requires that the goods be ranked by the degree of comparative cost. Each country exports the products in which it has the greatest comparative advantage. Conversely, each country imports the products in which it has the greatest comparative disadvantage.

Table 2. 5 and Table 2. 6 show the cost or price of five commodities in the United Kingdom and the United States. To determine which commodities will be exported and imported by the United States and the United Kingdom, we must first express all commodity prices in terms of the same currency and then compare prices in the two nations. For example, if the exchange rate between the dollar and the pound is one pound for two dollars. The dollar prices of the commodities in the U. K. are shown in Table 2.5.

Table 2.5 Commodity Dollar Prices in the United Kingdom

Commodity	A	B	C	D	E
Dollar Price in the U.K.	12	8	6	4	2

Suppose the corresponding commodity prices in the U.S. are shown in Table 2.6 as follows:

Table 2.6 Commodity Prices in the United States

Commodity	A	B	C	D	E
Dollar Price in the U.S.	2	4	6	8	10

At this exchange rate, the dollar price of commodities A, B are lower in the United States than in the United Kingdom; commodity C is equally priced in the two nations; and the dollar prices of commodities D and E are lower in the United Kingdom. As a result, the United States will export commodities A and B to the United Kingdom and import commodities D and E from the United Kingdom. Commodity C will not be traded.

Now assume that the exchange rate between the dollar and the pound is £1= $3, the dollar prices of the commodities in the two countries are shown in Table 2.7.

Table 2.7 Commodity Prices in the United States and United Kingdom

Commodity	A	B	C	D	E
Dollar Price in the U.S.	2	4	6	8	10
Dollar Price in the U.K.	18	12	9	6	3

At this higher exchange rate, the dollar prices of commodities A, B and C are lower in the U.S, while the dollar prices of commodities D and E are lower in the U.K. Thus the U.S. would export commodities A, B and C to the U.K. and import commodities D and E from the U.K.

Once the equilibrium exchange rate is established, we will be able to determine exactly which commodities are exported by the U.S. and which are exported by the U. K. Each nation will then have a comparative advantage in the commodities that it exports at the particular equilibrium exchange rate established.

The cutoff point between what is exported and what is imported also depends on the relative strength of international demand for the various products. The strength of demand and supply will determine the cutoff point between U. S. and U. K. production.

2.5.2 Comparative Advantage with More Than Two Countries

2.5.2 多国的比较优势

When many countries are included in a trading example, the trading country will find it advantageous to enter multilateral trading relationships.

Suppose that, instead of two countries and five commodities, we have two commodities (wheat and cloth) and five nations (A, B, C, D, and E). Table 2.7 ranks these nations from lowest to highest in terms of their internal P_W/P_C values. With trade, the equilibrium P_W/P_C will settle somewhere between 1 and 5. That is $1 < P_W/P_C < 5$.

If the equilibrium $P_W/P_C = 3$ with 3, Nations A and B will export wheat to Nations D and E in exchange for cloth. Nation C will not engage in international trade in this case because its pre-trade P_W/P_C equals the equilibrium P_W/P_C with trade. Given a trade equilibrium $P_W/P_C = 4$, Nations A, B and C will export wheat to Nation E in exchange for cloth and Nation D will not engage in international trade. If the equilibrium $P_W/P_C = 2$ with trade, Nation A will export wheat to all the other nations, except for Nation B, in exchange for cloth.

This discussion can easily be extended to any number of countries. However, generalizing our analysis to many commodities and many nations at the same time becomes cumbersome and is unnecessary. What is important at this point is that the same conclusions reached on the basis of our simple model with only two commodities and two nations still hold. **The Ricardian model shows that if we want to maximize total output in the world, then we should**

(1) fully employ all resources worldwide;

(2) allocate those resources within countries to each country's comparative advantage industries;

(3) allow the countries to trade freely thereafter.

李嘉图模型认为，欲使世界产量最大化，我们必须（1）在世界范围内使用资源；（2）根据比较优势分配资源；（3）允许国家之间进行自由贸易。

In this way, we might raise the well-being of all individuals despite differences in relative productivities. In this description, we do not predict that a result will carry over to the complex real world. Instead, we carry the logic of comparative advantage to the real world and ask how things would have to look to achieve a certain result (maximum output and benefits). In the end, we should not say that the model of comparative advantage tells us anything about what will happen when two countries begin to trade; instead, we should say that the theory tells us some things that can happen.

☞ Questions

☞ 本章习题

1. What are the three things that must be achieved to maximize world output?

2. Suppose that the unit labor requirements for wine and cheese are $a_{LC} = 6$ hrs./lb. and $a_{LW} = 4$ hrs./gal., respectively, and that labor hours applied to cheese and wine production are 60 and 80, respectively. What is total output of cheese and wine?

3. Suppose that the unit labor requirements for wine and cheese are $a_{LC} = 3$ hrs./lb. and $a_{LW} = 2$ hrs./gal., respectively, and that labor hours applied to cheese and wine production are 60 and 80, respectively. What would the total output of wine be if all the labor hours were shifted to produce wine?

4. Suppose that the unit labor requirements for wine and cheese are a_{LC} = 6 hrs./lb. and a_{LW} = 4 hrs./gal., respectively, and that total labor hours available for production are 60. Plot the production possibility frontier.

5. Suppose each country specialized in the wrong good. Depict an equilibrium using the free trade prices in each country to show why national welfare would fall in free trade relative to autarky.

Chapter 3

New Classical Theories of International Trade

第三章

新古典贸易理论

In this chapter, we extend our trade model. First, we explain the basis of comparative advantage. The Heckscher-Ohlin model, which is one of the most important models of international trade, expands upon the Ricardian model largely by introducing a second factor of production. **In its two-by-two-by-two variant, meaning two goods, two factors, and two countries, it represents one of the simplest general equilibrium models that allows for interactions across factor markets, goods markets, and national markets simultaneously.**

在两个国家两种商品两种生产要素模型中，产品市场要素市场以及各国市场同时实现均衡。

These interactions across markets are one of the important economics lessons displayed in the results of this model. With the H-O model, we learn how changes in supply or demand in one market can feed their way through the factor markets and, with trade, the national markets and influence both goods and factor markets at home and abroad. **In other words, all markets are everywhere interconnected.**

所有市场跨国界紧密联系。

Among the important results are that **international trade can improve economic efficiency but that trade will also cause a redistribution of income between different factors of production.** In other words, some will gain from trade, some will lose, but the net effects are still likely to be positive.

国际世界贸易提高经济效率的同时会影响不同生产要素之间的收入分配。

The end of the chapter discusses the specific factor model, which represents a cross between the H-O model and the immobile factor model. The implications for income distribution and trade are highlighted.

3.1 H-O Theory

3.1 H-O 理论

3.1.1 Development of H-O Theory

3.1.1 H-O 理论的发展

The factor proportions model was originally developed by two Swedish economists, Eli Heckscher and his student Bertil Ohlin, in the 1920s. Many elaborations of the model were provided by Paul Samuelson after the 1930s, and thus sometimes the model is referred to as the Heckscher-Ohlin-Samuelson (HOS) model. In the 1950s and 1960s, some noteworthy extensions to the model were made by Jaroslav Vanek, and so occasionally the model is called the Heckscher-Ohlin-Vanek model. Here we will simply call all versions of the model either the Heckscher-Ohlin (H-O) model, or simply the more generic "factor proportions model".

3.1.2 H-O Theory Is More Realistic?

3.1.2 H-O 理论更贴近现实吗？

The H-O model incorporates a number of realistic characteristics of production that are left out of the simple Ricardian model. Recall that in the simple Ricardian model only one factor of production, labor, is needed to produce goods and services. The productivity of labor is assumed to vary across countries, which implies a difference in technology between nations. It was the difference in technology that motivated advantageous international trade in the model.

The standard H-O model begins by expanding the number of factors of production from one to two. The model assumes that labor and capital are used in the production of two final goods. Here, capital refers to the physical machines and equipment that are used in production. Thus machine tools, conveyers, trucks, forklifts, computers, office buildings, office supplies, and much more are considered capital.

两种生产要素（资本和劳动力）的假定符合现实。

The assumption of two productive factors, capital and labor, allows for the introduction of another realistic feature in production: differing factor proportions both across and within industries. When one considers a range of industries in a country, it is easy to convince oneself that the proportion of capital to labor applied in production varies considerably. For example, steel production generally involves large amounts of expensive machines and equipment spread over perhaps hundreds of acres of land, but it also uses relatively few workers. (Note that relative here means relative to other industries.) In the tomato industry, in contrast, harvesting requires hundreds of migrant workers to hand-pick and collect each fruit from the vine. The amount of machinery used in this process is relatively small.

In the H-O model, we define the ratio of the quantity of capital to the quantity of labor used in a production process as the capital-labor ratio. We imagine, and therefore assume, that different industries producing different goods have different capital-labor ratios. It is this ratio (or proportion) of one factor to another that gives the model its generic name: **the factor proportions model.** 要素比例模型

In a model in which each country produces two goods, an assumption must be made as to which industry has the larger capital-labor ratio. Thus if the two goods that a country can produce are steel and clothing and if steel production uses more capital per unit of labor than is used in clothing production, we would say the steel production is **capital-intensive.** relative to clothing production. Also, if steel production is capital intensive, then it implies that clothing production must be **labor-intensive** relative to steel. 资本密集型 劳动密集型

Another realistic characteristic of the world is that countries have different quantities—that is, endowments—of capital and labor available for use in the production process. Thus some countries like the United States are well endowed with physical capital relative to their labor force. In contrast, many less-developed countries have much less physical capital but are well endowed with large labor forces. We use the ratio of the aggregate endowment of capital to the aggregate endowment of labor to define relative factor abundance between countries. Thus if, for example, the United States has a larger ratio of aggregate capital per unit of labor than France's ratio, we would say that the United States is capital-abundant relative to France. By implication, France would have a larger ratio of aggregate labor per unit of capital and thus France would be labor-abundant relative to the United States.

It is worth emphasizing here a fundamental distinction between the H-O model and the Ricardian model. Whereas the Ricardian model assumes that production technologies differ between countries, the H-O model assumes that production technologies are the same. The reason for the identical technology assumption in the H-O model is perhaps not so much because it is believed that technologies are really the same, although a case can be made for that. Instead, the assumption is useful in that it enables us to see precisely how differences in resource endowments are sufficient to cause trade and it shows what impacts will arise entirely due to these differences.

3.1.3 The Assumptions of H-O Theory

3.1.3 H-O 理论的假设

Perfect Competition

完全竞争

Perfect competition in all markets means that the following conditions are assumed to hold.

Many firms produce output in each industry such that each firm is too small for its output decisions to affect the market price. This implies that when choosing output to maximize profit, each firm takes the price as given or exogenous.

Firms choose output to maximize profit. The rule used by perfectly competitive firms is to choose the output level that equalizes the price (P) with the marginal cost (MC). That is, set P = MC.

Output is homogeneous across all firms. This means that goods are identical in all their characteristics such that a consumer would find products from different firms indistinguishable. We could also say that goods from different firms are perfect substitutes for all consumers.

There is free entry and exit of firms in response to profits. Positive profit sends a signal to the rest of the economy and new firms enter the industry. Negative profit (losses) leads existing firms to exit, one by one, out of the industry. As a result, in the long run economic profit is driven to zero in the industry.

Information is perfect. For example, all firms have the necessary information to maximize profit and to identify the positive profit and negative profit industries.

Two Countries 两个国家

The case of two countries is used to simplify the model analysis. Let one country be the United States, the other France. Note that anything related exclusively to France in the model will be marked with an asterisk.

Two Goods 两种商品

Two goods are produced by both countries. We assume a barter economy. This means that there is no money used to make transactions. Instead, for trade to occur, goods must be traded for other goods. Thus we need at least two goods in the model. Let the two produced goods be clothing and steel.

Two Factors 两种要素

Two factors of production, labor and capital, are used to produce clothing and steel. Both labor and capital are homogeneous. Thus there is only one type of labor and one type of capital. The laborers and capital equipment in different industries are exactly the same. We also assume that labor and capital are freely mobile across industries within the country but immobile across countries. Free mobility makes the Heckscher-Ohlin (H-O) model a long-run model.

Factor Constraints 要素存量既定

The total amount of labor and capital used in production is limited to the endowment of the country.

The labor constraint is $L_C + L_S = L$, where L_C and L_S are the quantities of labor used in clothing and steel production, respectively. L represents the labor endowment of the country. Full employment of labor implies the expression would hold with equality.

The capital constraint is $K_C + K_S = K$, where K_C and K_S are the quantities of capital used in clothing and steel production, respectively. K represents the capital endowment of the country. Full employment of capital implies the expression would hold with equality.

Endowments 要素禀赋

The only difference between countries assumed in the model is a difference in endowments of capital and labor.

A country is **capital-abundant** relative to another country if it has more capital endowment per labor endowment than the other country. Thus in this model the United States is capital abundant relative to France if $\frac{K}{L} > \frac{K^*}{L^*}$ where K is the capital endowment, L the labor endowment in the United States, K^* is the capital endowment, and L^* the labor endowment in France.

资本相对丰裕

Note that if the United States is capital-abundant, then France is labor-abundant since the above inequality can be rewritten to get $\frac{L^*}{K^*} > \frac{L}{K^*}$. This means that France has more labor per unit of capital for use in production than the United States.

Demand

需求

Factor owners are the consumers of the goods. The factor owners have a well-defined utility function in terms of the two goods. Consumers maximize utility to allocate income between the two goods.

3.1.4 General Equilibrium of H-O Theory

3.1.4 H-O 理论的一般均衡

The H-O model is a general equilibrium model. The income earned by the factors is used to purchase the two goods. The industries' revenue in turn is used to pay for the factor services. The prices of outputs and factors in equilibrium are those that equalize supply and demand in all markets simultaneously.

The H-O model assumes that the only differences between countries are these variations in the relative endowments of factors of production. It is ultimately shown that (1) trade will occur, (2) trade will be nationally advantageous, and (3) trade will have characterizable effects on prices, wages, and rents when the nations differ in their relative factor endowments and when different industries use factors in different proportions.

Factor Intensity and Factor Abundance

要素密集度和要素丰裕度

The production functions in Table 3.1 and Table 3.2 represent industry production, not firm production. The industry consists of many small firms in light of the assumption of perfect competition.

Production functions are assumed to be identical across countries within an industry. Thus both the United States and France share the same production function $f(L, K)$ for clothing and $g(L, K)$ for steel. This means that the countries share the same technologies. Neither country has a technological advantage over the other. This is different from the Ricardian model, which assumed that technologies were different across countries.

Table 3.1 Production of Clothing

United States	France
$Q_C = f(L_C, K_C)$	$Q_C^* = f(L^* C, K_C^*)$

Where

Q_C = quantity of clothing produced in the United States, measured in racks;

L_C = amount of labor applied to clothing production in the United States, measured in labo hours;

K_C = amount of capital applied to clothing production in the United States, measured in capital hours;

$f()$ = the clothing production function, which transforms labor and capital inputs into clothing output.

* All starred variables are defined in the same way but refer to the production process in France.

Table 3.2 Production of Steel

United States	France
$Q_S = g(L_S, K_S)$	$Q_S^* = g(L_S^*, K_S^*)$

Where

Q_S = quantity of steel produced in the United States, measured in tons;

L_S = ammount of labor applied to steel production in the United States, measured in labor hours;

K_S = amount of capital applied to steel production in the United States, measured in capital hours;

$g()$ = the steel production function, which transforms labor and capital inputs into steel output.

* All starred variables are defined in the same way but refer to the production process in France.

By taking the ratios of the unit factor requirements in each industry, we can define a capital-labor (or labor-capital) ratio. These ratios, one for each industry, represent the proportions in which factors are used in the production process. They are also the basis for the model's name.

First, $\frac{\alpha_{KC}}{\alpha_{LC}}$ is the capital-labor ratio in clothing production. It is the proportion in which capital and labor are used to produce clothing.

Similarly, $\frac{\alpha_{KS}}{\alpha_{LS}}$ is the capital-labor ratio in steel production. It is the proportion in which capital and labor are used to produce steel.

We say that steel production is capital-intensive relative to clothing production if $\frac{\alpha_{KS}}{\alpha_{LS}} > \frac{\alpha_{KC}}{\alpha_{LC}}$.

This means steel production requires more capital per labor hour than is required in clothing production. Notice that if steel is **capital-intensive**, clothing must be labor-intensive.

Clothing production is labor-intensive relative to steel production if $\frac{\alpha_{LC}}{\alpha_{KC}} > \frac{\alpha_{LS}}{\alpha_{KS}}$.

This means clothing production requires more labor per capital hour than steel production.

Factor intensity is a comparison of production processes across industries but within a country. Factor abundance is a comparison of endowments across countries.

Production Possibility Frontier 生产可能性边界

The production possibility frontier can be derived in the case of variable proportions by using the same labor and capital constraints used in the case of fixed proportions, but with one important adjustment. Under variable proportions, the unit factor requirements are functions of the wage-rental ratio (w/r). This implies that the capital-labor ratios (which are the ratios of the unit factor requirements) in each industry are also functions of the wage-rental ratio. If there is a change in the equilibrium (for some reason) such that the wage-rental rate rises, then labor will become relatively more expensive compared to capital. Firms would respond to this change by reducing their demand for labor and raising their demand for capital. In other words, firms will substitute capital for labor and the capital-labor ratio will rise in each industry. This adjustment will allow the firm to maintain minimum production costs and thus the highest profit possible. The labor constraint with full employment can be written as

$$\alpha_{LC}(w/\mathrm{r})Q_C + \alpha_{LC}(w/\mathrm{r})Q_S = L \qquad (3.1)$$

where αLc and αLw are functions of (w/r).

The capital constraint with full employment becomes

$$\alpha_{KC}(w/r)Q_C + \alpha_{KS}(w/r)Q_S = K \tag{3.2}$$

where α_{KC} and α_{KS} are functions of (w/r).

Under variable proportions, the production possibility frontier takes the traditional bowed-out shape, as shown in Figure 3.1. All points on the PPF will maintain full employment of both labor and capital resources. **The slope of a line tangent to the PPF (such as the line through point *A* in Figure 3.1) represents the quantity of steel that must be given up to produce another unit of clothing.** As such, the slope of the PPF is the opportunity cost of producing clothing. Since the slope becomes steeper as more and more clothing is produced (as when moving production from point *A* to point *B*), we say that there is increasing opportunity cost. This means that more steel must be given up to produce one more unit of clothing at point *B* than at point *A* in the figure. In contrast, in the Ricardian model the PPF was a straight line that indicated constant opportunity costs.

生产可能性边界上切线的斜率等于该点上增加一单位某一产品生产的机会成本。

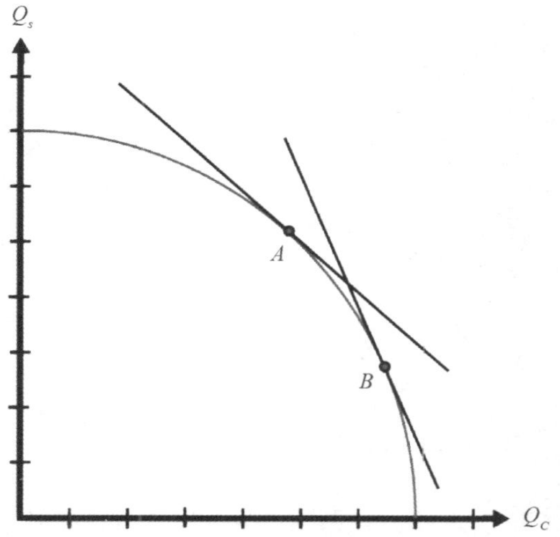

Figure 3.1 Production Possibility Frontier

Equilibrium at Autarky

封闭条件下的均衡

The H-O model assumes that the two countries (United States and France) have identical technologies, meaning they have the same production functions available to produce steel and clothing. The model also assumes that the aggregate preferences are the same across countries. The only difference that exists between the two countries in the model is a difference in resource endowments. We assume that the United States has relatively more capital per worker in the aggregate than does France. This means that **the United States is capital-abundant** compared to France. Similarly, **France, by implication, has more workers per unit of capital in the aggregate and thus is labor-abundant compared to the United States.** We also assume that **steel production is capital-intensive and clothing production is labor-intensive.**

美国相对于法国资本比较丰裕，法国相对于美国劳动力比较丰裕。服装是劳动密集型产品，钢铁是资本密集型产品。

The difference in resource endowments is sufficient to generate different *PPFS* in the two countries such that equilibrium price ratios would differ in autarky. To see why, imagine first that the two countries are identical in every respect. This means they would have the same *PPF* (depicted as the PPF_0 in Figure 3.2, the same set of aggregate indifference curves, and the same autarky equilibrium.

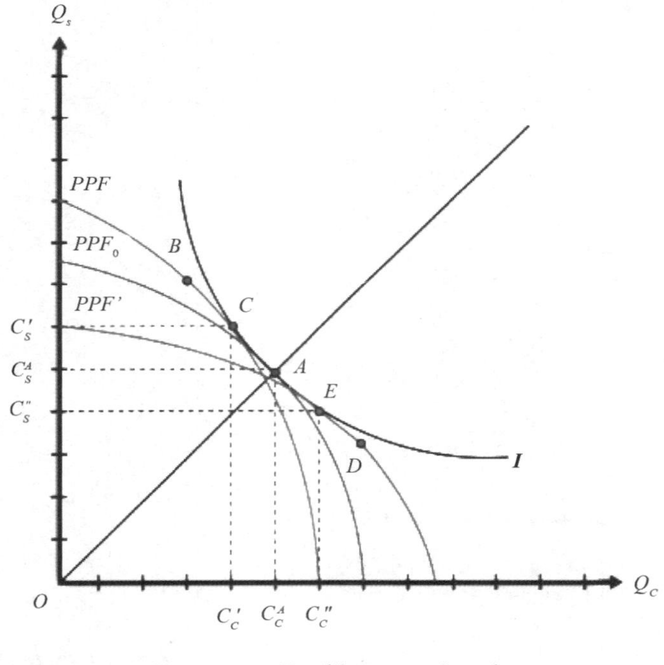

Figure 3.2　Equilibrium at Autarky

Given the assumption about aggregate preferences—that is, $U = C_C C_S$—the indifference curve I, will intersect the countries' *PPF* at point *A*, where the absolute value of the slope of the tangent line (not drawn), P_C/P_S, is equal to the slope of the ray from the origin through point A.

The United States experiences an increase in K and a decrease in L. Both changes will cause an increase in output of the good that uses capital intensively (i.e., steel) and a decrease in output of the other good (clothing). The U.S. PPF would shift from PPF_0 to PPF in Figure 3.2. Thus to find the autarky production point, we simply find the indifference curve that is tangent to the U.S. PPF. This occurs at point C on the new U.S. PPF along the original indifference curve I.

France experiences an increase in L and a decrease in K. These changes will cause an increase in output of the labor-intensive good (i.e., clothing) and a decrease in output of the capital-intensive good (steel). The French PPF would shift from PPF_0 to PPF'. The autarky production point, we simply find the indifference curve that is tangent to the French PPF, occurs at point E on the red French PPF along the original indifference curve I.

All of the above implies that as one country becomes labor abundant and the other capital abundant, it causes a deviation in their autarky price ratios. The country with relatively more labor (France) is able to supply relatively more of the labor-intensive good (clothing), which in turn reduces the price of clothing in autarky relative to the price of steel. The United States, with relatively more capital, can now produce more of the capital-intensive good (steel), which lowers its price in autarky relative to clothing. These two effects together imply that $\left(\frac{P_C}{P_S}\right)_{Aut}^{US} > \left(\frac{P_C}{P_S}\right)_{Aut}^{FR}$.

Any difference in autarky prices between the United States and France is sufficient to induce profit-seeking firms to trade. The higher price of clothing in the United States (in terms of steel) will induce firms in France to export clothing to the United States to take advantage of the higher price. The higher price of steel in France (in terms of clothing) will induce U.S. steel firms to export steel to France. Thus the United States, abundant in capital relative to France, exports steel, the capital-intensive good. France, abundant in labor relative to the United States, exports clothing, the labor-intensive good. This is the H-O theory. Each country exports the good intensive in the country's abundant factor.

Equilibrium with Trade

贸易后的均衡

The United States is assumed to be capital-abundant, which skews its PPF_{US} in the direction of steel production, the capital-intensive good. France is labor-abundant, which skews its PPF_{FR} in the direction of clothing production, the labor-intensive good. In free trade, each country faces the same price ratio, as shown in Figure 3.3.

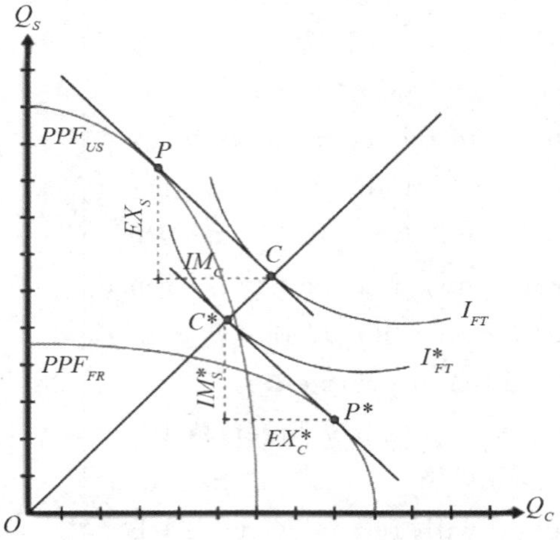

Figure 3.3　Free-Trade Equilibrium

The United States produces at point P. The tangent line at P represents the national income line for the U.S. economy. Consumption in the United States occurs where the aggregate indifference curve IFT, representing preferences, is tangent to the national income line at C. To reach the consumption point, the United States exports EX_S and imports IM_C.

France produces at point P^*. The tangent line at P^* represents the national income line for the French economy. Consumption in France occurs where the aggregate indifference curve I^*_{FT}, representing preferences, is tangent to the national income line at C^*. Note that since the United States and France are assumed to have the same aggregate homothetic preferences and since they face the same price ratio in free trade, consumption for both countries must lie along the same ray from the origin O_C. For France to reach its consumption point, it exports EX^*_C and imports IM^*_S. In order for this to be a free trade equilibrium in a two-country model, U.S. exports of steel must equal French imports of steel ($EX_S = IM_S^*$) and French exports of clothing must equal U.S. imports of clothing ($EX_C^* = IM_C$). In other words, the U.S. trade triangle formed by EX_S, IM_C, and the U.S. national income line must be equivalent to France's trade triangle formed by EX_C^*, IM_S^*, and the French national income line.

National Welfare Effects of Free Trade in the Heckscher-Ohlin Model

H-O模型下的自由贸易中的国家福利状况

The U. S. autarky production and consumption points are determined where the aggregate indifference curve is tangent to the U.S. PPF. This occurs at point A. The United States realizes a level of aggregate utility that corresponds to the indifference curve I_{Aut}.

The U.S. production and consumption points in free trade are P and C, respectively. In free trade, the United States realizes a level of aggregate utility that corresponds to the indifference curve I_{FT}. Since the free trade indifference curve I_{FT} lies to the northeast of the autarky indifference curve I_{Aut}, national welfare rises as the United States moves to free trade. France's autarky production and consumption points are determined by finding the aggregate indifference curve that is tangent to the French PPF. This occurs at point A^*. France realizes a level of aggregate utility that corresponds to the indifference curve I_{Aut}^*.

French production and consumption points in free trade are P^* and C^*, respectively. In free trade, France realizes a level of aggregate utility that corresponds to the indifference curve I_{FT}^*. Since the free trade indifference curve I_{FT}^* lies to the northeast of the autarky indifference curve I_{Aut}^*, national welfare rises as France moves to free trade.

This means that free trade will raise aggregate welfare for both countries relative to autarky. Both countries are better off with free trade.

3.2 The Stolper-Samuelson Theorem

3.2 斯托珀-萨缪尔森定理

3.2.1 Commodity Price and Factor Price

3.2.1 商品价格与要素价格

The Stolper-Samuelson theorem demonstrates how changes in

output prices affect the prices of the factors when positive production and zero economic profit are maintained in each industry. It is useful in analyzing the effects on factor income either when countries move from autarky to free trade or when tariffs or other government regulations are imposed within the context of a H-O model.

Due to the assumption of perfect competition in all markets, if production occurs in an industry, then economic profit is driven to zero. The zero-profit conditions in each industry imply

$$P_S = a_{LS}W + a_{KS}r \quad (3.3)$$

and

$$P_C = a_{LC}W + a_{KC}r \quad (3.4)$$

If the payments to factors for each ton produced equal the price per ton, then profit must be zero in the industry. The same logic is used to justify the zero-profit condition in the clothing industry.

We imagine that firms treat prices exogenously since any one firm is too small to affect the price in its market. Because the factor output ratios are also fixed, wages and rentals remain as the two unknowns. In Figure 3.4, we plot the two zero-profit conditions in wage-rental space.

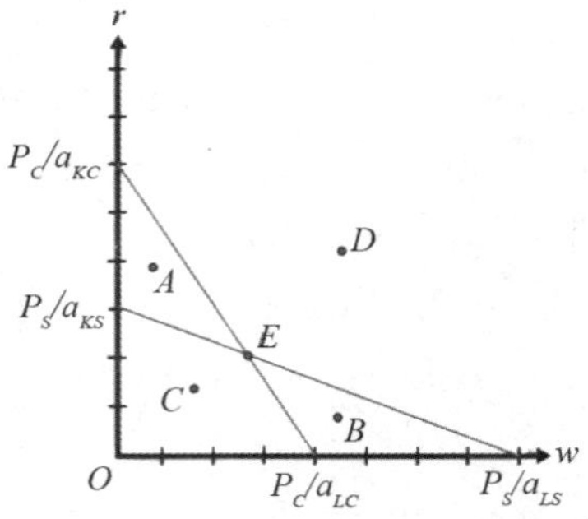

Figure 3.4 Zero Profit Lines in Clothing and Steel

The set of all wage and rental rates that will generate zero profit in the steel industry at the price P_S is given by the flatter blue line. At wage and rental combinations above the line, as at points A and D, the per-unit cost of production would exceed the price and profit would be negative. At wage-rental combinations below the line, as at points B and C, the per-unit cost of production would fall short of the price, and profit would be positive. Notice that the slope of the flatter line is $-\frac{P_S/a_{KS}}{P_S/a_{LS}}=-\frac{a_{LS}}{a_{LS}}$.

Similarly, the set of all wage-rental rate combinations that will generate zero profit in the clothing industry at price P_C is given by the steeper red line. All wage-rental combinations above the line, as at points B and D, generate negative profit, while wage-rental combinations below the line, as at A and C, generate positive profit. The slope of the steeper line is $-\frac{P_C/a_{KC}}{P_C/a_{LC}}=-\frac{a_{LC}}{a_{KC}}$.

The only wage-rental combination that can simultaneously support zero profit in both industries is found at the intersection of the two zero-profit lines—point E. This point represents the equilibrium wage and rental rates that would arise in an H-O model when the price of steel is P_S and the price of clothing is P_C.

3.2.2 The Stolper-Samuelson Theorem

3.2.2 斯托珀-萨缪尔森定理

Now, suppose there is an increase in the price of one of the goods. Say the price of steel, P_S, rises. This could occur if a country moves from autarky to free trade or if a tariff is placed on imports of steel. The price increase will cause an outward parallel shift in the blue zero-profit line for steel, as shown in Figure 3.5. The equilibrium point will shift from E to F, causing an increase in the equilibrium rental rate from r_1 to r_2 and a decrease in the equilibrium wage rate from w_1 to w_2. Only with a higher rental rate and a lower wage can zero profit be maintained in both industries at the new set of prices. Using the slopes of the zero-profit lines, we can show that $\frac{a_{LC}}{a_{KC}}>\frac{a_{LS}}{a_{KS}}$, which means that clothing is labor-intensive and steel is capital-intensive. Thus, when the price of steel rises, the payment to the factor used intensively in steel production (capital) rises, while the payment to the other factor (labor) falls.

If the price of clothing had risen, the zero-profit line for clothing would have shifted right, causing an increase in the equilibrium wage rate and a decrease in the rental rate. Thus an increase in the price of clothing causes an increase in the payment to the factor used intensively in clothing production (labor) and a decrease in the payment to the other factor (capital).

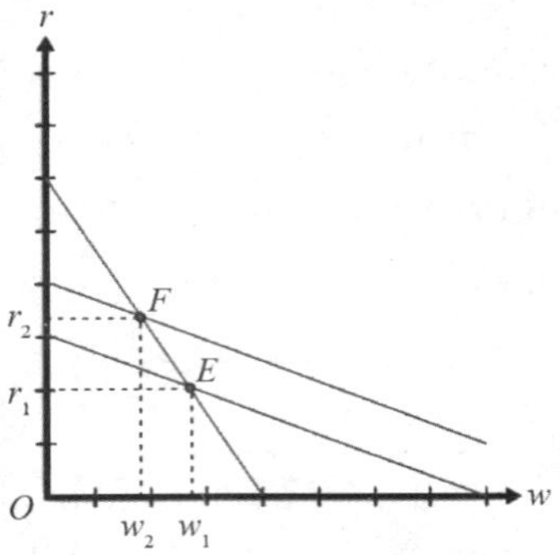

Figure 3.5 Graphical Depiction of Stolper-Samuelson Theorem

This gives us the Stolper-Samuelson theorem: an increase in the price of a good will cause an increase in the price of the factor used intensively in that industry and a decrease in the price of the other factor.

3.2.3 The Distributive Effects of Free Trade in the H-O Model

3.2.3 H-O 理论中贸易的收入分配效应

The term "distributive effects" refers to the distribution of income gains, losses, or both across individuals in the economy. In the Heckscher-Ohlin (H-O) model, there are only two distinct groups of individuals: those who earn their income from labor (workers) and those who earn their income from capital (capitalists). In actuality, many individuals may earn income from both sources. For example, a worker who has deposits in a pension plan that invests in mutual funds has current wage income, but changes in rental rates will affect his or her future capital income. This person's income stream thus depends on both the return to labor and the return to capital.

For the moment, we shall consider the distributive effects on workers who depend solely on labor income and capitalists who depend solely on capital income. Later we shall consider what happens if individuals receive income from both sources.

To measure gains or losses to workers and capitalists, we must evaluate the effects of free trade on their real incomes. Increases in nominal income are not sufficient to know whether an individual is better off since the price of exportable goods will also rise when a country moves to free trade. By assessing the change in real

衡量劳动所有者和资本所有者的得失，我们必须评估自由贸易对他们实际收入的影响。

income, we can determine how the purchasing power of workers and capitalists is affected by the move to free trade.

Suppose there are two countries, the United States and France, producing two goods, clothing and steel, using two factors, capital and labor, according to an H-O model. Suppose steel production is capital-intensive and the United States is capital abundant. This implies that clothing production is labor-intensive and France is labor-abundant.

If these two countries move from autarky to free trade, then, according to the H-O theorem, the United States will export steel to France and France will export clothing to the United States. Also, the price of each country's export good will rise relative to each country's import good. Thus in the United States, P_S/P_C rises, while in France P_C/P_S rises.

如果这两个国家从封闭状态到自由贸易，根据 H-O 理论，美国将出口钢铁到法国，法国将出口服装到美国。此外，每个国家出口商品的价格相对于每个国家的进口商品都会增加。

In the United States, $\left(\frac{Ps}{Pc}\right) \Longrightarrow P_S > P_C$—that is, if the ratio of prices rises, it must mean that the percentage change in P_S is greater than the percentage change in P_C. Then applying the magnification effect for prices implies $r > P_S > P_C > w$.

This in turn implies that

$$\frac{r}{Ps}\uparrow, \frac{r}{Pc}\uparrow \frac{w}{Ps}\downarrow, \frac{w}{Pc}\downarrow$$

which means that the real rent in terms of both steel and clothing rises and the real wage in terms of both steel and clothing falls.

These results imply that both countries will experience a redistribution of income when moving from autarky to free trade. Some individuals will gain from trade, while others will lose. Distinguishing the winners and losers more generally can be done by referring to the fundamental basis for trade in the model. Trade occurs because of differences in endowments between countries. The United States is assumed to be capital-abundant, and when free trade occurs, capitalists in the United States benefit. France is assumed to be labor-abundant, and when free trade occurs, workers in France benefit. Thus, in the H-O model, **a country's relatively abundant factor gains from trade, while a country's relatively scarce factor loses from trade.**

一国的丰富要素将从贸易中获益，稀缺要素则从贸易中受损。

3.3 Factor-price Equalization

3.3 要素价格均等化

The Heckscher-Ohlin model generates several important conclusions for a country that moves from autarky to free trade: **Aggregate national welfare rises**—this is displayed as achieving a higher level of utility on a set of national indifference curves. Income is redistributed among individuals within the economy—this is shown by applying the magnification effect for prices to the price changes that arise in moving from autarky to free trade. **It is shown that the real income of a country's relatively abundant factor rises while the real income of a country's relatively scarce factor falls.**

一国整体福利提高

一国丰富要素的实际报酬提高则稀缺要素的实际报酬将下降。

In autarky, the two countries face different prices for the output goods. The difference in prices alone is sufficient to cause a deviation in wages and rents between countries because it affects the marginal productivity. However, in addition, in a variable proportions model the difference in wages and rents also affects the capital-labor ratios in each industry, which in turn affects the marginal products. **All of this means that for various reasons the wage and rental rates will differ between countries in autarky.**

因为不同原因，封闭条件下两国的工资和地租有所差异。

Once free trade is allowed in outputs, output prices will become equal in the two countries. Since the two countries share the same marginal productivity relationships, it follows that only one set of wage and rental rates can satisfy these relationships for a given set of output prices. **Thus free trade will equalize goods' prices and wage and rental rates.**

自由贸易将使两国的商品价格、工资和地租均等。

Since the two countries face the same wage and rental rates, they will also produce each good using the same capital-labor ratio. However, because the countries continue to have different quantities of factor endowments, they will produce different quantities of the two goods.

In the real world, it is difficult to know whether production technologies are different, similar, or identical. Supporting identical production technology, one could argue that state-of-the-art capital can be moved anywhere in the world. On the other hand, one might counter by saying that just because the equipment is the same doesn't mean the workforces will operate the equipment similarly. There will likely always remain differences in organizational abilities, workforce habits, and motivations.

3.4 The Rybczynski Theorem

3.4 罗伯津斯基定理

3.4.1 The Relationship Between Endowments and Outputs

3.4.1 要素禀赋与产出

The Rybczynski theorem was developed in 1955 by the Polish-born English economist Tadeusz Rybczynski. **It states that at constant relative goods prices, a rise in the endowment of one factor will lead to a more than proportional expansion of the output in the sector which uses that factor intensively, and an absolute decline of the output of the other good.** In the context of the Heckscher-Ohlin model of international trade, open trade between two regions often leads to changes in relative factor supplies between the regions. This can lead to an adjustment in the quantities and types of outputs between the two regions. The Rybczynski theorem explains the outcome from an increase in one of these factors' supply as well as the effect on the output of a good which depends on an opposing factor.

在相对商品价格不变的情况下，一个要素增加，将导致密集使用该要素的产品产量增加，而另一个产品的产量则绝对下降。

3.4.2 The Rybczynski Theorem

3.4.2 罗伯津斯基定理

The theorem is useful in analyzing the effects of capital investment, immigration, and emigration within the context of an H-O model.

The relationship between input and output

$$aL_1 y_1 + aL_2 y_2 = L, \ (i.e., L_1 + L_2 = L) \qquad (3.5)$$

$$aK_1 y_1 + aK_2 y_2 = K. \ (i.e., K_1 + K_2 = K) \qquad (3.6)$$

The above equations show that the sum of the inputs used in the two industries must add up to the nation's input supplies.

$$(L_1, K_1) + (L_2, K_2) = (L, K) \qquad (3.7)$$

An increase in the endowment of labor increases the production of labor-intensive good and decreases the production of the other good (capital-intensive good). The cone of diversification can be used to illustrate Rybczynski theorem in the output space.

An increase in the endowment of one factor results in either an ultra-export or import biased growth.

Figure 3.6 depicts that production occurs initially on the PPF at point *Q*.

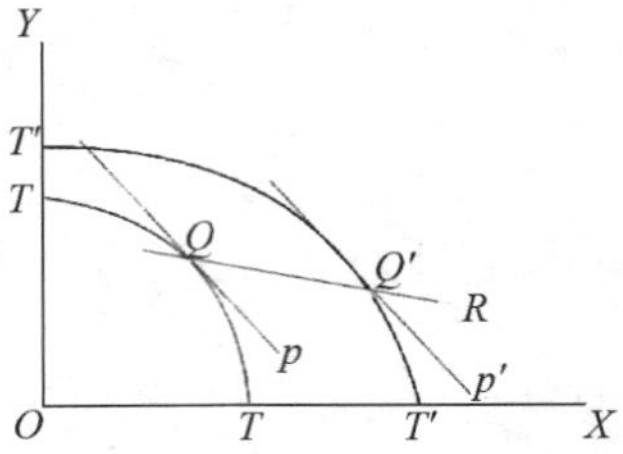

Figure 3.6 Graphical Depiction of Rybczynski Theorem

Next, suppose there is an increase in the labor endowment. This will cause an outward parallel shift in the labor constraint. The PPF and thus production will shift to point Q'. If the endowment of capital rose, the capital constraint would shift out, causing an increase in capital-intensive production and a decrease in labor-intensive production. Recall that since the labor constraint is steeper than the capital constraint, steel is capital intensive and clothing is labor intensive.

This means that, in general, an increase in a country's endowment of a factor will cause an increase in output of the good that uses that factor intensively and a decrease in the output of the other good.

3.4.3 Export-biased Growth

If an increase in a country's endowment of a factor will cause an increase in output of the good, which is the country's exportable goods, it is called export-biased growth.

If the country is small, it does not affect the international price ratio. We then examine the case of a large country, one whose trade can have an impact on the relative international price ratio (that is, an effect on the price the country receives for its exports, the price it pays for its imports, or both).

In a large country, the expansion of exportable goods will reduce the price of the goods in the world market and then worsen the terms of trade of this nation.

一个大国，偏向于出口的增长会降低出口产品在国际市场上的价格并恶化其贸易条件。

Immiserizing Growth

悲惨增长

Immiserizing growth is a theoretical situation first proposed by Jagdish Bhagwati, in 1958, where economic growth could result in a country being worse off than before the growth. If growth is heavily export biased it might lead to a fall in the terms of trade of the exporting country. In rare circumstances this fall in the terms of trade may be so large as to outweigh the gains from growth. If so, this situation would cause a country to be worse off after growth than before. This result is only valid if the growing country is able to influence world prices. Harry G. Johnson had, independently, worked out conditions for this result in 1955.

Three conditions seem crucial for immiserizing growth to occur:

1. The country's growth must be strongly biased toward expanding the country's supply of exports and the increase in export supply must be large enough to have a noticeable impact on world prices.

2. The foreign demand for the country's exports must be price inelastic, so that an expansion in the country's export supply leads drop in the international price of the export product.

3. Before the growth, the country must be heavily engaged in trade, so that the welfare loss from the decline in the terms of trade is great enough to offset the gains from being able to produce more.

It may seem foolish for a nation to undergo an expansion that makes itself worse off. Countries that export a diversified selection of export products do not seem to be at much risk of experiencing immiserizing growth.

3.5 The Leontief Paradox

3.5 里昂惕夫之谜

Does H-O Model Explain Actual Trade Patterns?

H-O 模型能解释实际的贸易模式吗?

Wassily W. Leontief was the first economist to attempt to test the H-O theory empirically.

In 1953, Leontief found that the United States, the most capital-abundant country in the world, exported commodities that were more labor-intensive than capital-intensive, in contradiction with H-O theory. Leontief used this result to infer that the United States should adapt its competitive policy to match its economic realities.

In 1971, Robert Baldwin showed that U.S. imports were 27% more capital-intensive than U.S. exports in the 1962 trade data, using a measure similar to Leontief's.

In 1980, Edward Leamer questioned Leontief's original methodology for comparing factor contents of an equal dollar value of imports and exports (i. e. on real exchange rate grounds). However, he acknowledged that the U.S. paradox still appears in Baldwin's data for 1962 when using a corrected method comparing factor contents of net exports and domestic consumption.

A 1999, survey of the econometric literature by Elhanan Helpman concluded that the paradox persists, but some studies in non-US trade were instead consistent with the H-O theory.

In 2005, Kwok & Yu used an updated methodology to argue for a lower or zero paradox in U.S. trade statistics, though the paradox is still derived in other developed nations.

Leontief's Paradox

里昂惕夫之谜

Leontief's tests failed to confirm H-O theory. So we got the Leontief paradox.

Leontief's paradox in economics is that a country with a higher capital-per worker has a lower capital/labor ratio in exports than in imports.

里昂惕夫之谜表明资本丰富的国家出口劳动密集型产品。

Explanations for the Paradox

里昂惕夫之谜的解释

Economists have tested the H-O theory in several ways. The most fruitful response to the paradox was to introduce their factors of production besides just capital and labor. We should make use of the fact that there are different kinds of labor, different kinds of natural resources, different kinds of capital, and so forth. The post-Leontief studies showed that the United States was also abundant in farmland and highly-skilled labor. And the United States was indeed a net exporter of products that use these factors intensively, as H-O predicts.

Linder states that demand plays a more important role than comparative advantage as a determinant of trade—with the hypothesis that countries which share similar demands will be more likely to trade.

3.6 Specific Factor Model

3.6 特定要素模型

The specific factor (SF) model was originally discussed by Jacob Viner, and it is a variant of the Ricardian model. Hence the model is sometimes referred to as the Ricardo-Viner model. The model was later developed and formalized mathematically by Ronald Jones (1971) and Michael Mussa (1974). Jones referred to it as the two-good, three-factor model. Mussa developed a simple graphical depiction of the equilibrium that can be used to portray some of the model's results. It is this view that is presented in most textbooks.

The model's name refers to its distinguishing feature—that one factor of production is assumed to be "specific" to a particular industry. **A specific factor is one that is stuck in an industry or is immobile between industries in response to changes in market conditions.** A factor may be immobile between industries for a number of reasons. Some factors may be specifically designed (in the case of capital) or specifically trained (in the case of labor) for use in a particular production process. In these cases, it may be impossible, or at least difficult or costly, to move these factors across industries.

特定要素指市场条件发生变化但是不能在部门间自由流动的要素。

The SF model is designed to demonstrate the effects of trade in an economy in which one factor of production is specific to an industry. The most interesting results pertain to the changes in the distribution of income that would arise as a country moves to free trade.

3.6.1 Basic Assumptions

3.6.1 基本假设

The SF model assumes that an economy produces two goods using two factors of production, capital and labor, in a perfectly competitive market. One of the two factors of production, typically capital, is assumed to be specific to aparticular industry—that is, it is completely immobile. The second factor, labor, is assumed to be freely and costlessly mobile between the two industries. Because capital is immobile, one could assume that capital in the two industries is different, or differentiated, and thus is not substitutable in production. Under this interpretation, it makes sense to imagine that there are really three factors of production: labor, specific capital in Industry 1, and specific capital in Industry 2.

These assumptions place the SF model squarely between an immobile factor model and the H-O model. In an immobile factor model, all the factors of production are specific to an industry and cannot be moved. In an H-O model, both factors are assumed to be freely mobile—that is, neither factor is specific to an industry. Since the mobility of factors in response to any economic change is likely to increase over time, **we can interpret the immobile factor model results as short-run effects, the SF model results as medium-run effects, and the H-O model results as long-run effects.**

固定要素模型是短期理论，特定要素模型是中期理论而H-O理论是长期理论。

Production of Good 1 requires the input of labor and capital specific to Industry 1. Production of Good 2 requires labor and capital specific to Industry 2. There is a fixed endowment of sector-specific capital in each industry as well as a fixed endowment of labor. **Full employment of labor is assumed**, which implies that the sum of the labor used in each industry equals the labor endowment. **Full employment of sector-specific capital is also assumed**; however, in this case the sum of the capital used in all the firms within the industry must equal the endowment of sector-specific capital.

充分就业

资本充分使用

The model assumes that firms choose an output level to **maximize profit, taking prices and wages as given.** The equilibrium condition will have firms choosing an output level, and hence a labor usage level, such that the market-determined wage is equal to the value of the marginal product of the last unit of labor. The value of the marginal product is the increment of revenue that a firm will obtain by adding another unit of labor to its production process. It is found as the product of the price of the good in the market and the marginal product of labor. Production is assumed to

利润最大化，价格和工资既定

display diminishing returns because the fixed stock of capital means that each additional worker has less capital to work with in production. This means that each additional unit of labor will add a smaller increment to output, and since the output price is fixed, the value of the marginal product declines as labor usage rises. When all firms behave in this way the allocation of labor between the two industries is uniquely determined.

The production possibility frontier (PPF) will exhibit increasing opportunity costs. This is because expansion of one industry is possible by transferring labor out of the other industry, which must therefore contract. Due to the diminishing returns to labor, each additional unit of labor switched will have a smaller effect on the expanding industry and a larger effect on the contracting industry. This means that the graph of the PPF in the SF model will look similar to the PPF in the variable proportion H-O model. However, in relation to a model in which both factors were freely mobile, the SF model PPF will lie everywhere inside the H-O model PPF. This is because the lack of mobility of one factor inhibits firms from taking full advantage of efficiency improvements that would be possible if both factors can be freely reallocated.

生产可能性边界上的机会成本递增。

3.6.2 Specific Factor Model Results

3.6.2 特定要素模型的推论

The SF model is used to demonstrate the effects of economic changes on labor allocation, output levels, and factor returns. Many types of economic changes can be considered, including a movement to free trade, the implementation of a tariff or quota, growth of the labor or capital endowment, or technological changes. This section will focus on effects that result from a change in prices. In an international trade context, prices might change when a country liberalizes trade or when it puts into place additional barriers to trade.

When the model is placed into an international trade context, differences of some sort between countries are needed to induce trade. The standard approach is to assume that countries differ in the amounts of the specific factors used in each industry relative to the total amount of labor. This would be sufficient to cause the

PPFs in the two countries to differ and could potentially generate trade. Under this assumption, **the SF model is a simple variant of the H-O model.** However, the results of the model are not sensitive to this assumption. Trade may arise due to differences in endowments, differences in technology, differences in demands, or some combination. The results derive as long as there is a price change, for whatever reason.

特定要素理论是H-O理论的变形。

So suppose, in a two-good SF model, that the price of one good rises. If the price change is the result of trade liberalization, then the industry whose price rises is in the export sector. The price increase would set off the following series of adjustments. **First, higher export prices would initially raise profits in the export sector since wages and rents may take time to adjust.** The value of the marginal product in exports would rise above the current wage, and that would induce the firms to hire more workers and expand output. However, to induce the movement of labor, the export firms would have to raise the wage that they pay. Since all labor is alike (the model assumes labor is homogeneous), the import-competing sector would have to raise its wages in step so as not to lose all of its workers. **The higher wages would induce the expansion of output in the export sector (the sector whose price rises) and a reduction in output in the import-competing sector.** The adjustment would continue until the wage rises to a level that equalizes the value of the marginal product in both industries.

出口商品价格的提高会增加出口部门的利润，工资和地租也会随之调整。

高工资会使出口部门的产出增加而与进口相竞争的部门产出下降。

The return to capital in response to the price change would vary across industries. In the import-competing industry, lower revenues and higher wages would combine to reduce the return to capital in that sector. However, in the export sector, greater output and higher prices would combine to raise the return to capital in that sector.

资本报酬会因部门不同而不同。

The real effects of the price change on wages and rents are somewhat more difficult to explain but are decidedly more important. Remember that absolute increases in the wage, or the rental rate on capital, does not guarantee that the recipient of that income is better off, since the price of one of the goods is also rising. Thus the more relevant variables to consider are the real returns to capital (real rents) in each industry and the real return to labor (real wages).

Ronald Jones (1971) derived a magnification effect for prices in the case of an increase in the price of an export good and a decrease in the price of an import good, as when a country moves to free trade, the magnification effect predicts the following impacts:

The real return to capital in the export industry will rise with respect to purchases of both exports and imports.

The real return to capital in the import-competing industry will fall with respect to purchases of both exports and imports.

The real wage to workers in both industries will rise with respect to purchases of the import good and will fall with respect to purchases of the export good.

两个行业的工人的实际工资相对于进口商品的购买量将上升，而相对于出口商品的购买量则会下降。

This result means that when a factor of production, like capital, is immobile between industries, **a movement to free trade will cause a redistribution of income.** Some individuals—owners of capital in the export industry—will benefit from free trade. Other individuals—owners of capital in the import-competing industries—will lose from free trade. Workers, who are freely mobile between industries, may gain or may lose since the real wage in terms of exports rises while the real wage in terms of imports falls. If workers' preferences vary, then those individuals who have a relatively high demand for the export good will suffer a welfare loss, while those individuals who have a relatively strong demand for imports will experience a welfare gain.

贸易开放后收入会重新分配。

Notice that the clear winners and losers in this model are distinguishable by industry. As in the immobile factor model, the factor specific to the export industry benefits, while the factor specific to the import-competing industry loses.

需要注意的是，该模型中的得失与所处的部门相关。在固定要素模型中，出口部门的要素受益，而与进口相竞争的部门要素受损。

☞ Summary

☞ 本章总结

1. Variable proportions imply that the PPF becomes bowed out and continuous, consisting of many output combinations that can be produced with full employment of labor and capital.

2. The H-O theorem states that trade is motivated by price differences and a country will export that good that is intensive in the country's abundant factor. In the standard case, a country will

produce more of its export good and less of its import good but will continue to produce both.

3. A capital-abundant (labor-abundant) country exports the capital-intensive (labor-intensive) good because that product price is initially higher in the labor-abundant (capital-abundant) country.

4. The line tangent to the free trade production point on the PPF represents the national income line and has a slope equal to the terms of trade. The consumption point in free trade equilibrium is found as the tangency point of the highest national indifference curve along the national income line tangent to the production point. The pattern of trade is shown as the exports and imports needed to move from the production point to the consumption point.

5. In the H-O model, when countries implement free trade, output prices, wages, and rents on capital change. If a country is abundant in capital (labor), then a movement to free trade will increase real rents (wages) and decrease real wages (rents). In other words, income is redistributed from workers (capital owners) to capital owners (workers). Because labor and capitalare assumed to be homogeneous factors, workers (capital owners) in both industries realize identical real income effects.

The redistribution of income in the H-O model is based on which factor an individual owns, not on which industry an individual works in (as it is in the immobile factor model).

6. The factor-price equalization theorem says that when the product prices are equalized between countries as they move to free trade in the H-O model, then the prices of the factors (capital and labor) will also be equalized between countries.

7. Factor-price equalization arises largely because of the assumption that the two countries have the same technology in production.

8. The Rybczynski theorem shows there is a positive relationship between changes in a factor endowment and changes in the output of the product that uses that factor intensively. The Rybczynski theorem shows there is a negative relationship between changes in a factor endowment and changes in the output of the product that does not use that factor intensively.

9. The specific factor (SF) model is designed to evaluate the real-world phenomenon that some factors of production are more mobile between industries than others. It does that by assuming that one factor (capital) cannot move between industries, while the other factor (labor) can freely move. In all other respects, the SF model is like the H-O model.

10. The SF model shows that upon opening to free trade, the real rents in the exports industry rise, real rents in the import-competing industry fall, and real wages in both industries may rise or fall.

☞ Questions

☞ 本章习题

1. Consider an H-O economy in which there are two countries (United States and France), two goods (wine and cheese), and two factors (capital and labor). Suppose a decrease in the price of cheese causes a decrease in the wage rate in the U.S. economy. Which factor is used intensively in cheese production in France? Which H-O theorem is used to get this answer? Explain.

2. "The factor-price equalization theorem indicates that with free trade the real wage earned by labor becomes equal to the real rental rate earned by landowners." Is this correct or not? Why?

3. The empirical results that Leontief found in his tests are viewed as a paradox. Why?

Chapter 4

Modern Trade Theory

第四章

现代贸易理论

In our analysis of international trade you have learned why countries have a comparative advantage in producing different types of goods. The United States has a comparative advantage in machines and India in cloth because the two countries are endowed with different factor proportions. Comparative advantage based on the factor-proportions theory is the foundation of our understanding of the gains from specialization and trade. With this foundation we can determine the impact that trade has on factor prices and a country's distribution of income.

However, a large share of international trade is not based on comparative advantage that results from different factor endowments. Countries also trade essentially the same goods with one another. This is known as intra-industry trade.

然而，越来越多的国际贸易行为并非建立在比较优势和要素禀赋的基础上，而是更多地出现在了同一个行业内部。这就是所谓的产业内贸易。

4.1 Inter-industry Trade and Intra-industry Trade

4.1 行业间贸易和行业内贸易

Example of intra-industry trade are not hard to find in the real world. Computers made by IBM are exported to countries around the world at the same time that Americans import computers made by Hitachi, NEC, and other foreign companies. Similarly, while Boeing exports commercial aircraft, some American airline companies have purchased aircrafts made by Airbus, a European manufacturer. Despite these examples, the extent to which intra-industry trade occurs is an open empirical question.

Much of inter-industry trade takes place between nations having vastly different resource endowments (such as developing countries and industrially developed countries) and can be explained by the principle of comparative advantage(H-O model).

Although some inter-industry specialization occurs, this in general has not been the type of specialization that industrialized countries took in the post-World War Ⅱ era. Rather than emphasizing the entire industries, industrial countries have adopted a narrowed form of specialization. They have practiced intra-industry specialization, focusing on the production of particular products or groups of products within a given industry (for example, subcompact autos rather than autos). With intra-industry specialization, the opening up of trade will not generally result in the elimination or wholesale contraction of the entire industries within a nation; instead, the range of products produced and sold by each nation changes.

Advanced industrial countries have increasingly been emphasizingintra-industry trade—two-way trade in a similar commodity.

Example of intra-industry trade are not hard to find in the real world. Computers made by IBM are exported to countries around the world at the same time that Americans import computers made by Hitachi, NEC, and other foreign companies. Similarly, while Boeing exports commercial aircraft, some American airline companies have purchased aircrafts made by Airbus, a European manufacturer. Despite these examples, the extent to which intra-industry trade occurs is an open empirical question.

In the Ricardian and H-O models, a country would not simultaneously export and import the same product. The existence of intra-industry trade appears to be incompatible with the models of comparative advantage previously discussed. Intra-industry trade involves flows of goods with similar factor requirements. Countries that are net exporters of manufactured goods embodying sophisticated technology also purchase such goods from other countries. Much of intra-industry trade is conducted among industrial countries, especially those developed countries with similar resource endowments. The industries where intra-industry trade takes place tend to be oligopolies, with a few large firms covering most of the markets.

What Leads to These Intra-industry Trade?

Intra-industry trade includes trade in homogeneous goods as well as in differentiated products. For homogeneous goods, the reasons for intra-industry trade are easy to grasp. A nation may export and import the same product because of transportation costs.

Another reason for intra-industry trade in homogeneous goods is seasonal factors. The seasons in the Southern Hemisphere are opposite to those in the Northern Hemisphere. Brazil may export seasonal items (such as agricultural products) to the United States at one time of the year and import them from the United States at another time during the same year.

Although some intra-industry trade occurs in homogeneous products, available evidence suggests that most intra-industry occurs in differentiated products. Within manufacturing, the levels of intra-industry trade appear to be especially high in machinery, chemicals, and transportation equipment. A significant share of the output of modern economies consists of differentiated products within the same broad product group. Within the automobile industry, a Ford is not identical to a Honda, aToyota, or a Chevrolet. Two-way trade flows can occur in differentiated products within the same broad product group.

For industrial countries, intra-industry trade in differentiated manufactured goods often occurs when manufacturers in each country produce for the "majority" consumer tastes within their country while ignoring "minority" consumer tastes. This unmet need is fulfilled by imported products. For example, most Japanese consumers prefer Toyotas to General Motors vehicles; yet some Japanese consumers purchase vehicles from General Motors, while Toyotas are exported to the United States. Intra-industry trade expands the range of choices available to consumers in each country.

Intra-industry trade in differentiated products can also be explained by overlapping demand segments in trading nations. We will discuss this theory in the following sections. When U. S. manufacturers look overseas for markets, they often find them in countries having market segments that are similar to the market

什么原因导致产业内贸易发生?

产业内贸易包括同质产品贸易和差异产品贸易。对于同质产品，产业内贸易的原因很容易理解。由于运输成本，一个国家可以进出口同一种产品。

同质产品的产业内贸易的另一个原因是季节性因素。

尽管一些产业内贸易发生在同质产品中，但现有证据表明，大多数产业内贸易发生在差异化产品中。在制造业中，机械、化工和运输设备的行业内贸易水平似乎特别高。

segments in which they sell in the United States, for example, luxury automobiles sold to high-income buyers. Nations with similar income levels can be expected to have similar tastes, and thus sizable overlapping market segments, as envisioned by Linder's theory of overlapping demand; they would be expected to engage heavily in intra-industry trade.

Besides marketing factors, economies of scale associated with differentiated products also explain intra-industry trade. A nation may enjoy a cost advantage over its foreign competitors by specializing in a few varieties and styles of a product (for example, subcompact autos with a standard transmission and optional equipment), while its foreign competitor enjoys a cost advantage by specializing in other variants of the same product (subcompact autos with automatic transmission, air-conditioning, cassette player, and other optional equipment). Such specialization permits longer production runs, economies of scale, and decreasing unit cost. We will also discuss the details about the economies of scale in the following sections.

4.2 Product Life Cycle Theory

4.2 产品生命周期理论

Another explanation for the occurrence of intra-industry trade between countries is **the product life cycle** theory. In this case, changes in technology or a new product design can change the pattern of imports and exports. For many manufactured goods, comparative advantage may shift over time from one country to another. The basic idea behind the product cycle is that developed countries tend to specialize in producing new goods based on technological innovations, whereas the developing countries tend to specialize in the production of already well-established goods.

产品生命周期是指产品从被发明到产品特性随着时间推移为消费者和生产者熟悉而变得标准化的过程。

The theory of the product cycle is that as each good moves through its product cycle, there will be changes in the geographical location of where and how the good is produced. In the first stage of the product life cycle, manufacturers of a "new" product need to be close to a high-income market in order to receive consumer feedbacks. Generally, firms target the initial small-scale production at a

产品生命周期理论认为，每一种商品都会在生产周期当中进行移动。在第一阶段，生产新产品的厂商需要靠近高收入消费者以便获得消费者的反馈。

consumer base with substantial income in their domestic market, such as the United States. At this point, both the product design and the production process are still evolving. The product may need to be improved or the production process may need to be adjusted to determine the most efficient method of production. These design and production enhancements usually require specialized scientific and engineering inputs that are available only in developed countries. During this stage of the product cycle, both consumption and production of a "new" product are likely to occur in a relatively high-income and high-cost-of-production country. Over time, the firm will perfect the product and the production process. At this point, the product's consumption and production increases. Aside from serving the domestic market, the firm will begin to export the new product to other countries where there is additional demand from high-income consumer.

In the second stage of the product cycle, the product matures as it becomes more standardized in terms of size, features, and the production process. If foreign demand is sufficiently large, the firm may find it more profitable to produce the product in other high-income markets rather than export it. In some circumstances, the country where the product was originally developed may begin importing the product from other high-income countries where production costs are lower.

在产品生命周期的第二阶段，随着生产越来越标准化，产品变得成熟起来。

In the third stage of the product cycle, the product and the production process have become so standardize that profit maximization leads firms to produce in the lowest-cost production site. At this point, the standardized production processes can be moved to developing countries where using semi-skilled labor in assembly-type operations keeps production cost low. The innovating country now becomes an importer of the product. In the innovating country, attention moves on to a new product at the early stage of its product cycle. Examples of products that have experienced a typical product cycle include radios, TVs, VCRs, and semiconductor chips. The product may have started as a "new" and somewhat unique product in the first stage. In the last stage, the product has become a standardized product so that factor abundance and low production costs determine the pattern of

在产品生命周期的第三个阶段，商品和生产过程的标准化使得企业在最低的成品水平上生产以获得利润最大化。

production and trade.

How does the product life cycle relate to comparative advantage? The answer is simple. Early in a product's life, the country that invents the product has a comparative advantage. As the country exports the good to the rest of the world, and as the product becomes increasingly more standardized, it is possible for competing firms in other countries to gain market share, if these firms have a cost advantage in large-scale manufacturing. In such instance, comparative advantage shifts from the inventing country to countries where manufacturing cost are lower.

The product life cycle model is a model that has limited applicability. It represents an attempt to explain trade in manufactured products that requires some degree of technical sophistication in their invention, design, and development. In some cases, the theory seems to fit the facts. For instance, color television was invented in the United States, and in the early days of the product, the United States produced and exported this good. Over time, the production of color television has shifted almost entirely to countries such as Japan, and Republic of Korea (ROK).

For other sophisticated products, such as computers and aircrafts, the model seems to do less well. The United States, which took the lead in the development of these goods, still retains a substantial comparative advantage despite that both are now relatively mature products. These examples point to the fundamental weakness of the product life cycle model: its inability to generalize its predictions on the timing of changes in the location of comparative advantage.

4.3 Theory of Overlapping Demands

4.3 重叠需求理论

Another explanation of intra-industry trade focused on the importance of demand characteristics in various countries. The home market effect has implications for another theory of trade, the so-called theory of overlapping demands.

In the early 1960s, the economies Staffan Linder used the concept of overlapping demands to suggest that similarities between countries could be the basis of trade, even though factor prices were the same in both countries.

According to Linder, the factor-endowment theory has considerable explanatory power for trade in primary products (natural resources) and agricultural goods. But it does not explain trade in manufactured goods because the main force influencing such trade is domestic demand condition. Because much of international trade involves manufactured goods, demand conditions play an important role in explaining overall trade patterns.

林德认为，要素禀赋理论只揭示了初级产品和农产品的贸易动力，并未对工业产品的国际贸易动机进行解释，这是因为影响工业产品贸易的主要因素是国内需求状况。由于大部分国际贸易商品属于工业产品，因此需求结构对于解释贸易模式具有非常重要的作用。

Linder states that firms within a country are generally motivated to manufacture goods for which there is a large domestic market. This market determines the set of goods that these firms will have to sell when they begin to export. The foreign markets with greatest export potential will be found in nations with consumer tasters similar to those of domestic consumers. A nation's exports are thus an extension of production for the domestic market.

According to the overlapping demands hypothesis, trade in manufactured goods is likely to be greatest among countries with similar tastes and income levels. Linder argues that firms within a country are primarily oriented toward producing a specific variety of a good for which there is a large home market. As such, a country's tastes and preferences determine the specific variety of the product its firms will produce and could then export to foreign consumers. The most promising foreign markets for these exports will be found in countries with tastes and income levels similar to those of the country in which the products are produced. Each country will produce products that primarily serve its home market, but part of the output will be exported to other countries where there is a receptive market.

根据重叠需求理论，工业产品贸易更有可能发生在偏好和收入水平相似的国家之间。

For example, a U. S. automobile firm will produce an automobile that satisfies the tastes and preferences of mostU. S. consumers. However, there will be a small number of U. S. consumers that do not prefer the domestic version. In Sweden and Germany, automobile producers will produce an automobile that satisfies the tastes and preferences of most Swedish and German consumers, respectively. However, it is likely that in both countries there will be a small number of consumers that do not prefer the Swedish and German versions. In all three countries there are some consumers who are not able to purchase the variety of automobile that they prefer. The hypothesis of overlapping demands indicates that in this case, U.S. producers could produce for their domestic market and export automobiles to Swedish and German consumers who prefer the U.S. automobile. In addition, Swedish and German producers would be able to export automobiles to U.S. consumers who prefer German and Swedish automobiles. These sorts of overlapping demands can lead to intra-industry trade.

Going further, Linder contends that tastes of consumers are conditioned strongly by their income levels. Thus, a country's average or per capita income will yield a particular pattern of tastes. Countries with high per capita incomes will demand high-quality manufactured goods (luxuries), while countries with low per capita incomes will demand lower-quality goods (necessities).

In general, the theory of overlapping demands can explain the large and growing amount of trade in similar but differentiated goods. These conclusions concerning trade patterns between countries are interesting because they are not based on or predicted by the factor-proportions theory. Everything else equal, the theory suggests that trade will be more intense between countries that have similar tastes, preferences, and incomes.

The Linder hypothesis explains which types of nations will most likely trade with each order. Nations with similar per capita incomes will have overlapping demand structures and will likely consume similar type of manufactured goods. Wealthy (industrial) nations will be more likely to trade with other wealthy nations, and poor (developing) nations will be more likely to trade with other poor nations.

Linder does not rule out all trade in manufactured goods between wealthy and poor nations. Because of unequal income distribution within nations, there will always be some overlapping of demand structure; some people in poor nations are wealthy, and some people in wealthy nations are poor. However, the potential for trade in manufactured goods is small when the extent of demand overlap is small.

Linder's theory is in rough accord with the facts. A high proportion of international trade in manufactured goods takes place among the relatively high-income (industrial) nations: Japan, Canada, the United States, and the European nations. Moreover, much of this trade involves the exchange of similar products: Each nation exports products that are much like the products it imports. However, Linder's theory is not borne out by developing country trade. The bulk of lower-income, developing countries tend to have more trade with high-income countries than with other lower-income countries.

4.4 Economies of Scale

4.4 规模报酬

Although comparative advantage theory has great appeal, it has little ability to explain why regions with similar productivity levels trade to the extent they do—why Europe and the United States, for example, trade in such great volume. Nor does it shed light on intra-industry trade; the fact that Germany and Japan will trade automobiles with each other.

In response to these weakness, economists developed a new theory of trade in the 1980s. This "new trade theory" is founded on the notion of **increasing-returns to scale**, also known as economies of scale. The increasing-returns explanation for trade dose not attempt to replace the comparative advantage explanation; it just supplements it.

规模报酬递增，是指投入的同比例增加而引起更大比例的产出提高的现象。

According to increasing-returns to scale trade theory, nations with similar factor endowments, and thus negligible comparative-advantage differences, may nonetheless find it beneficial to trade because they can take advantage of massive economies of scale, a phenomenon prevalent in a number of industries. In the automobile and pharmaceutical industries, for example, the first unit is very expensive to produce, but each subsequent unit costs much less than the one before because the large setup costs can be spread across all units. Companies such as Toyota and Honda reduce costs by specializing in machinery and labor and obtaining quantity

根据规模报酬递增理论，具有相似的要素禀赋，且比较优势差异不大的国家仍然可以通过庞大的经济规模的优势从国际贸易中有所获利。

discounts in the purchase of inputs.

Increasing-returns to scale trade theory asserts that a nation can develop an industry that has economies of scale, produce that good in great quantity at low average costs, and then trade those low-cost goods to other nations. By doing the same for other increasing-returns goods, all trading partners can take advantage of economies of scale through specialization and exchange.

Economies of scale thus provide additional cost incentive for specialization in production. Instead of manufacturing only a few units of each and every product that domestic consumer desire to purchase, a country specializes in the manufacture of large amounts of a limited number of goods and trades for the remaining goods. Specialization in a few products allows a manufacturer to benefit from longer production runs, which lead to decreasing average costs.

A key aspect of increasing-returns to scale trade theory is the home market effect: countries will specialize in products for which there is large domestic demand. Why? By locating close to its largest domestic demand, an increasing-scale industry can minimize the cost of shipping its products to its customers while still taking advantage of economies of scale. That is, auto companies will locate in Germany rather than France if it's clear that Germany are likely to buy more cars. That way the company can produce low-cost cars and not have to pay much to ship them to its largest market.

But the home market effect also has a disturbing implication. If increasing-scale industries tend to locate near their largest markets, what happens to small market areas? Other things equal, they're likely to become deindustrialized as factories and industries move to take advantage of scale economies and low transportation costs. Thus, trade could lead to small countries and rural areas becoming peripheral to the economic core, the backwater suppliers of commodities. As Canadian critics phrased it, "With free trade, Canadians would become hewers of wood and drawers of water." However, other things are not strictly equal: comparative-advantage effects exist alongside the influence of increasing returns, so the eventual result of open trade is not a foregone conclusion.

4.5 Reciprocal Dumping Model

4.5 互相倾销模型

The analysis of dumping suggest that price discrimination can actually give rise to international trade. Suppose, there are two monopolies, each producing the same good, one at Home and one in Foreign. To simplify the analysis, assume that these two firms have the same marginal cost. Suppose also that there are some costs of transportation between the two markets, so that if the firms charge the same price there will be no trade. In the absence of trade, each firm's monopoly would be uncontested.

If we introduce the possibility of dumping, however, trade may emerge. Each firm will limit the quantity it sells in its home market, recognizing that if it tries to sell more it will drive down the price on its existing domestic sales. If a firm can sell a little bit in the other market, however, it will add to its profit even if the price is lower than in the domestic market, because the negative effect on the price of existing sales will fall on the other firm, not on itself. So each firm has an incentive to "raid" the other market, selling a few units at a price that (net of transportation costs) is lower than the home market price but still above marginal cost.

如果我们引入倾销的可能性，贸易就可能出现。每家公司都会限制其在国内市场的销售数量，因为他们意识到，如果试图销售更多的产品，就会压低现有国内销售的价格。然而，如果一家公司能在另一个市场销售一点，即使价格低于国内市场，其利润也会增加，因为对现有销售价格的负面影响将落在另一家公司身上，而不是自己身上。因此，每家公司都有动机"突袭"另一个市场，以低于本国市场价格（扣除运输成本）但仍高于边际成本的价格出售一些产品。

If both firms do this, however, the result will be the emergence of trade even though there was (by assumption) no initial difference in the price of the good in the two markets, and even though there are some transportation costs. Even more peculiarly, there will be two-way trade in the same product. For example, a cement plant in country A might be shipping cement to country B while a cement plant in B is doing the reverse. The situation in which dumping leads to two-way trade in the same product is known as reciprocal dumping. This may seem like a strange case, and it is admittedly rare in international trade for exactly identical goods to be shipped in both directions at once. However, the reciprocal dumping effect probably tends to increase the volume of trade in goods that are not quite identical.

Is such peculiar and seemingly pointless trade socially desirable? The answer is ambiguous. It is obviously wasteful to ship the same good, or close substitutes, back and forth when transportation is costly. However, notice that the emergence of reciprocal dumping in our story eliminates what were initially pure monopolies, leading to some competition. The increased competition represents a benefit that may offset the waste of resources in transportation. The net effect of such peculiar trade on a nation's economic welfare is therefore uncertain.

☞ Key Terms

☞ 关键术语

intra-industry trade, homogeneous, product life cycle theory, theory of overlapping demands, reciprocal dumping model

产业内贸易、同质的、产品生命周期理论、需求重叠理论、相互倾销理论

☞ Questions

☞ 本章问题

1. Distinguish between inter-industry and intra-industry trade.

2. What are the major determinants of intra-industry trade in homogeneous products?

3. What is meant by economies of scale? Explain the difference between internal and external economies of scale.

4. How can economies of scale be a basis for trade?

5. State the product cycle theory of trade and identify the various stages of production.

6. What goods might be examples of products that are currently going through or have gone through the various stages of the product cycle?

7. Explain how overlapping demands between countries could lead to trade.

8. What would Linder's theory suggest about the future prospects of developing countries in exporting goods to developed countries?

Chapter 5

International Factor Movements Theory

Up to this point we have been concerned entirely with international trade. That is, we have focused on the causes and effects of international exchanges of goods and services. Movement of goods and services is not, however, the only form of international integration. This chapter is concerned with another form of integration, international movements of factors of production, or factor movements. Factor movements include labor migration, the transfer of capital via international borrowing and lending, and the subtle international linkages involved in the formation of multinational corporations.

The principles of international factor movements do not differ in their essential from those underlying international trade in goods. Both international borrowing and lending and international labor migration can be thought of as analogous in their causes and effects to the movement of goods.

Although there is a fundamental economic similarity between trade and factor movement, however, there are major differences in the political context. A labor-abundant country may under some circumstances import capital-intensive goods; under other circumstance it may acquire capital by borrowing abroad. A capital-abundant country may import labor-intensive goods or begin employing migrant workers. A country that is too small to support firms of efficient size may import goods from where large firms have an advantage or allow those goods to be produced locally by subsidiaries of foreign firms. In each case the alternative strategies may be similar in their purely economic consequences but radically different in their political acceptability.

Overall, international factor movement tends to raise even more political difficulties than international trade. Thus, factor

第五章

国际要素流动理论

之前我们将视角关注于国际贸易。也就是说，我们关注了商品和服务国际交换的原因及效果。商品和服务的流动已经不再是国际资源整合的唯一形式。本章将考虑另一种整合形式：要素的国际流动。要素流动包括劳动移民、资本移动或国际借贷，以及以跨国公司为形态的国际联系。

movements are subject to more restrictions than trade in goods. Immigration restrictions are nearly universal. Until the 1980s several European countries, such as France, maintained controls on capital movements even though they had virtually free trade in goods with their neighbors. Investment by foreign-based multinational corporations is regarded with suspicion and tightly regulated throughout the world. The result is that factor movements are probably less important in practice than trade in goods, which is why we took an analysis of trade in the absence of factor movements as our starting point. Nonetheless, factor movements are very important, and it is valuable to spend a chapter on their analysis.

5.1 International Movement of Labor

5.1 劳动力的国际流动

We begin our discussion with an analysis of the effects of labor mobility. In the modern world, restriction on the flow of labor are legion—just about every country imposes restrictions on immigration. Thus, labor mobility is less prevalent in practice than capital mobility. It remains important, however, that it is also simple in some ways to analyze than capital movement, for reasons that will become apparent later in the chapter.

5.1.1 Motives for International Labor Movement

5.1.1 国际劳动力流动的动机

Up to this point, we have modeled economic growth as originating from within the growing country. Countries can also grow because they receive factor inputs from other countries. Consider the case of the United States. It is estimated that about 70 million people migrated to the United States from foreign countries between 1820 and 2004. This influx of new population helped expand the labor force of the United States just at the time when other factors, such as land (through purchase, conquest, and expropriation) and capital (through domestic-and foreign-sourced investment), were also growing. Thus, immigration played a large part in the emergence of the United States as a leading world economy by the end of the 19th-century.

The United States is not the only country to have experienced large inflows of migrants. For instance, between 1960 and 1980, Canada, Australia, and New Zealand took in 5.7 million immigrants, roughly one-third of the permanent world immigration during this period. Moreover, because these countries have much smaller populations, the proportion of immigrants to total population is much higher there than it is in the United States.

In addition to moves that migrants view as essentially permanent, a considerable amount of temporary immigration occurs today. These temporary moves are often the result of specific policies instituted by governments in host countries. Under these programs, workers from foreign (source) countries are invited to relocate in host countries for short time spans to work in various industries. Beginning in the 1960s and extending through at least 1975, rich Western European countries invited guest workers (or **gastarbeiter**) from neighboring poorer countries, such as Italy, Spain, Portugal, Turkey, Greece, and Yugoslavia. All in all, about 6.3 million workers were invited to move to Western Europe, and they composed a substantial proportion of the work forces there. The number of workers participating in this program tended to reduce by substantial proportions the work forces in the source countries. Portugal, for example, exported more than 10 percent of its labor force. In addition to the guest worker programs in Western Europe, the OPEC countries of the Middle East have imported a large number of workers from countries such as Egypt, Jordan, Pakistan, India, and even ROK. And, for many years, migrant workers from Mexico have crossed the border to work in the United States during agriculture harvests.

外来工人/客籍工人，指被允许暂时在另一个国家的特定经济部门工作的外国工人。

Migration occurs for many reasons and follows a variety of paths. Most international relocations happen because the migrant is seeking at least one of three things: better economic conditions, refuge from political tyranny or devastation, or reunion with other family members. Much of the migrant flow, such as in the guest worker programs, is from poor countries to rich countries. These flows are largely motivated by the opportunities workers have to earn higher wages and to enjoy the benefits of greater job security. Poor country to poor country and rich country to rich country flows are also relatively common. Rich country to poor country flows are not.

Migrants possess different skills. Much of the rich country to rich country migration that occurs involves skilled labor. A substantial amount of migration from poor countries to rich countries also involves skilled labor. The process whereby skilled workers leave their homeland and relocate abroad is known as brain drain. The notion of a brain drain became an important focus of study in the 1960s. Back then, the concern was that Europe's most skilled workers, including its best scientists, doctors, and engineers, were abandoning Europe for the United States, Canada, and elsewhere. Today, that flow has diminished and in some instances may have reversed its direction. More recently, concern has grown that rich industrialized countries may be draining skilled labor from poor developing countries, where, at the margin, the contribution of skilled labor to economic development may be quite high.

Because of relatively higher wage levels and general standards of living, poor country to rich country movements of low-skilled workers are a common phenomenon. This pattern of migration describes well the flows of workers from Southern and Eastern Europe to the United States in the early part of the 12th-century and the migration of workers from Mexico and Southeast Asia to the United States today. The outflow of unskilled workers has sometimes been described as a brawn drain.

Three points should be noted about this redistribution of the world's labor force.

1. It leads to a convergence of real wage rates. Real wages rise at home, fall in foreign.

2. It increases the world's output as a whole.

3. Despite this gain, some people are hurt by the change. Those who would originally have worked at home receive higher real wages, but those who would originally have worked in foreign receive lower real wages. Landowners in Foreign benefit from the larger labor supply, but landowners in home are made worse off. As in the case of the gains from international trade, then, international labor mobility, while allowing everyone to be better off in principle, leaves some groups worse off in practice.

对于世界劳动力的重新分配，有三个观点值得注意。

1. 世界劳动力的重新分配导致了均等化的实际工资率。国内实际工资上涨，国外实际工资下降。

2. 世界劳动力的重新分配增加了世界的整体产出。

3. 尽管世界整体产出增加，但仍有些人会因这一变化而有所损失。

5.1.2 Other Welfare Effects of International Labor Movement

We have just seen that a very simple model tells us quite a lot about both why international factor movements occur and what effect they have. Labor mobility in our simple model is driven by international differences in resources; also like trade, it is beneficial in the sense that it increases world production, yet is associated with strong income distribution effects that make those gains problematic.

Let us consider briefly how the analysis is modified when we add some of the complications we have assumed away.

We need to remove the assumption that the two countries produce only one good. Suppose, then, that the countries produce two goods, one more labor intensive than the other. Home can in a sense export labor and import land by exporting the labor-intensive good and importing the land-intensive good. It is possible in principle for such trade to lead to a complete equalization of factor prices without any need for factor mobility. If this happened, it would of course remove any incentive for labor to move from Home to Foreign.

In practice, while trade is indeed a substitute for international factor movement, it is not a perfect substitute. Complete factor price equalization is not observed in the real world because countries are sometimes too different in their resources to remain unspecialized; there are barriers to trade, both natural and artificial; and there are differences in technology as well as resources between countries.

We might wonder on the other side whether factor movements remove the incentive for international trade. Again the answer is that while in a simple model movement of factors of production can make international trade in goods unnecessary, in practice there are substantial barriers to free movement of labor, capital, and other potential mobile resources. And some resources cannot be brought together—Canadian forests and Caribbean sunshine cannot migrate.

Extending the simple model of factor mobility, then, does not change its fundamental message. The main point is that trade in factors is, in purely economic terms, very much like trade in

5.1.2 国际劳动力流动的其他福利影响

我们已经通过一个简单的模型了解到为什么国际要素流动会发生，以及什么因素影响了国际要素流动。

我们需要去掉诸如只有两个国家只生产一种产品这样的假设，转而假定，众多国家生产两种商品，其中一种比另一种更加劳动力密集。

goods; it occurs for much the same reasons and produces similar results.

5.2 International Movement of Capital

5.2 资本的国际流动

劳动力不是唯一的可以跨越国界进行流动的要素，资本——不仅是金融形态的也包括物理形态的——也可以完成跨国流动。

Labor is not the only factor that flows across international boundaries. Capital, both in financial and in physical form, does as well. In fact, international flows of capital have become an everyday fact of life in the international economy and, because of their enormous size, are probably much more important than labor flows in influencing rates of economic growth and the location of economic activity.

5.2.1 Motives for International Capital Movement

5.2.1 资本国际流动的动机

Again, we consider the case of the United States. Throughout the 19th-century, it was a capital-importing country. Other countries—most notably the United Kingdom—lent a substantial proportion of the financial capital that enabled the construction of railroads, factories, and communication systems, thereby helping to propel the U. S. economy to the status of an industrial giant. Imports of European-made capital goods (in exchange for U. S. agriculture products) also helped promote the development of the U.S. industrial base.

Even though, of late, the United States has been importing more capital than it has been exporting, the United States still supplies substantial amounts of capital to the rest of international transfer of capital known as direct foreign investment. This happens when a domestic (e.g. U.S.) firm acquires ownership of or control over the operations of a foreign subsidiary firm. According to U.S. definitions, a (parent) firm is said to directly invest abroad if it has a direct or indirect ownership interest of 10 percent or more in a foreign business enterprise (foreign affiliate corporation). American firms have engaged indirect foreign investment by setting up (or buying previously existing) production and marketing facilities in foreign countries, or by becoming minority owners of competing foreign corporations. Firms that own and operate capital in one or more foreign countries are known as multinational corporations(MNCs).

Virtually all of America's most well-known corporations, such as Ford, General Motors, IBM, McDonald's and Coca-Cola, are MNCs. Many lesser-known American companies are **MNCs** as well. In 2003, worldwide sales of U. S. MNCs totaled almost $10 trillion, and worldwide employment of U.S. MNCs stood at 30.1 million people. The American (parent corporation) shares of these totals were $6.6 trillion in sales and 21.7 million employees, respectively. Table 5.1 provides detail on an industry-by-industry breakdown of MNC activity, as measured by employment, both in the United States and in foreign locations. Clearly, the manufacturing sectors account for the largest share of MNC employment both in the United States and overseas. Within this category, a considerable fraction of overseas employment is in the transportation equipment sector, largely employees of U. S. automakers in foreign assembly plants.

跨国公司 (multinational corporations, MNCs),指在两个或两个以上国家设立生产或营销机构开展经营的企业。

Table 5.1 Employment of Non-bank U.S. MNCs in 2003

Industries	Worldwide	Parent	Affiliate	Affiliates Employment a Percentage Total
All Industries	30,065.2	21,701.2	8,363.0	27.8
Mining	303.7	144.2	159.5	52.5
Utilities	417.3	347.2	70.1	16.8
Manufacturing	12,415.1	8,152.9	4,262.2	34.3
Wholesale Trade	1,573.6	781.4	792.2	50.3
Information	2,198.5	1,854.6	343.9	15.6
Finance (except banks) and Insurance	1,680.3	1,383.7	296.6	17.7
Professional Services	1383.0	946.4	436.6	31.6
Other	10,093.7	8,090.8	2,002.9	19.8

Source:史蒂文·赫斯特德,迈克克·梅尔文.国际经济学[M].7版.姜文学,译注.大连:东北财经大学出版社,2008:286.

Table 5.2 provides some information on the location of foreign affiliate of U.S. MNCs, again measured by levels of employment.

According to this table, almost 70 percent of foreign U.S. MNCs employment is in developed countries, with the greatest share in Western Europe. The greatest amount of U.S. MNCs employment in developing countries is found in Latin America.

Table 5.2 Employment of U.S. MNC Foreign Affiliates, by Area, 2003

Number of Employees(thousand)		Number of Employees(thousand)	
All Countries	8,363.9	Developing Countries	2,914.8
Developed countries	5,449.1	Latin America	1,592.0
Canada	1,067.2	Middle East	52.4
France	556.8	Asia and Pacific	1,179.6
Germany	584.3	Africa	90.8
United Kingdom	1,171.3	Mexico	827.1
Japan	238.7	India	103.7
Australia, New Zealand, and South Africa	379.3	ROK	78.1

Source：史蒂文・赫斯特德，迈克尔・梅尔文.国际经济学[M]. 7 版. 姜文学，译注.大连：东北财经大学出版社，2008：287.

Foreign MNCs exist, and mostly operate in the United States. The U.S. companies that are affiliates of foreign MNCs sold \$2.3 trillion in goods and services in 2000 and employed more than 6.4 million people. European-based corporations accounted for the greatest share of U.S. affiliate employment (66 percent). United Kingdom and Japanese-based firms were the largest employers of workers in the United States, with 17 percent and 14 percent, respectively. Canadian firms accounted for almost 11 percent.

Why some firms choose to become MNCs is an interesting and unresolved question in economics. Clearly, firms that operate in foreign countries are at a disadvantage relative to their locally based foreign competitors. That is, they face additional costs, including the costs of coordinating activities over long distances, that their competitors do not incur. Economic theory suggests, then, that there must be special advantages to being multinational, or else these firms would cease such operations. What sort of special advantages might there be? First, MNCs might have access to special technology. Control over this technology would enable the

MNC to compete successfully with local firms. A second possibility is that there may be increasing returns to scale that accrue to a firm that operates plants in many locations.

As we noted in our discussion of NAFTA, some have argued that trade liberalization between rich and poor countries will induce firms in high-wage countries to relocate their manufacturing operations to low-wage countries. In the process, employment would fall in high-wage countries and production would be replaced by imports from low-wage countries. This practice is known as outsourcing. The numbers in Tables 5.1 and 5.2 suggest that, to date, U.S. MNCs have not made widespread use of this practice.

5.2.2 Direct Foreign Investment

5.2.2 跨国直接投资

In the last section we focused on international borrowing and lending. This is a relatively simple transaction, in that the borrowing makes no demands on the lender other than that of repayment. An important part of international capital movement, however, takes a different form, that of **direct foreign investment**. By direct foreign investment we mean international capital flows in which a firm in one country creates or expands a subsidiary in another. The distinctive feature of direct foreign investment is that it involves not only a transfer of resources but also the acquisition of control. That is, the subsidiary does not simply have a financial obligation to the parent company; it is part of the same organizational structure.

跨国直接投资，指在投资人以外的国家所经营的企业拥有持续利益的一种投资，其目的在于获得对该企业经营管理的发言权。

Multinational firms are often a vehicle for international borrowing and lending. Parent companies often provide their foreign subsidiary with capital, in the expectation of eventual repayment. To the extent that multinational firms provide financial to their foreign subsidiaries, direct foreign investment is an alternative way of accomplishing the same things as international lending. This still leaves open the question, however, of why direct investment rather than some other way of transferring funds is chosen. In any case, the existence of multinational firms does not necessarily reflect a net capital flow from one country to another. Multinationals sometimes raise money for the expansion of their subsidiaries in the country where the subsidiary operates rather than in their home country. Furthermore, there is a good deal of two-way foreign direct investment among industrial countries, U.S. firms expanding their European subsidiaries at the same time as European firms expand their U.S. subsidiaries.

The point is that while multinational firms sometimes act as a vehicle for international capital flows, it is probably by a mistake to view direct foreign investment as primarily an alternative way for countries to borrow and lend. Instead, the main point of direct foreign investment is to allow the formation of multinational organizations. That is, the extension of control is the essential purpose.

But why do firms seek to extend control? Economists do not have as fully developed a theory of multinational enterprise as they do of many other issues in international economics. There is some theory on the subject, however, which we now review.

5.2.3 The Theory of Multinational Enterprise

5.2.3 跨国公司理论

The basic necessary elements of a theory of multinational firms can best be seen by looking at an example. Consider the European operations of American auto manufacturers. Ford and General Motors, for example, sell many cars in Europe, but nearly all those cars are manufactured in plants in Germany, Britain, and Spain. This arrangement is familiar, but we should realize that there are two obvious alternatives. On one side, instead of producing in Europe, the U.S. firms could produce in the United States and export to the European market. On the other side, the whole market could be served by European producers such as Volkswagen and Renault. Why, then, do we see this particular arrangement, in which the same firms produce in different countries?

The modern theory of multinational enterprise starts by distinguishing between the two questions of which this larger question is composed. First, why is a good produced in two (or more) different countries rather than one? This is known as the question of **location**. Second, why is production in different locations done by the same firm rather than by separate firms? This is known, for reason that will become apparent in a moment, as

区位

the question of **internalization**. We need a theory of location to explain why Europe does not import its automobiles from the United States; we need a theory of internalization to explain why Europe's auto industry is not independently controlled. 内部化

The theory of location is not a difficult one in principle. The location of production is often determined by resources. Aluminum mining must be located where the bauxite is, aluminum smelting near cheap electricity. Minicomputer manufacturers locate their skill-intensive design facilities in Massachusetts or northern California and their labor-intensive assembly plants in Ireland or Singapore. Alternatively, transport costs and other barriers to trade may determine location. American firms produce locally for the Europe market partly to reduce transport costs; since the models that sell well in Europe are often quite different from those that sell well in the United States, it makes sense to have separate production facilities and to put them on different continents. As these examples reveal, the factors that determine a multinational corporation's decision about where to produce are probably not much different from those that determine the pattern of trade in general.

The theory of internalization is another matter. Why not have independent auto companies in Europe? We may note first that there are always important transactions between a multinational's operations in different countries. The output of one subsidiary is often an input into the production of another; or technology developed in one country may be used in others; or management may usefully coordinate the activities of plants in several countries. These transactions are what tie the multinational firm together, and the firm presumably exists to facilitate these transactions. But international transactions need not be carried out inside a firm. Components can be sold in an open market, and technology can be licensed to other firms. Multinationals exist because it turns out to be more profitable to carry out these transactions within a firm rather than between firms. This is why the motive for multinationals is referred to as "internalization".

We have defined a concept, but we have not yet explained what gives rise to internalization. Why are some transactions more profitable conducted within a firm rather than between firms? There are a variety of theories, none as well-grounded either in theory or in evidence as our theories of location. We may note two influential views, however, about why activities in different countries may usefully be integrated in a single firm.

The first view stresses the advantages of internalization for technology transfer. Technology, broadly defined as any kind of economically useful knowledge, can sometimes be sold or licensed. There are important difficulties in doing this, however. Often the technology involved in, say, running a factor has never been written down; it is embodied in the knowledge of a group of individuals and cannot be packaged and sold. Also, it is difficult for a prospective buyer to know how much the knowledge is worth—if the buyer knew as much as the seller, there would be no need to buy. Finally, property rights in knowledge are often hard to establish. **If a European firm licenses technology to a U.S. firm, other U. S. firms may legally imitate that technology. All these problems may be reduced if a firm, instead of selling technology, sets about capturing the returns from the technology in other countries by setting up foreign subsidiaries.**

国际化的第一个优势在于技术的传递。

如果欧洲的公司允许美国的公司使用技术，其他美国公司则可以模仿该项技术。如果欧洲公司设立海外分支机构而非出售技术，它就可以从其他国家那里获得该项技术的收益。

The second view stresses the advantage of internalization for vertical integration. If one firm (the "upstream" firm) produces a good that is used as an input for another firm (the "downstream" firm), a number of problems can result. For one thing, if each has a monopoly position, they may get into a conflict as the downstream firm tries to hold the price down while the upstream firm tries to raise it. There may be problems of coordination if demand or supply is uncertain. Finally, a fluctuating price may impose excessive risk on one or the other party. If the upstream and downstream firms are combined into a single "vertically integrated" firm, these problems may be avoided or at least reduced.

国际化的第二个优势在于垂直一体化。

It should be clear that these views are by no means as rigorously worked out as the analysis of trade carried out elsewhere in this book. The economic theory of organizations—which is what we are talking about when we try to develop a theory of multinational corporations—is still in its infancy. This is particularly unfortunate because in practice multinationals are a subject of heated controversy—praised by some of generating economic growth, accused by others of creating poverty.

5.3 Economic Analysis of International Labor and Capital Movement

5.3 跨国劳动力和资本流动的经济学分析

In this section, we end our discussion of international flows of factors by developing and analyzing a simple model that allows one to understand some of the economic implications of these flows. The model we develop is sufficiently general to allow us to apply it to international flows either of labor or of capital. For concreteness, however, we shall discuss labor migration. We leave as an exercise the application of this model to the study of international capital mobility.

We begin by assuming that there is one country, America, that produces one good Y (or GDP), by means of fixed amount of capital and labor. The first thing we want to establish is the level of labor demand in America under this situation. We define the **marginal product of labor** (MP_L) in America as the additional amount (in physical units) of output that can be produced with the additional of one more worker to the production process. What are the properties of the MP_L? Recall that we have assumed that there is a fixed stock of capital in America. If the capital stock is fixed, it seems plausible that, as more and more workers are added to the production process, the MP_L will exhibit diminishing returns to labor. (That is, the increase in output due to an increase in labor will become smaller and smaller. This will occur because a fixed amount of machines is being shared by a larger and larger workforce.)

劳动边际产量，指的是每增加一单位的劳动力所带来的产出的增加量（实物量）。劳动（边际）收益递减，指在其他条件不变的情况下，随着劳动力的增加，劳动的边际产量递减。

Suppose that Y sells for P dollars per unit in the output market and that the market is competitive. Then, we define the **value marginal product of labor** (VMP_L) as the amount of money producers receive from selling the amount that was produced because the last worker was hired. In other words,

$$VMP_L = P \times MP_L \tag{5.1}$$

劳动边际产品价值，指的是劳动边际产量的货币价值。

where VMP_L represents the marginal revenue to producers from hiring the last worker.

Let's now consider the profit-maximizing decision by producers in determining their labor input. Suppose the going wage rate for workers is W; W can be thought of as the marginal cost of the last worker. The profit-maximizing rule, then, is simple. Producers should hire workers until the marginal cost of the last worker equals the marginal revenue when that worker was hire. That is, firms should equate marginal revenue with marginal cost.

Given information on the value of P and values of MP_L for different levels of employment, it is possible to develop a graph of the VMP_L. Such a graph appears in Figure 5.1. This curve slopes downward, reflecting the diminishing marginal product of labor. The VMP_L curve can be thought of as the demand-for-labor curve. We denote the fixed supply of workers in the economy by distance OA in the diagram. The interaction of demand and supply in the labor market determines the wage rate W'. Note, then, that the rectangular area defined by $OW'ZA$ is total value of labor earnings in the economy. This is determined by the fact that there are OA workers, each earning OW'. The remaining area under the VMP_L curve, the triangle $W'TZ$, represents payments to the other factor of production, capital. How do we know this? Recall that at any point the height of the VMP_L curve represents the marginal revenue earned by producers because that worker was hired. The worker was paid \$$OW'$. The remainder is the amount left over that is available to pay owners of the capital stock also used in the production process. The combined areas represent total labor income and total income paid to capital owners, in other words, the value of GDP.

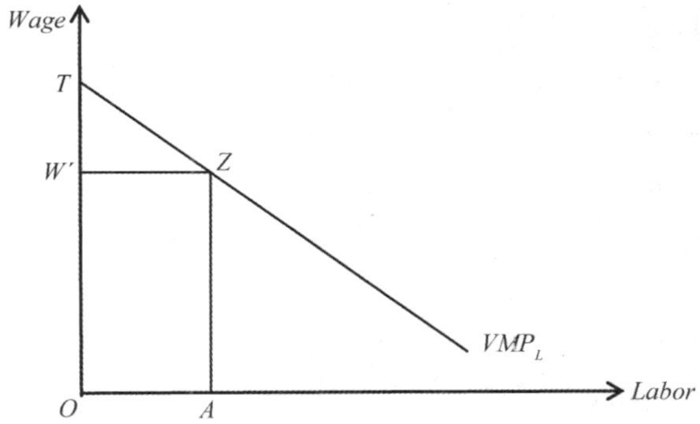

Figure 5.1 Distribution of Income Between Labor and Capital

We are now in the position to consider migration. Let's assume that America allows an inflow of foreign workers and that these workers are as skilled as their American counterparts. The obvious effect of this policy is to increase the supply of labor. We denote this increase by the distance AB in Figure 5.2. There are several economic implications to the immigration of foreign workers.

First, as the diagram shows, there is a wage effect. Because of the expansion in the supply of labor (and the assumption that everything else, including the capital stock, has been held constant), wages are driven down to W''. There is also an output effect. The expansion in the labor force means that more goods can be produced. The value of expanded production is shown in the diagram as the area of the trapezoid $AZZ''B$. Of this amount, the triangle $ZZ'Z''$ represents payments to capital, while the rectangle $ABZ''Z'$ represents the wages paid to foreign workers.

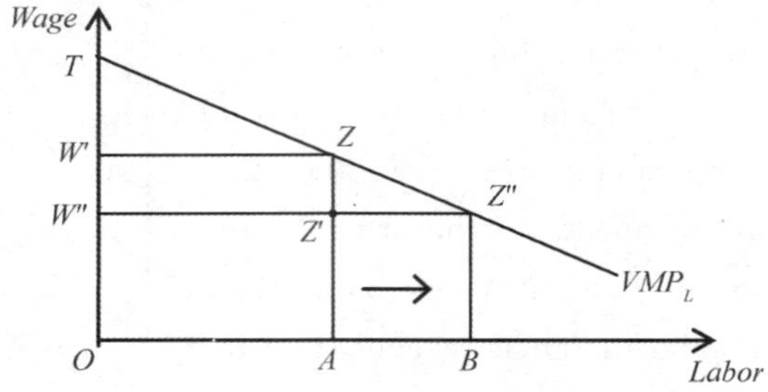

Figure 5.2 The Economic Effects of Labor Immigration

Finally, there is an income-redistribution effect. Domestic labor experiences a drop in the wage rate from OW' to OW'', and total domestic labor earnings fall from $OW'ZA$ to $OW''Z'A$. The difference between the areas of these two rectangles represents the value of lost earnings to domestic labor. This amount is not lost to the economy, however. Rather, it reverts to capital owners (assumed to be domestic residents). Capital owners benefit from the immigration of foreign labor because the resulting expansion in output leads to a more intensive use of capital and therefore to a rise in rental rates.

Thus, it is clear that even though foreign labor immigration leads to greater domestic output, not everyone in the society benefits from this inflow. Domestic labor loses. Domestic capital owners gain. Exactly the opposite occurs in the source country.

This can be seen from the diagram by considering an outflow of workers equivalent to the distance AB. In this case, labor has become somewhat more scare. Its wage rises and total output falls. Capitalists in the labor-exporting country are made worse off because of this emigration of labor from their country.

We can draw several conclusions from this analysis. First, if we were to generalize the results of this model to many goods and factors of production, the following result holds: international factor flows tend to lower the returns of those factors in the host country that most directly substitute for this factor and tend to raise the returns of other factors. This could mean that some types of labor in the host country could benefit from foreign migration. For instance, an influx of foreign unskilled labor into the United States may result in higher incomes for (domestic) skilled workers. Second, because factor flows have effects on the distributions of income in host and source countries, these countries often impose policies to limit factor flows. Such policies include restrictions on immigration and limits on capital outflows. The former are more common in rich countries, while the latter are more common in poor countries.

☞ Key Terms

☞ 关键术语

international factor movements theory, gastarbeiter, multinational corporations (MNCs), outsourcing, direct foreign investment, location, internalization, vertical integration, marginal product of labor (MP_L), value marginal product of labor (VMP_L)

国际要素流动理论、客籍工人、跨国公司、外包跨国直接投资、区位、内部化、劳动边际产量、劳动边际产品价值

☞ Questions

☞ 本章习题

1. At home and in foreign countries there are two factors of production, land and labor, used to produce only one good. The land supply in each country and the technology of production are the same. The marginal product of labor in each country depends on employment as follows:

Number of Workers Employed	Marginal Product of Last Worker
1	20
2	19
3	18
4	17
5	16
6	15
7	14
8	13
9	12
10	11
11	10

Initially, there are 11 workers employed at home, but only 3 workers in foreign countries.

Find the effect of free movement of labor from home to foreign countries on employment, production, real wages, and the income of landowners in each country.

2. Explain the analogy between international borrowing and lending and ordinary international trade.

3. Suppose that A is a small open economy that takes world prices as given. What would be the effect on wages and rents in A if it were to experience an inflow of foreign capital? Use a diagram to explain your answer. Which groups would favor this capital inflow? Which would oppose it? Explain.

4. Which of the following is a direct foreign investment, and which is not?

(1) A Saudi businessman buys a New York apartment building.

(2) The same businessman buys \$10 million of IBM stock.

(3) A French company merges with an American company; stockholders in the U.S. company exchange their stock for share in the French firm.

(4) An Italian firm builds a plant in Russia and manages the plant as a contractor to the Russian government.

Chapter 6

Tariffs

第六章

关　税

We have seen that free trade maximizes world output and benefits all nations. **However, practically all nations impose some restrictions on the free flow of international trade. In this chapter, we analyze the theories for trade protection, such as infant industry argument, terms of trade argument, the domestic market failure argument. Then, we will analyze the effects of a tariff on production, consumption, trade, and welfare of the nation imposing the tariff and its trade partner(s).**

现实世界中，所有的国家都对自由贸易设置一些限制。本章我们将分析一些贸易保护的理论，例如幼稚产业理论、贸易条件参数、国内市场失灵等，并分析关税对关税设置国和它的贸易伙伴国在生产、消费和国家福利方面的影响。

6.1 Theories for Trade Protection

6.1 贸易保护理论

We have now concluded our discussion on various forms of protection available to countries. A clear implication of this discussion has been that under many circumstances, protection is harmful to national welfare. If this is so, why do governments impose protection? Putting the question in another way, are there any circumstances where protection is a valid means to a particular policy goal? As we demonstrate in the following sections, the answer to the last question is yes. In particular, protection is an appropriate policy to use to achieve certain economic and non-economic outcomes. However, as we also demonstrate, protection is never the most economically efficient policy to achieve the objectives of the government.

6.1.1 Infant Industry Argument

6.1.1 幼稚产业理论

One of the oldest justifications for protection is the infant industry argument. It's built on the notion that certain industries require temporary protection from foreign competition to grow and prosper. This may be because the initial costs of production tend to be high. **However, given time and access to a protected market, firms will expand production and learn the techniques necessary to lower their costs and to be internationally competitive. In fact, after some time, the protection can be removed, and if the government has made the right choices regarding whom to protect, the industry will thrive.**

幼稚产业理论认为，在新兴产业能够参与世界市场的生产和营销竞争之前，需要对其进行临时性的保护，使其扩大产能，学习必要的技术。事实上，一段时间后，这种保护可以取消，如果政府在保护哪个产业方面做出了正确的选择，这个产业就会兴旺发达。

There are a number of problems with the logic of the infant industry argument. First, it presupposes that protected firms will work to lower costs, even though they are destined to face increased foreign competition if they are successful. It would seem more likely that protecting the infant industry provides the infant with an incentive never to grow up.

Second, even if the industry responds by improving its productivity, the argument seems to imply that governments are better able to pick winners than the private market is. After all, it is not uncommon for industries to lose money when they first get started. One of the functions of the financial sector is to provide firms with funds to produce until they become profitable. Moreover, when the initial funding comes from private sources, domestic residents are not subject to the higher prices that are the inevitable result of government-imposed protection.

The validity of the infant industry argument is better confined to those situations where the government is in a superior position to support the development of certain industries. Such a situation comes about on occasion in developing countries when the infant industry is one whose growth will lead to an expansion of the infrastructure of the economy. That is, sometimes firms must build roads, expand airports, extend public utility services, teach workers certain generally applicable work habits, and the like before production can take place. When these improvements are made, the society benefits, but the industry may never be compensated for the expense it has incurred in the process. Protection is one means to ensure that the industry is compensated for providing these services to the economy.

Despite the points just discussed, infant industry protection may not be the most efficient way to encourage certain industries to develop and grow within an economy. Clearly, as was the case with national defense protection, if the goal is to expand production, then a production subsidy with free trade is more efficient than protection. Moreover, if what the government wants is expanded infrastructure (e.g., improved roads, harbors, airports, or better-trained workers), then under almost all circumstances it would be more efficient for the government to provide these goods directly rather than to impose protection so that they might be provided by the private sector.

6.1.2 Terms of Trade Argument

6.1.2 贸易条件论

One argument for deviating from free trade comes directly out of cost-benefit analysis: **for a large country that is able to affect the prices of foreign exporters, a tariff lowers the price of imports and thus generates a terms of trade benefit. This benefit must be set against the costs of the tariff, which arise because the tariff distorts production and consumption incentives. It is possible, however, that in some cases the terms of trade benefits of a tariff outweigh its costs, so there is a terms of trade argument for a tariff.**

对于有能力影响国外出口商价格的大国，关税可以降低进口商品的价格，带来贸易条件上的收益。这一收益必须与关税的成本相抵，这些成本来自关税对生产和消费激励的扭曲。在一些情况下，贸易条件会使得关税的收益超过其成本，这被称为关税的贸易条件论。

For a sufficiently small tariff rate, the terms of trade benefits must outweigh the costs. Thus at small tariff rates a large country's welfare is higher than with free trade (Figure 6.1). As the tariff rate increases, however, the costs eventually grow more rapidly than the benefits and the curve relating national welfare to the tariff rate turns down. A tariff rate that completely prohibits trade (t_p in Figure 6.1) leaves the country worse off than with free trade; further increases in the tariff rate beyond t_p have no effect, so the curve flattens out.

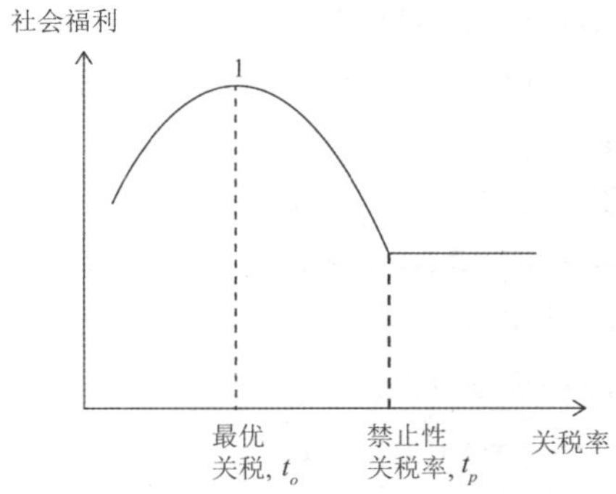

Figure 6.1 The Tariff and the Country's Welfare

For a large country, there is an optimum tariff rate t_p at which the marginal gain from improved terms of trade just equals the marginal efficiency loss from production and consumption distortion.

At point 1 on the curve in Figure 6.1, corresponding to the tariff rate t_o, national welfare is maximized. The tariff rate t_o that maximizes national welfare is the **optimum tariff.** (By convention, the phrase optimum tariff is used to refer to the tariff justified by a terms of trade argument rather than to the best tariff given all possible considerations.) The optimum tariff rate is always positive but less than the prohibitive rate (t_p) that would eliminate all imports.

最优关税，指使一国因贸易条件改善而减少带来的损失，并使净收益实现最大化的关税水平，也即使一国福利水平达到最高的关税水平，其税率称为最优关税率。

What policy would the terms of trade argument dictate for export sectors? Since an export subsidy worsens the terms of trade, and therefore unambiguously reduces national welfare, the optimal policy in export sectors must be a negative subsidy, that is, a tax on exports that raises the price of exports to foreigners. Like the optimum tariff, the optimum export tax is always positive but less than the prohibitive tax that would eliminate exports completely.

The policy of Saudi Arabia and other oil exporters has been taxing their exports of oil, raising the price to the rest of the world. Although oil prices fell in the mid-1980s, it is hard to argue that Saudi Arabia would have been better off under free trade.

The terms of trade argument against free trade has some important limitations, however. Most small countries have very little ability to affect the world prices of either their imports or exports, so that the terms of trade argument is of little practical importance. For large countries like the United States, the problem is that the terms of trade argument amounts to an argument for using national monopoly power to extract gains at other countries' expense. The United States could surely do this to some extent, but such a predatory policy would probably bring retaliation from other large countries. A cycle of retaliatory trade moves would, in turn, undermine the attempts at international trade policy coordination described later in this chapter.

The terms of trade argument against free trade, then, is

intellectually impeccable but of doubtful usefulness. In practice, it is emphasized more by economists as a theoretical proposition than it is used by governments as a justification for trade policy.

6.1.3 Domestic Market Failure Argument

6.1.3 国内市场失灵论

Leaving aside the issue of terms of trade, the basis theoretical case for free trade rested on cost-benefit analysis using the concepts of consumer and producer surplus. Many economists have made a case against free trade based on the counterargument that these concepts, producer surplus in particular, do not properly measure costs and benefits.

Why might producer surplus not properly measure the benefits of producing a good? We consider a variety of reasons in the next two chapters: **the possibility that the labor used in a sector would otherwise be unemployed or underemployed, the existence of defects in the capital or labor markets that prevent resources from being transferred as rapidly as they should be to sectors that yield high returns, and the possibility of technological spillovers from industries that are new or particularly innovative. These can all be classified under the general heading of domestic market failures.** That is, each of these examples is one in which some market in the country is not doing its job right—the labor market is not clearing, the capital market in the country is not doing its job right, and so on.

为什么生产者剩余不能用于衡量生产一种商品的收益?可能资本或劳动力市场中存在阻碍生产要素快速流动的因素;或者部分劳动力如果不被用于某一产业就将处于失业或半失业的状态;又或者一个全新的或具有创新特征的行业存在技术溢出效应。这些现象的原因被总结为国内市场失灵。

Suppose, for example, that the production of some goods yields experience that will improve the technology of the economy as a whole but that the firms in the sector cannot appropriate this benefit and therefore do not take it into account in deciding how much to produce. Then there is a marginal social benefit to additional production that is not captured by the producer surplus measure. This marginal social benefit can serve as a justification for tariff or other trade policies.

The domestic market failure argument against free trade is a particular case of a more general concept known in economics as the theory of the second best. This theory states that a hand-off policy is desirable in one market only if all other markets are working properly. If they are not, a government intervention that appears to distort incentives in one market may actually increase welfare by offsetting the consequences of market failures elsewhere. For example, if the labor market is malfunctioning and fails to deliver full employment, a policy of subsidizing labor-intensive industries, which would be undesirable in a full-employment economy, might turn out to be a good idea. It would be better to fix the labor market, for example, by making wages more flexible, but if for some reason this cannot be done, intervening in other markets may be a "second-best" way of alleviating the problem.

When economists apply the theory of the second best to trade policy, they argue that imperfections in the internal functioning of an economy may justify interfering in its external economic relations. This argument admits that international trade is not the source of the problem but suggests nonetheless that trade policy can provide at least a partial solution.

6.1.4 Strategic Trade Policy and Industrial Policy

Strategic trade policy is an advanced argument developed in favor of an activist trade policy and protectionism. According to this argument, a nation can create a comparative advantage (through temporary trade protection, subsides, tax benefits, and cooperative government-industry programs) in such fields as semiconductors, computers, telecommunications, and other industries that are deemed crucial to future growth in nation. These high-technology industries are subject to high risks, require large-scale production to achieve economies of scale, and give rise to extensive external economies when successful. Strategic trade policy suggests that by encouraging such industries, the nation can reap the large external economies that result from them and enhance its further growth prospects. This is similar to the infantindustry argument in developing nations, expect that it is advanced for industrial nations to acquire a comparative advantage in some crucial high-tech industries.

Examples of strategic trade and industrial policy (an activist policy by the government to stimulate the development and growth of some industries, usually a high-tech one, in an industrial nation) are semiconductors in the 1970s and 1980s in Japan and the development of the Concorde (the supersonic aircraft) and Airbus

6.1.4 战略贸易政策与工业政策

战略贸易政策的提出是为了支持积极的贸易政策和保护主义。基于这一观点，在半导体、计算机、通信等关系到国家未来发展的关键行业，一国可以通过临时的贸易保护、补贴、税收优惠和合作的政府产业项目创造出比较优势。

in Europe in the 1970s. Semiconductors in Japan are usually given as the textbook case of a successful strategic trade and industrial policy. The market for semiconductors (such as computer chips) was dominated by the United States in the 1970s. Starting in the mid-1970s, Japan's powerful Ministry of Trade and Industry (MITI) targeted the development of this industry by financing research and development, granting tax advantages for investments in the industry, and fostering government-industry cooperation, while protecting the domestic market from foreign (especially the United States) competition.

These policies are credited for Japan's success in nearly wrestling control of the semiconductor market from the United States in the mid-1980s. Most economists remain skeptical, however, and attribute Japan's stunning performance in this field primarily to other forces, such as greater educational emphasis on science and mathematics, higher rates of investment, and a willingness to take a long-run view of investments rather than stressing quarterly profits, as in the United States. In Europe, the Concorde was a technological feat but a commercial disaster, and Airbus Industrie would not have survived without heavy government subsidies.

There are also serious difficulties in carrying out strategic trade and industrial policies. First, it is extremely difficult to pick winners (i.e., choose the industries that will provide large external economies in the future) and devise appropriate polices to successfully nurture them. Second, since most leading nations undertake strategic trade polices at the same time, their efforts are largely neutralized, so that the potential benefits to each may be small. Third, when a country does achieve substantial success with a strategic trade policy, this comes at the expense of other countries (i.e., it is a beggar-thy-neighbor policy), who are likely to retaliate. Faced with all these practical difficulties, even supporters of strategic trade policies grudgingly acknowledge that free trade is still the best policy, after all. That is, free trade may be suboptimal in theory, but it is optimal in practice.

While generally opposing industrial targeting and strategic trade policies domestically, the United States did retaliate against countries that adopted these policies to the detriment of U. S. economic interests. An example was the semiconductor agreement that the United States negotiated with Japan in 1991 discussed earlier. On a broader scale, the United States and Japan engaged in negotiations (called the Structural Impediment Initiative, or SII) during the mid-1980s aimed, among other things, at opening the entire Japanese distribution system more widely to U. S. firms. During the 1990s, the United States also demanded a sharp reduction in subsidies granted to Airbus Industrie by the governments of France, Germany, England, and Spain, to agriculture by the European Union, and since the turn of the new century on subsidies for Airbus's development of its new super jumbo aircraft. Furthermore, the United States has requested that other countries, such as Brazil, China, and India, remove excessive restrictions against specific U.S. exports and demanded protection for its intellectual property (such as patented materials) from unauthorized and uncompensated use.

6.2 Tariffs

6.2 关税

The conclusion of the principle of comparative advantage presented so far is that free trade and specialization lead to the most efficient use of world resources. With specialization, the level of world output is maximized. Not only do free trade and specialization enhance world welfare, but they can also benefit each participating nation. Every nation can overcome the limitations of its own productive capacity to consume a combination of goods that exceeds the best it can produce in isolation.

Despite the power of the free trade argument, however, free trade policies may not be favored. Policy makers are torn between the appeal of greater global efficiency made possible by free trade and the needs of the voting public whose main desire is to preserve short-run interests such as employment and income. The benefits of free trade may take years to achieve and are spread out over wide segments of society, whereas the costs of free trade are immediate and fall on specific groups (for example, workers in the import-competing industry).

Researchers at Harvard University have investigated the factors that make people more likely to favor or oppose free trade. Analyzing a survey of more than 28,000 people in 23 countries, they found the expected result that well-educated people in well-educated countries are more likely to favor free trade, while workers in industries exposed to foreign competition in any country are more likely to be against it. Surprisingly, however, even well-educated workers in poorer nations tend to be against free trade. This opposition, from those who might be expected to be allies of globalization, may make it more difficult to extend free trade. The researchers also found that high levels of nationalism and patriotism are associated with support for protectionism. It implies that continuing global conflicts, which foster nationalist fervor at home and abroad, could undermine the support of free trade.

This part considers barriers to free trade. In particular, it focuses on the role that tariffs play in the global trading system.

6.2.1 Types of Tariffs

6.2.1 关税的类型

A **tariff** is a tax that is imposed by a government on imports or exports. Such taxes are extremely common throughout the world. They also have a long history. Virtually every country of the world imposed tariffs on at least some products. The United States has tariffs on a wide variety of imported items. It does not, however, impose tariffs on exports. This practice was forbidden in the original articles of the Constitution. Many countries do put a tax on their exports, such as Brazil on its coffee exports.

关税，指一国政府对进口或出口进行的征税。

As we are about to demonstrate, **tariffs have several effects on the economy where they are imposed. For instance, tariffs have a revenue effect. That is, they are a mechanism for raising government revenue.** Tariffs also have a **protective effect**. Consider an import tariff: since the tariff is applied only on imported products, foreign producers incur a cost not borne by domestic competitors. And to the extent that foreign producers pass on these higher costs to local consumers in the form of higher prices, domestic producers of similar products may find it easier to compete against their foreign rivals. Because tariffs typically provide this protective effect,

关税对经济的影响有以下几个方面。收入效应，指征收关税带来的政府税收收入的增加。保护效应，指征收关税带来的国内企业生产规模的扩大。

advocates of tariffs, and for that matter other forms of trade barriers, are often described as protectionists.

Generally, both the revenue and the protective effects of a tariff will operate at the same time. However, there are special cases when only one of these effects is present. For instance, a tariff that is imposed on an import when no domestic producer exists would be a pure revenue tariff. A prohibitive tariff is one that is so high that no goods are imported and thus is an example of a purely protective tariff—in such a circumstance no government revenue is collected.

Governments in developed economies rarely, if ever, rely on tariffs as a major source of government revenue. Consequently, it is difficult to point to an example of a pure revenue tariff collected by the United States or other major industrialized economies. On the other hand, the governments in developing economies depend heavily on trade taxes as a source of revenue. Therefore, examples of pure revenue tariffs abound. Tariffs in developed economies primarily exist because of their protective effect.

Next, note that for every product there are three possible tariffs. The first column, known as Column 1 General Rates of Duty, is duty category most commonly utilized by customs officials. Tariffs from this category are applied to goods from countries to which the United States has granted **most favored nation status** (MFN). If the United States (or any other country) grants another country MFN status, it agrees to charge tariffs against that country's goods that are no higher than those imposed against the goods of any other country.

最惠国地位,指一国承诺对享受最惠国待遇国家的货物征收的关税不高于其他任何国家。

Now, consider the numbers in this column of tariffs. These rates illustrate the ways in which tariffs are calculated. For instance, **tariffs may be ad valorem**, which means that the tax is collected as a percentage of the value of the product. Most of the U.S. tariff code is expressed in ad valorem terms. For example, the MFN U.S. Tariff rate on imported peach preserves is 17 percent, but the MFN rate on prepared palm hearts is only 0.9 percent. Imported peach products compete with many domestic varieties, and the tariff on these products is high; few American food processors produce canned palm hearts, and the tariff on these

从价税(ad valorem tariff),指按货物售价的百分率征收的关税。

products is almost zero.

Tariffs may be specific. That is, the tariff may be a fixed amount of money per unit of goods traded—regardless of the value of an individual unit. **Tariffs may be compound.** Such tariffs have both specific and ad valorem components.

从量税(specific tariff),指对一单位货物征收固定金额的关税。

混合税(compound tariff),指对货物同时征收从价税和从量税。

Countries that have not been granted MFN status are charged tariffs based on Column 2 Rates of Duty. These rates are substantially higher (sometimes 200 or 300 percent higher) than MFN rates. For instance, the non-MFN tariff on processed strawberry products is 35 percent, almost three times the MFN rate.

The third set of rates, known as Column 1 Special Rates of Duty, are tariffs even lower than MFN rates, which are applied to certain products from many developing countries or to products from countries with whom the United States has negotiated special trade agreements. An example of the first is the **generalized system of preference** (GSP), which was instituted by the United States in the early 1970s. Other industrialized countries (or regions), including Canada, the European Union (EU), and Japan, have their own GSP programs, many instituted about the same time or before the date of the U.S. plan. The idea behind the GSP is that by charging lower tariffs on such products, the United States will have an incentive to expand their purchases from the preference-receiving countries. In turn, expanded exports should improve the standards of living for these countries (and raise the demand for imports from industrialized countries such as the United States).

普遍优惠制,指发达国家对来自某些发展中国家的货物征收优惠低关税的制度。

In addition to special tariffs applied to goods from developing countries, the United States grants tariff concessions to countries with whom it has negotiated preferential trade agreements. In early 2006, the United States had agreements in place with Canada and Mexico (NAFTA), Australia, Chile, Israel, Jordan, Morocco, and Singapore and had negotiated an agreement with five Central American countries, Costa Rica, Dominican Republic, El Salvador, Honduras, and Nicaragua, and with some tariffs going to zero only after a considerable phasing-in period.

6.2.2 Effective Rate of Protection

6.2.2 有效保护率

It is tempting to assume that domestic producers with high import tariffs receive a high degree of protection, and domestic producers with low import tariffs receive a low degree of protection. However, such a simple relationship between tariff rates and the degree of protection does not necessarily hold. To determine the actual degree of protection an industry receives, one must not only consider the tariff on the final good but also any tariffs on the intermediate inputs that the industry uses to produce the final good. This means that we need to consider the impact of tariffs on the value of the product produced domestically. A measure that accounts for the importance of these items is called the effective rate of protection.

For example, consider two DVD players. One is produced in the United States, the other is produced in a foreign country. Assume that both DVD players sell for \$100 in the United States under conditions of free trade. Further, assume that half of the value of the foreign and domestically produced DVD players—\$50—is imported components from a third country, and domestic and foreign production—value-added—accounts for the other half of the cost of the DVD players—\$50. Now, suppose that a 20-percent tariff is imposed on the imported DVD player and this tariff raises the imported price of the DVD player to \$120—\$100 for the DVD player and \$20 for the tariff. The tariff rate is 20 percent, but what is the **effective rate of protection** for U.S. producers of DVD players? The effective rate of protection provided to the domestic DVD player producers by the 20-percent tariff on imports of finished DVD players is equal to the percentage increases in domestic value-added made possible by the tariff. Domestic value-added before the tariff was \$50 and domestic value added after the tariff is \$70.

关税的有效保护率(ERP)，指关税使保护对象的单位产出增加值在征税后提高的百分比，其衡量的是某国通过关税对某一行业的保护程度。

The domestic value-added after the tariff can be determined in one of two ways. First, it can be calculated as the difference between the tariff-inclusive price—\$120—and the price of the imported components—\$50. Second, it can be calculated as the sum of the tariff—\$20—plus the domestic value-added before the tariff—\$50.

征收进口关税后的价值增加额有两种测算方法，其一是含税价格与进口投入品价格之差；其二是总关税加上征收进口关税前的价值增加额。

The percentage change in the domestic value-added is determined as \$20/\$50 or 40 percent. In this case, a 20-percent tariff rate allows domestic value-added to rise by 40 percent, and this measures the effective rate of protection for domestic producers. Table 6.1 shows the impact of the tariff on U.S. value-added in detail. A 20-percent tariff rate does not always imply an effective rate of protection of 40 percent. **The relationship between the tariff rate and the effective rate of protection depends on the percentage of imported components used in the production process and the presence or absence of tariffs on the imported components and the final good.**

名义关税税率与有效保护率的关系取决于进口投入品的关税率与最终产品的关税率之间的关系。

Table 6.1 The Effective Rate of Protection

	Under Free Trade		With a 20-percent Tariff	
	Foreign DVD Player	Domestic DVD Player	Foreign DVD Player	Domestic DVD Player
Component Parts	\$50	\$50	\$50	\$50
Assembly Cost (Value-added)	50	50	50	70
Tariff			20	
Price	100	100	120	120

The general formula for determining the effective rate of protection is:

决定关税有效保护率的通用公式为：$ERP=(T_f-aT_c)/(1-a)$。

$$\boldsymbol{ERP=(T_f-aT_c)/(1-a)}$$

In our example, T_f is the tariff rate on the imported final product—the DVD player; a is the percentage of imported components used in producing the final product (\$50/\$100)=0.5; and T_c is the tariff rate on the imported components used to produce a DVD player. For example, if the imported components were taxed (tariff) at 10 percent, and DVD players faced a 20-percent tariff, then the effective rate of protection would be 30 percent (i.e., $(0.20-0.5\times0.1)/(1-0.5)$). Because the effective rate of protection is determined by the interaction of three variables, the potential outcome is ambiguous, and the effective rate of protection can even be negative. This occurs when the tariff on imported components multiplied by the percentage of imported inputs into the production process is larger than the tariff on the final good.

The tariffs on final goods in the U.S. tariff schedule are

frequently small. However, a seemingly small nominal tariff coupled with a large percentage of the product coming from imported inputs can yield a large effective rate of protection. This phenomenon is so common that it is referred to as tariff escalation. The tariff schedules of many developed countries are structures in such a way as to have low tariffs on imported inputs coupled with higher tariffs on the final goods. In effect, the effective rate of protection on final products in developed countries is frequently higher than the nominal tariff posted in the tariff schedule. This tariff escalation encourages the final processing of imported inputs to occur in developed countries. This **structure of protection** discourages the processing of intermediate products into final goods in the foreign country where the intermediate products are produced. A consistent complaint of developing countries is that this structure of protection hinders their ability to transform raw materials into intermediate of final goods. Although the magnitude of this effect may be debatable, the existence of it is not. Any time the tariff escalates with the stage of processing, foreign producers who wish to produce the final product with local inputs are being discriminated against. Because these producers are frequently in developing countries, the escalation of tariffs in developed countries makes the world distribution of income more unequal than if there were no tariffs at all.

保护结构

6.2.3 Tariff Welfare Effects

6.2.3 关税的福利分析

To analyze the economic impact of commercial policies including tariffs, it is necessary to develop some new tools of analysis. In particular, we are going to leave our general equilibrium framework to concentrate on the market for a specific product. To avoid confusion with our earlier notation, let's consider the market for grapes (G) in country A. In Figure 6.2 we illustrate the demand curve for grapes (labeled D_G). This curve is the sum of individual demand curves for all the residents of country A. It tells us the maximum amount that people in A would be willing to pay for a given quantity of grapes (good G). For instance, if a monopolist controlled the supply of grapes in A and could sell his or her product 1 unit at a time to the highest bidder, he or she could receive P_1 for the first unit sold, P_2 for the second unit sold, and so on. It is seldom the case, however, that products are sold in such a fashion. Rather, one price exists in the market so that all individuals pay the same, even if some were willing to pay more.

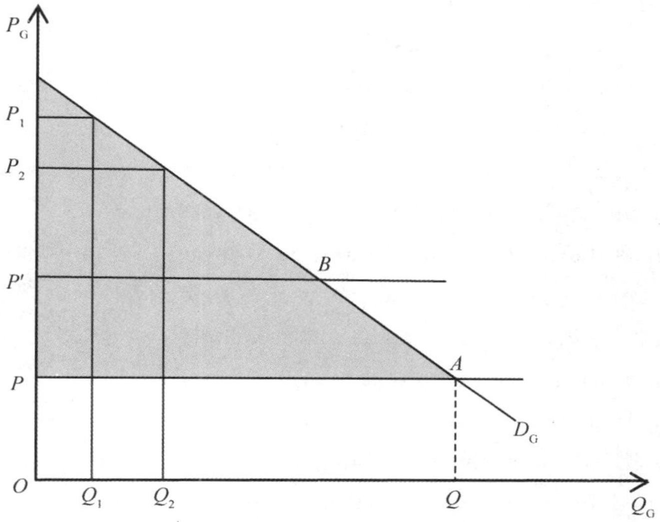

Figure 6.2 Consumer Surplus

Consider Figure 6.2 again. Suppose that P is the market price. The quantity purchased in the market would be Q unit. Total expenditure (price times quantity) would be represented by the rectangle $OPAQ$. If, on the other hand, there had been a monopolist selling each unit for what the market would bear, the amount spent on grapes would have been the entire area under the demand curve up to Q units. The difference between what individuals would be willing to pay and the amount that they actually pay is known as consumer surplus. In the diagram it is the shaded triangle whose base begins at the market price.

Consumer surplus has an important and useful interpretation. It represents the amount of money people would have been willing to spend but did not have to spend to purchase a particular product. Thus, it provides us with a convenient measure of the gains to consumers from being able to transact in markets. Note that consumer surplus varies inversely with price. That is, if the market price of grapes were to rise to P', consumer surplus would fall.

消费者剩余，指消费者在购买某数量商品时所愿意支付的金额与他实际支付金额之间的差异。

Lower market prices increase the amount of consumer surplus.

Let us turn our attention now to the other side of the market—producers. Consider Figure 6.3. There, we illustrate the market supply curve for domestic producers (labeled S_G). This curve tells us the minimum amount of money producers would accept to place a given quantity of grapes on the market. For instance, to sell 1 unit the market price must be at least P_0. Again, suppose that the market price is P. If so, then for all units supplied to the market up to Q, the industry receives a price in excess of the minimum required to produce and market those units. The difference between what the industry receives and that minimum amount is known as **producers surplus** (shown in the graph as the shaded area). Producers surplus can also be thought of as profits plus revenue to cover the fixed costs of production. This is true because the height of the supply curve at any level of output tells us the additional (or marginal) cost to producers of making that unit. As such, it is the variable cost of that unit. In the graph, the area under the supply curve up to point Q represents total variable costs, while that area plus the shaded area represents total revenue. Thus, the shaded area is the difference between total revenue and total variable costs, or total fixed costs plus short-run profits.

生产者剩余，指生产者从市场上实际支付的价格与生产者愿意接受的最低价格之间的差异。

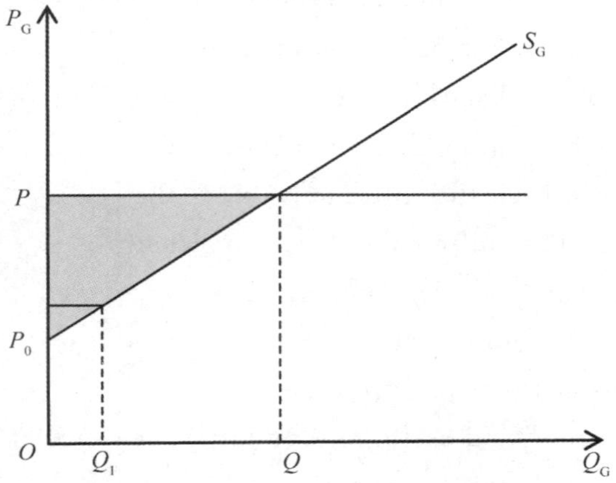

Figure 6.3 Producers Surplus

6.3 Effect of a Tariff on Consumer and Producer Surplus

6.3 关税对消费者剩余和生产者剩余的影响

The increase in the price of commodity X from $P_X = \$1$ to $P_X = \$2$ as a result of the 100 percent tariff imposed by the nation on its imports of commodity X leads to a reduction in consumer surplus and an increase in producer surplus. These are examined in Figure 6.4 and then used in the next section to obtain a monetary measure of the costs and benefits of the tariff.

The left panel of Figure 6.4 shows that the loss of consumer surplus resulting from the tariff is equal to the shaded area $AGHB = \$90$. The reason for this is as follows. Before the imposition of the tariff, consumers in the nation consume $100X$ at $P_X = \$1$. Consumers pay for each unit as much as they are willing to pay for the last, or 100th, unit of commodity X (given by point B on D_X). Consumers, however, receive more satisfaction and would therefore be willing to pay higher prices for earlier units of commodity X, as indicated by the height of the demand curve for each unit of the commodity consumers buy.

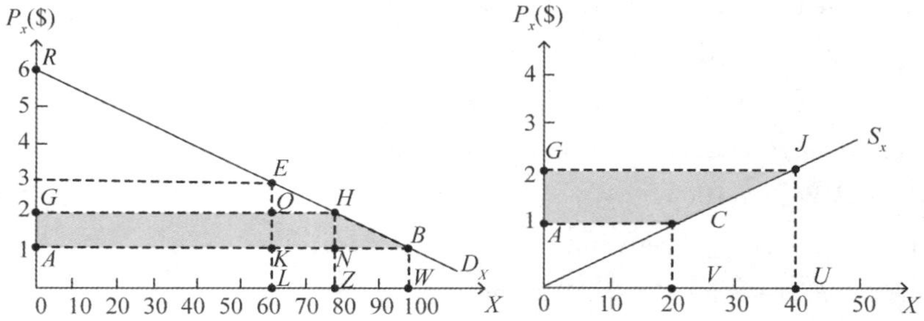

Figure 6.4 Effect of Tariff on Consumer and Producers Surplus

Source：多米尼克・萨尔瓦多.国际经济学[M]. 9 版. 北京：清华大学出版社,2008：121.

The left panel shows that a tariff that increases the price of commodity X from $P_X = \$1$ to $P_X = \$2$ results in a reduction in consumer surplus from $ARB = \$250$ to $GRH = \$160$, or by the shaded area $AGHB = \$90$. The right panel shows that the tariff increases producer surplus by the shaded area $AGJC = \$30$.

The difference of what consumers would be willing to pay for each unit of the commodity (indicate by the height of D_X at that point) and what they actually pay for that unit (the same as for the last unit that they purchase) is called consumer surplus. Thus, consumer surplus (the difference between what consumers are willing to pay for a specific amount of a commodity and what they actually pay for it) is the difference between what consumers would be willing to pay for each unit of the commodity and what they actually pay. Graphically, consumers surplus is measured by the area under the demand curve above the going price.

For example, the left panel of Figure 6.4 shows that consumers in the nation would be willing to pay $LE=\$3$ for the 60th unit of commodity X. Since they only pay $1, they receive a consumer surplus of $KE=\$2$ on the 60th unit of commodity X they purchase. Similarly, for the 80th unit of commodity X, consumers would be willing to pay $ZH=\$2$. Since they only pay $ZN=\$1$, they receive a consumer surplus of $NH=\$1$ on the 80th unit of X that they purchase. For the 100th unit of commodity X, consumers would be willing to pay $WB=\$1$. Since this is equal to the price that they actually pay, the consumer surplus for the 100th unit of X is zero. With the total of 100X being purchased at $P_X=\$1$ in the absence of the import tariff, the total consumer surplus in the nation is equal to $ARB=\$250$ ($5 times 100 divided by 2). This is the difference between what consumers would have been willing to pay ($ORBW=\$350$) and what they actually pay for 100X ($OABW=\$100$).

When the nation imposes a 100 percent import tariff, the price of commodity X rises from $P_X=\$1$ to $P_X=\$2$ and purchases of commodity X fall from 100X to 80X. With the tariff, consumers pay $OGHZ=\$160$ for 80X. The consumer surplus thus shrinks from $ARB=\$250$ (with $P_X=\$1$ before the tariff) to $GRH=\$160$ (when $P_X=\$2$ with the tariff), or by $AGHB=\$90$ (the shaded area in the left panel of Figure 6.4). The imposition of the 100 percent import tariff by the nation thus leads to a reduction in consumer surplus.

The right panel of Figure 6.4 shows that the increase in rent or producers surplus resulting from the tariff is given by shaded area

$AGJC = \$30$. The reason for this is as follows. At free trade $P_X = \$1$, domestic producers produce $20X$ and receive $OACV = \$20$ in revenues. With the tariff and $P_X = \$2$, they produce $40X$ and receive $OGJU = \$80$. Of the $\$60$ increase ($AGJC + VCJU$) in the revenue of producers, $VCJU = \$30$ (the unshaded area under the S_X curve between $20X$ and $40X$) represents the increase in their costs of production, while the remained (shaded area $AGJC = \$30$) represents the increase inrent or producers surplus (a payment that need not be made in the long run in order to induce producers to supply a specific amount of a commodity of factor services). This is defined as a payment that need not to be made in the long run in order to induce domestic producers to supply the additional $20X$ with the tariff. The increase in rent of producer surplus resulting from the tariff is sometimes referred to as the subsidy effect of the tariff.

6.3.1 Costs and Benefits of a Tariff in a Small Nation

6.3.1 小国关税的成本和收益

The concept and measure of consumer and producer surplus can now be used to measure the costs and benefits of the tariff in the monetary terms in the nation. These are shown in Figure 6.5.

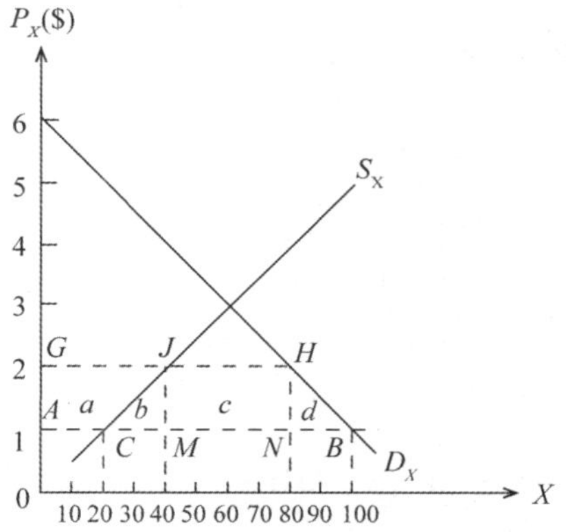

Figure 6.5 Cost and Benefits of a Tariff in a Small Nation

Figure 6.5 shows that when the nation imposes a 100 percent import tariff, the price of commodity X increases from $P_X = \$1$ to $P_X = \$2$, consumption falls from $AB = 100X$ to $GH = 80X$, production increases from $AC = 20X$ to $GJ = 40X$, imports decline from $CB = 80X$ to $JH = 40X$, and the government of the nation collects $MJHN = \$40$ in import duties. Furthermore, consumer surplus declines by $AGHB = \$90$, and producer surplus increases by $AGJC = \$30$.

Figure 6.5 shows that of the reduction of the consumer surplus of $AGHB = a + b + c + d = \$90$, $MJHN = c = \$40$ is collected by the government as tariff revenue, $AGJC = a = \$30$ is redistributed to domestic producers of commodity X in the form of increased producer surplus or rent, while the remaining \$20 (the sum of the areas of triangles $CJM = b = \$10$ and $BHN = d = \$10$) represents the **protection cost, or dead-weight loss** (the real losses in a nation's welfare because of inefficiencies in production an distortions in consumption resulting from a tariff), to the economy.

保护成本，或称无谓损失指因未达到有效率生产而造成的国家福利的实际损失，由关税造成的消费扭曲。

The production component ($CJM = b = \$10$) of the protection cost arises because, with the tariff, some domestic resources are transferred from the more efficient production of exportable commodity Y (not shown in the figures) to the less efficient production of importable commodity X in the nation. The consumption component ($BHN = d = \$10$) of the protection cost arises because the tariff artificially increases P_X in relation to P_Y and distorts the pattern of consumption in the nation.

Thus, the tariff redistributes income from domestic consumers (who pay a higher price for the commodity) to domestic producers of the commodity (who receive the higher price) and from the nation's abundant factor (producing exportable) to the nation's scarce factor (producing importable). This leads to inefficiencies. By dividing the loss of consumer surplus by the number of jobs "saved" in the industry because of the tariff (or equivalent rate of protection), we can calculate the cost per domestic job saved.

6.3.2 Cost and Benefits of a Tariff in a Large Nation

6.3.2 大国的关税成本和收益

We now examine the effects of an import tariff in a large nation—defined as a nation that affects the world price of the commodity by its trading. We will see that part of the tariff will fall on domestic consumers (in the form of the higher price they pay for the import commodity) and part will fall on foreign producers (in the form of the lower price they receive for the commodity). The reason is that the decline in the demand for the import of the commodity by a large nation (as a result of the increase in price due to the tariff) is significant and leads to a reduction in the price that foreign producers can charge for the commodity. The incidence or burden of import tariff then falls partly on consumers in the large nation imposing the tariff and partly on foreign producers that export the commodity. This is shown in Figure 6.6.

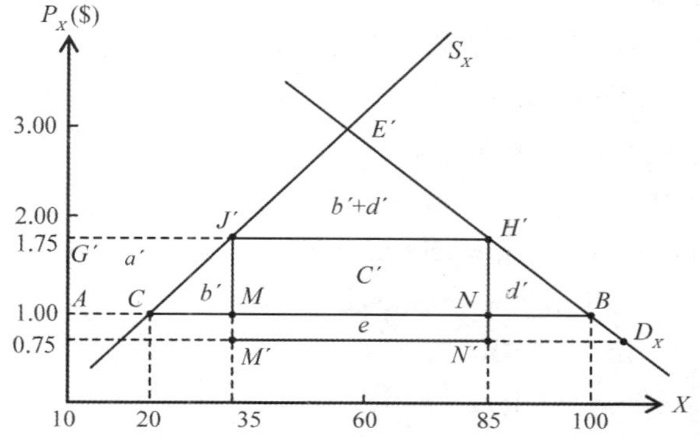

Figure 6.6 Cost and Benefits of a Tariff in a Large Nation

Figure 6.6 is similar to Figure 6.5, except that the vertical or price axis has been expanded. The free trade price of commodity X is still \$1.00, and the nation still imposes a \$1.00 import tariff. But now, because the nation is large, the price that domestic consumers pay for the commodity increases only to \$1.75 (instead of \$2.00 when the nation is small), and foreign producers of the commodity receive \$0.75 instead of \$1.00. The \$1.00 difference between the price of \$1.75 paid by domestic consumers and the \$0.75 price received by foreign producers is collected by the government of the nation imposing the import tariff.

We can now measure the costs and benefits of the tariff on the large nation imposing the tariff. Since the price of the imported commodity increases for domestic consumers from \$1.00 to \$1.75, the loss of consumer surplus is equal to $AG'H'B=a'+b'+c'+d'$, of which a' is the increase in producer's surplus, c' is the tariff revenue collected by the government from domestic consumers, and $b'+d'$ is the protection cost, or dead-weight loss, of the tariff to the nation. Now the welfare loss to the nation is $b'=$ \$5.625(15 times \$0.75, divided by 2) plus $d'=$ \$5.625, for a total of \$11.25. Note that since the price for domestic consumers increases only by \$0.75, the protection of dead-weight loss of the tariff is less than for the small nation (where the price of the import commodity increased by the full \$1.00 value of the import tariff and the welfare loss was \$20).

From Figure 6.6, we see that government of the large nation also collects \$0.25 on each of the $J'H' = 50X$ imported from foreign producers (in the form of the lower price that they now receive) for a total of $MM'N'N = e = \$12.50$. This is the **terms of trade effect of the tariff** (the reduction in the price of the import commodity that results when a large nation imposes an import tariff). Since the tariff revenue that the government collects from foreign producers ($e = \$12.50$) exceeds the protection cost or dead-weight loss of the tariff ($b' + d' = \$11.25$), the large nation as a whole is better off with the tariff than without the tariff.

关税的贸易条件效应，指一个大国征收进口关税导致进口商品价格的降低。

Had the opposite been the case, the large nation would have experienced a net welfare loss. It all depends on which of the two effects is larger. In general, the more elastic or flatter are the demand and supply curves of the importable commodity in the nation imposing the tariff, the smaller is the burden or incidence of a tariff on domestic consumers and the larger is the burden on foreign producers, and the more likely it is that the large nation will experience a net welfare gain from the tariff.

☞ Key Terms

theories for trade protection, infant industry argument, terms of trade argument, optimum tariff, domestic market failure, strategic trade policy, tariff, revenue effects, protective effects, most favored nation (MFN) status, ad valorem tariff, specific tariff, compound tariff, generalized system of preference (GSP), effective rate of protection (ERP), structure of protection, consumer surplus, producers surplus, protection cost, dead-weight loss, trade effect of the tariff

☞ 关键术语

贸易保护理论、幼稚产业理论、贸易条件参数、最优关税、国内市场失灵、战略性贸易政策、关税、收入效应、保护效应、最惠国地位、从价税、从量税、混合税、普遍优惠制、关税的有效保护率、保护结构、消费者剩余、生产者剩余、保护成本、无谓损失、关税的贸易条件效应

☞ Questions

☞ 本章习题

1. Describe a revenue tariff, a specific tariff, an ad valorem tariff, and a compound tariff.

2. Describe consumer and producer surplus.

3. Describe the economic effects that occur when a small country imposes a tariff.

4. Show how a tariff reduces the welfare of consumers by a larger amount than it increases the welfare of producers.

5. Explain the economic effects of a tariff that is imposed by a large country.

6. What is the infant industry argument for protection? How must this argument be qualified?

7. What is meant by strategic trade and industrial policy? Why is it relevant today?

Chapter 7

Non-tariff Trade Barriers

第七章

非关税贸易壁垒

7.1 An Introduction to Non-tariff Trade Barriers

7.1 非关税贸易壁垒简介

Although tariffs have historically been the most important form of trade restriction, there are many other types of trade barriers, such as import quotas, voluntary export restraints, and anti-dumping actions. After World War II, as the global economy recovers and develops, there is a universal cut in tariffs, and tariff barriers as a trade protection effect has been much less than in the past. Instead, various non-tariff barriers (NTBs) have been adopted to restrict imports as an important means of protecting domestic industries and markets. They are considered in this chapter.

7.2 Import Quota

7.2 进口配额

Instead of imposing a tax on an imported commodity, as under the tariff, the government may directly restrict the volume of permissible imports to a certain maximum level. **An import quota is a direct restriction on the quantity of a good imported.** For example, the amount of wheat imported by China in 2017 was limited to 9.636 million tons. The limits are presumably below what would be imported under free-market conditions, for otherwise there would be no need for the quota. Indeed, if free-market demand for imports falls below the quota, the quota becomes ineffective or non-binding. Thus, a government-imposed quota of 2 million cars is non-binding if only 1 million cars would be imported in the

进口配额是对进口商品在数量上的直接限制。

absence of restrictions. To administer the quota the government distributes import licenses to importers, allowing each one to import the commodity up to a prescribed limit. The importer is not free to import any quantity above that limit, regardless of market demand.

It is important to avoid having the misconception that import quotas somehow limit imports without raising domestic prices. The truth is that an import quota always raises the domestic price of the imported good. When imports are limited, the immediate result is that at the initial price, the demand for the good exceeds domestic supply plus imports. This causes the price to be bid up until the market clears. In the end, an import quota will raise domestic prices by the same amount as a tariff that limits imports to the same level (except in the case of domestic monopoly, in which the quota raises prices even more).

The difference between a quota and a tariff is that with a quota, the government receives no revenue. When a quota instead of a tariff is used to restrict imports, the money that would have appeared with a tariff as government revenue is collected by whoever receives the import licenses. License holders are thus able to buy imports and resell them at a higher price in the domestic market. The profits received by the holders of import licenses are known as quota rents. In assessing the costs and benefits of an import quota, it is crucial to determine who gets the rents. When the rights to sell in the domestic market are assigned to governments of exporting countries, as is often the case, the transfer of rents abroad makes the costs of a quota substantially higher than the equivalent tariff.

7.3 Export Subsidy

7.3 出口补贴

出口补贴是指向出口货物的企业或个人支付的补贴。

An export subsidy is a payment to a firm or individual that ships a good abroad. Like a tariff, an export subsidy can be either specific (a fixed sum per unit) or ad valorem (a proportion of the value exported). When the government offers an export subsidy, shippers will export the good up to the point at which the domestic price exceeds the foreign price by the amount of the subsidy.

The effects of an export subsidy on prices are exactly the reverse of those of a tariff (Figure 7.1). The price in the exporting country rises from P_W to P_S, but because the price in the importing country falls from P_W to P_S^*, the price increase is less than the subsidy.

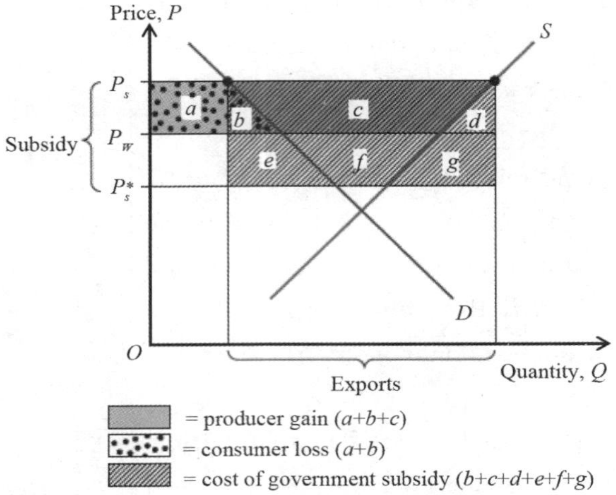

Figure 7.1 Effects of an Export Subsidy

An export subsidy raises prices in the exporting country while lowering them in the importing country. In the exporting country, consumers are hurt, producers gain, and the government loses because it must expend money on the subsidy. The consumer loss is the area $a + b$; the producer gain is the area $a + b + c$; the government subsidy (the amount of exports times the amount of the subsidy) is the area $b+c+d+e+f+g$. The net welfare loss is therefore the sum of the areas $b+d+e+f+g$. Of these, b and d represent consumption and production distortion losses of the same kind that a tariff produces. In addition, and in contrast to a tariff, the export subsidy worsens the terms of trade because it lowers the price of the export in the foreign market from P_W to P_S^*. This leads to the additional terms of trade loss $e + f + g$, which is equal to $P_W - P_S^*$ times the quantity exported with the subsidy. So, an export subsidy unambiguously leads to costs that exceed its benefits.

7.4 Dumping

Dumping is the sale of a commodity abroad at a price lower than in the home country. Often it is a result of a monopolist discriminating between the domestic and foreign markets. The word identical makes it difficult to establish the existence of dumping because in making international price comparisons, full allowance must be made for differences in specifications, including packaging and other superficial features. International standards exist for judging whether a commodity has been dumped.

Government export subsidies are a form of dumping discussed in the preceding section. Our concern here is with dumping by private companies unrelated to government subsidies. It is customary to distinguish among three types of dumping: **Sporadic dumping is disposal on foreign markets of an occasional surplus or overstock; it is tantamount to a domestic sale, and its effects are negligible. Predatory dumping occurs when a large home-based firm sells abroad at a reduced price in order to drive out competitors and gain control over the market, at which time it intends to reintroduce higher prices and use its newly acquired monopoly power to exploit that market.** Potential rivals may then be discouraged from entering the field by the fear of a repeated performance on the part of the monopolist. This is the most harmful form of dumping.

Persistent dumping is a direct outgrowth of profit-maximizing behavior by monopolists. Consider a manufacturer who holds a monopoly position on the domestic market, where he is also protected from import competition by transport cost or government restrictions. In foreign markets, on the other hand, he faces the competition of producers from the host country as well as from third countries. In economic terms, this situation implies that the demand elasticity is lower on the home market, where the consumers cannot turn to competing brands, than on foreign markets, where they can. The availability of close substitutes on foreign markets makes consumers highly responsive to price change in either direction. In other words, in terms of lost sales, the cost

7.4 倾销

倾销指的是以低于国内售价的价格在国外销售一种商品。

偶然性倾销指的是把偶尔的尾货或库存在国外市场销售处理；这与在国内市场促销类似，其影响微乎其微。

掠夺性倾销指的是一家大型国内公司通过降低售价驱逐竞争对手，获取市场支配地位，然后再利用其新获取的垄断力量引入更高价格掠夺市场。

持续性倾销指的是垄断厂商追求利润最大化行为。

to the producer of charging a high price is lower at home than abroad. To maximize his overall net return, he would charge a lower price abroad where he must meet competition than that charged at home where competitive pressure is lacking. Such dumping is harmful to the producers in the country receiving the dumped product, but this damage may be more than offset by the benefit to its consumers from the lower price.

One condition necessary for all forms of dumping is a separation of the domestic and foreign markets; otherwise, it is always possible for a foreign purchaser to resell the product on the home market and cut into the monopolist's profit. Thus, dumping is essentially price discrimination applied to the international arena. Indeed, it is easier to practice price discrimination internationally than nationally, because the domestic market cannot be fragmented into separate markets, while both transport costs and government restrictions often form an effective barrier between the domestic and foreign markets.

In actual practice it is difficult to distinguish the various types of dumping. Although predatory dumping is demonstrably harmful to the importing country, the same cannot be said of persistent dumping, which lowers the price to consumers. Yet government policy, often formulated under pressure from import-competing industries, applies to all of them. The most common measure to counteract dumping in the importing country is the imposition of ananti-dumping import duty. Such a duty, sanctioned by the WTO, is allowed for in the American tariff legislation, but its imposition requires elaborate proceedings: to prove the existence of dumping and to demonstrate the harm done to the competing domestic industry.

Over 1,100 anti-dumping measures are in force mainly by the United States, EU, Canada, and Australia, but also by developing countries, such as China and India. Recent examples are the U.S. tariff on steel products imposed in 2002, a U.S. tariff imposed on Chinese furniture in 2004, a U.S. tariff on shrimp imports from six countries imposed in 2004, and a Mexican duty on the U.S. beef levied in 2003. Sometimes an exporting country agrees to curtail its exports in order to avoid such duties. For example, in 1999 Russia limited steel exports to the United States. Average anti-dumping duties is high, and the very filing of a petition often discourages exports, thereby distorting world trade. Much to the chagrin of the U.S. trading partners and the WTO, the U.S. Senate passed (in 2000) the Byrd Amendment which allows U.S. companies, rather than the government, to keep the proceeds of the dumping levies. About $800 million were disbursed to U.S. companies in 2000—2004. In retaliation the WTO allowed the U.S. trading partners to impose duties on U.S. goods worth up to $150 million in any year.

A form of dumping called diversionary input dumping occurs when imports are made of materials that were dumped in the country where the final goods were manufactured. In 1988 the U.S. Trade Act mandated the administration to negotiate the banning of such dumping.

7.5 Voluntary Export Restraints

The voluntary export restraint (VER) is a variant on the import quota. It's also known as a voluntary restraint agreement (VRA). **A VER is a quota on trade imposed from the exporting country's side instead of the importer's.** The most famous example is the limitation on auto exports to the United States enforced by Japan after 1981.

Voluntary export restraints are generally imposed at the request of the importer and are agreed to by the exporter to forestall other trade restrictions. As we will see in Chapter 10, certain political and legal advantages have made VERs preferred instruments of trade policy in some cases. From an economic point of view, however, a voluntary export restraint is exactly like an import quota where the licenses are assigned to foreign governments and is therefore very costly to the importing country.

A VER is always more costly to the importing country than a tariff that limits imports by the same amount. The difference is that what would have been revenue under a tariff becomes rents earned by foreigners under the VER, so that the VER clearly produces a loss for the importing country.

7.5 自愿出口限制

自愿出口限制可看作是进口配额的一种变体。它是出口国(而不是进口国)对其出口到进口国的商品数量施加的限制。

A study of the effects of the three major U.S. voluntary export restraints of the 1980s—in textiles and apparel, steel, and automobiles—found that about two-thirds of the cost to consumers of these restraints was accounted for by the rents earned by foreigners.

In other words, the bulk of the cost represents a transfer of income rather than a loss of efficiency. This calculation also emphasizes that, from a national point of view, VERs are much more costly than tariffs. Given this fact, the widespread preference of governments for VERs over other trade policy measures requires some careful analysis.

Some voluntary export agreements cover more than one country. The most famous multilateral agreement is the Multi-Fiber Arrangement, which limited textile exports from 22 countries until the beginning of 2005. Such multilateral voluntary restraint agreements are known by yet another three-letter abbreviation: OMA, for "orderly marketing agreement".

7.6 Local Content Requirements

7.6 国产化要求

A local content requirement is a regulation that requires some specified fraction of a final good to be produced domestically. In some cases this fraction is specified in physical units, like the U.S. oil import quota in the 1960s. In other cases the requirement is stated in value terms, by requiring that some minimum share of the price of a good represent domestic value added. Local content laws have been widely used by developing countries trying to shift their manufacturing base from assembly back into intermediate goods. In the United States, a local content bill for automobiles was proposed in 1982 but was never acted on.

国产化要求指的是在最终产品中必须有一个明确规定的比例是本国生产的。

From the point of view of the domestic producers of parts, a local content regulation provides protection in the same way an import quota does. From the point of view of the firms that must buy locally, however, the effects are somewhat different. Local content does not place a strict limit on imports. Instead, it allows firms to import more, provided that they also buy more domestically. This means that the effective price of inputs to the firm is an average of the price of imported and domestically produced inputs.

Suppose that an automobile sells on the world market for \$8,000 and that the parts out of which that automobile is made sell for \$6,000. And to purchase the same parts domestically would cost \$10,000 but that assembly firms are required to use 50 percent domestic parts. Then they will face an average cost of parts of \$8,000 (0.5 × \$6,000 + 0.5 × \$10,000), which will be reflected in the final price of the car.

The important point is that a local content requirement does not produce either government revenue or quota rents. Instead, the difference between the prices of imports and domestic goods in effect gets averaged in the final price and is passed on to consumers.

An interesting innovation in local content regulations has been to allow firms to satisfy their local content requirement by exporting instead of using parts domestically. This is sometimes important. For example, U.S. auto firms operating in Mexico have chosen to export some components from Mexico to the United States, even though those components could be produced in the United States more cheaply, because doing so allows them to use less Mexican content in producing cars in Mexico for Mexico's market.

7.7 Other Trade Policy Instruments

7.7 其他贸易政策工具

There are many other ways in which governments influence trade. We list some of them briefly.

Export credit subsidies. This is like an export subsidy except that it takes the form of a subsidized loan to the buyer. The United States, like most other countries, has a government institution, the Export-Import Bank, which is devoted to providing at least slightly subsidized loans to aid exports.

出口信贷补贴类似于出口补贴，不过它采用对买方实施贷款补贴的方式。

National procurement. Purchases by the government or strongly regulated firms can be directed toward domestically produced goods even when these goods are more expensive than imports. The classic example is the European telecommunications industry. The nations

国家采购指政府或被强力管制的企业被规定购买本国生产的商品，即使这些商品比进口商品更昂贵。

of the European Union in principle have free trade with each other. The main purchasers of telecommunications equipment, however, are phone companies—and in Europe, these companies have until recently all been government-owned. These government-owned telephone companies buy from domestic suppliers even when the suppliers charge higher prices than suppliers in other countries. The result is that there is very little trade in telecommunications equipment within Europe.

Red-tape barriers. Sometimes a government wants to restrict imports without doing so formally. Fortunately or unfortunately, it is easy to twist normal health, safety, and customs procedures in order to place substantial obstacles in the way of trade. The classic example is the French decree in 1982 that all Japanese video cassette recorders had to pass through the tiny customs house at Poitiers—effectively limiting the actual imports to a handful.

进口环节壁垒，指政府以公众健康、安全和海关手续等理由对进口商品贸易造成实质障碍。

☞ Key Terms

import quota, export subsidy, dumping, voluntary export restraints, local content requirements, export credit subsidies, national procurement, red-tape barriers

☞ 关键术语

进口配额、出口补贴、倾销、自愿出口限制、国产化要求、出口信贷补贴、国家采购、进口环节壁垒

☞ Questions

☞ 本章习题

1. Suppose the China automobile industry is seeking protection from foreign imports. Compare and contrast (in terms of equivalence and related topics) the following measures of restricting automobile imports: (1) a tariff, (2) a quota, and (3) voluntary export restraints. Use graphs as needed.

2. Evaluate the following statements:

(1) As instruments of protection go, a tariff is less harmful to a country than a quota, and a quota is less harmful than a VER.

(2) Protection is an expensive and inefficient way to create jobs.

3. Answer the following questions:

(1) Define dumping and explain the three types of dumping.

(2) Show with a diagram how persistent dumping may arise.

Is this analysis equivalent to that of domestic price discrimination?

(3) What conditions are required for dumping to exist?

(4) What would an industry have to demonstrate in order to obtain protection from dumping? What form of protection is available?

4. Suppose that workers involved in manufacturing are paid less than all other workers in the economy. What would be the effect on the real income distribution within the economy if there were a substantial tariff levied on manufactured goods?

5. If tariffs, quotas, and subsidies each cause net welfare losses, why are they so common, especially in agriculture, among the industrialized countries such as the United States and the members of the European Union?

6. Is import protection a good way to save jobs? Why or why not? What are local content requirements?

Chapter 8

Trade Policies for Developing Nations

It is a commonly accepted practice to array all nations according to real income and then draw a dividing line between the advanced and developing ones. Included in the category of advanced nations are those of North America and Western Europe, plus Australia, New Zealand, and Japan. Most nations of the world are classified as developing, or less developed, nations. The developing nations are most of those in Africa, Asia, Latin America, and the Middle East. Table 8.1 provides basic economic and social indicators for selected nations in 2011. In general, advanced nations are characterized by relatively high levels of gross domestic product per capita, longer life expectancies, and higher levels of adult literacy. Most of the world's population live in the poorer developing countries.

Table 8.1 Basic Economic and Social Indicators for Selected Nations, 2011

Nations	Gross National Income Per Capita*	Life Expectancy /Years	Adult Literacy /%
Switzerland	52,530	83	99
United States	50,120	79	99
Japan	34,890	83	99
Chile	19,820	79	97
Mexico	15,770	77	93
Algeria	7,550	71	73
Indonesia	4,440	70	92
Guinea	940	56	30
Burundi	540	53	67

* Converted into international dollars using purchasing-power-parity rates. An international dollar has the same purchasing power as a U.S. dollar has in the United States.

Source: the World Bank. http://www.worldbank.org/data.

第八章

发展中国家的贸易政策

当前，一种被普遍接受的做法是，根据实际收入把所有的国家排序，并分为发达国家和发展中国家。发达国家（人均收入高的国家）包括北美和西欧国家，再加上澳大利亚、新西兰和日本。世界上大多数的国家都是发展中（欠发达）国家。发展中国家包括非洲、亚洲、拉丁美洲和中东的绝大多数国家。

Although international trade can provide benefits to domestic producers and consumers, some economists maintain that the current international trading system hinders economic development in the developing nations. They believe that conventional international trade theory based on the principle of comparative advantage is irrelevant for these nations. This chapter examines the reasons some economists provide to explain their misgivings about the international trading system. The chapter also considers policies aimed at improving the economic conditions of the developing nations.

8.1 Developing-nation Trade Characteristics

8.1 发展中国家贸易特征

If we examine the characteristics of developing-nation trade, we find that developing nations are highly dependent on advanced nations. A majority of developing nations' exports go to the advanced nations, and most developing nations' imports originate in advanced nations. Trade among developing nations is relatively minor, although it has increased in recent years.

如果考察发展中国家贸易的特点，我们就会发现发展中国家高度依赖发达国家。

Another characteristic is the composition of developing nations' exports, with its emphasis on primary products (agricultural goods, raw materials, and fuels). Of the manufactured goods that are exported by developing nations, many (such as textiles) are labor intensive and include only modest amounts of technology in their production.

另一个特点是，发展中国家的出口主要是初级产品（农产品、原材料和燃料）。在发展中国家出口的制成品中，多是劳动密集型的（如纺织品），其生产中只包含了少量的技术。

In the past three decades, the dominance of primary products in developing-nation trade has lessened. Many developing nations have been able to increase their exports of manufactured goods and services relative to primary products. These nations include China, India, Mexico, ROK, Bangladesh, Sri Lanka, Turkey, Morocco, Indonesia, Vietnam, and so on. Nations that have integrated into the world's industrial markets have realized significant poverty reduction.

How have developing nations been able to move into exports of manufactured products? Investments in both people and factories have played a role. The average education level and capital stock per worker have risen sharply throughout the developing world. Also, improvements in transport and communications, in conjunction with developing nation reforms, allowed the production chain to be broken into components, with developing nations playing a key role in global production sharing. Also, the liberalization of trade barriers in developing nations after the mid-1980s increased their competitiveness. This increase was especially true for manufactured goods and processed primary products. Developing nations are gaining ground in higher technology exports. Nevertheless, they have been frustrated about modest success in exporting these goods to advanced nations.

Many developing nations with a total population of around 2 billion people still have not integrated strongly into the global industrial economy; many of these nations are in Africa or used to be members of the Soviet Union. Their exports usually consist of a narrow range of primary products. These nations have often been handicapped by poor infrastructure, inadequate education, rampant corruption, and high trade barriers. Also, transport costs to advanced nation markets are often higher than the tariffs on their goods, so that transport costs are even more of a barrier to integration than the trade policies of rich nations. For these developing nations, incomes have been falling and poverty has been rising in the past 20 years. It is important for them to diversify exports by breaking into global markets for manufactured goods and services where possible. Why are some countries so much poorer than others?

8.2 The Problem of Developing Nations

8.2 发展中国家的难题

Tensions Between Developing Nations and Advanced Nations

发展中国家与发达国家之间的紧张关系

In spite of the trade frustrations of developing nations, most scholars and policymakers today agree that the best strategy for a poor country is to develop to take advantage of international trade. In the past two decades, many developing nations saw the wisdom of this strategy and opened their markets to international trade and foreign investment. Ironically, in spite of scholars' support for this change, the advanced world has sometimes maintained its own barriers to imports from these developing nations. Why is this so?

延伸思考 8.1

Think of the world economy as a ladder. On the bottom rungs are developing nations that produce mainly textiles and other low-tech goods. Toward the top are the United States, Japan, and the other advanced nations that manufacture sophisticated software, electronics, and pharmaceuticals. Up and down the middle rungs are all the other nations, producing everything from memory chips, autos, to steel. From this perspective, economic development is simple: everyone attempts to climb to the next rung. This process works well if the topmost nations can create new industries and products, adding another rung to the ladder: older industries can move overseas while new jobs are generated at home. But if innovation stalls at the highest rung, then Americans must compete with lower wage workers in developing nations.

A predicament faced by developing nations is that in order to make progress, they must displace producers of the least advanced goods that are still being produced in the advanced nations. If Zambia is going to produce textiles and apparel, it will compete against American and European producers of these goods. As producers in advanced nations suffer from import competition, they tend to seek trade protection in order to avoid it. However, this protection denies critical market access to developing nations, thwarting their attempts to grow. Thus, there is a bias against their catching up to the advanced nations.

Those who are protected in advanced nations from competition with developing nations tend to include those who are already near the bottom of the advanced nations' income distributions. Many of these people work in labor-intensive industries and have limited skills and low wages. Income redistribution programs ought to aid, not hinder, these people. To some extent, advanced nations face a tradeoff between helping their own poor and helping the world's poor. Critics note that the world as a whole needs to treat all poor as its own and those international institutions ought to ensure fairness to all who are in poverty. The World Trade Organization (WTO) is responsible for preventing advanced nations' trade policies from tilting too far in favor of their own people and against the rest of the world. This is why recent WTO meetings have been filled with tensions between poor and rich nations.

Providing developing nations with greater access to the markets of advanced nations will not solve all the developing nations' problems. They face structural weaknesses in their economies that are compounded by nonexistent or inadequate institutions and policies in the fields of law and order, sustainable macroeconomic management, and public services.

8.2.1 Trade Problems of The Developing Nations

8.2.1 发展中国家的贸易难题

The theory of comparative advantage maintains that all nations can enjoy the benefits of free trade if they specialize in production of those goods in which they have a comparative advantage and exchange some of them for goods produced by other nations. Policy makers in the United States and many other advanced nations maintain that the market-oriented structure of the international trading system furnishes a setting in which the benefits of comparative advantage can be realized. They claim that the existing international trading system has provided widespread benefits and that the trading interests of all nations are best served by pragmatic, incremental changes in the existing system. Advanced nations also maintain that to achieve trading success, they must administer their own domestic and international economic policies.

On the basis of their trading experience with advanced nations, some developing nations have become dubious of the distribution of trade benefits between themselves and advanced nations. They have argued that the protectionist trading policies of advanced nations hinder the industrialization of many developing nations. Accordingly, developing nations have sought a new international trading order with improved access to the markets of advanced nations. **Among the problems that have plagued developing nations have been unstable export markets, worsening terms of trade, and limited access to the markets of advanced nations.**

困扰发展中国家的难题包括：出口市场不稳定，贸易条件恶化，以及发达国家市场准入受限。

8.2.2 Unstable Export Markets

8.2.2 出口市场不稳定

One characteristic of some developing nations is that their exports are concentrated in only one or a few primary products. This situation is shown in Table 8.2 that illustrates the dependence of selected developing nations on a single primary product. A poor

发展中国家有一个特点：它们的出口集中在一种或少数几种主要产品上。

harvest or a decrease in market demand for that product can significantly reduce export revenues and seriously disrupt domestic income and employment levels.

Table 8.2 Developing Nation Dependence on Primary Products, 2012

Nations	Major Export Product	Percentage of Total Exports
Nigeria	Oil	95
Saudi Arabia	Oil	90
Venezuela	Oil	82
Benin	Cotton	81
Burundi	Coffee	80
Malawi	Tobacco	70
Zambia	Copper	62
Ethiopia	Coffee	60

Source: the World Bank Group, Data and Statistics: Country at a Glance Tables. http://www.worldbank.org/data; Central Intelligence Agency, World Factbook. www.cia.gov.

延伸思考 8.2

Economists maintain that a key factor underlying the instability of primary-product prices and producer revenues is the low price elasticity of the demand and supply schedules for products such as tin, copper, and coffee. Recall that the price elasticity of demand (supply) refers to the percentage change in quantity demanded (supplied) resulting from a one percent change in price. To the extent that demand and supply schedules are relatively inelastic, suggesting that the percentage change in price exceeds the percentage change in quantity, a small shift in either schedule can induce a large change in price and revenues.

经济学家们认为，导致初级产品价格及其生产者收入不稳定的关键因素是这些产品（比如锡、铜和咖啡）需求和供给的低价格弹性。

Figure 8.1 illustrates the supply and demand schedules for coffee, pertaining to the market as a whole. Assume that these schedules are highly inelastic. The market is in equilibrium at point A, where the market supply schedule S_0 intersects the market demand schedule D_0. The revenues of coffee producers total \$22.5 million, determined by multiplying the equilibrium price (\$4.50) times the quantity of pounds sold (5 million).

Referring to Figure 8.1(a), suppose that decreasing foreign incomes cause the market demand curve for coffee to decrease to

D_1. With the supply of coffee being inelastic, the decrease in demand causes a substantial decline in market price, from \$4.50 to \$2.00 per pound. The revenue of coffee producers falls to \$8 million. Part of this decrease represents a fall in producer profit. We conclude that coffee prices and earnings can be highly volatile when market supply is inelastic.

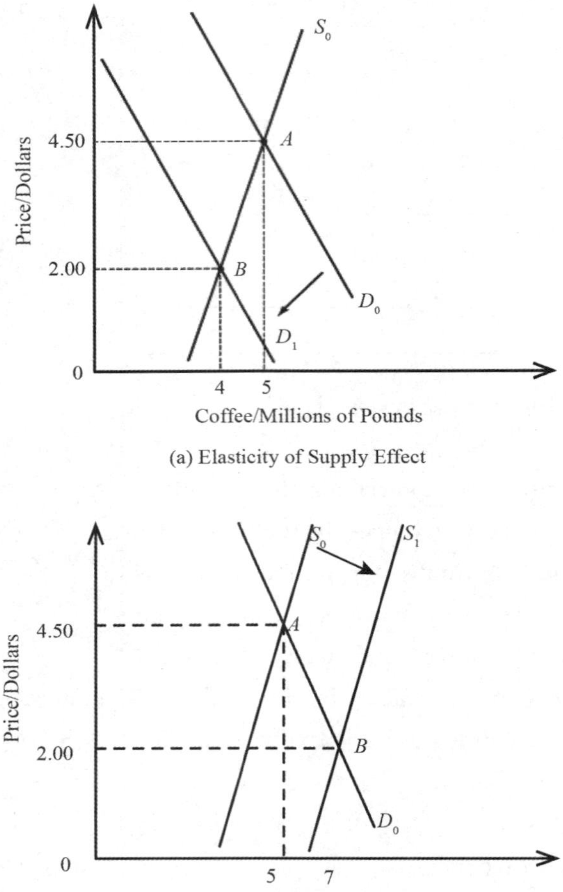

(a) Elasticity of Supply Effect

(b) Elasticity of Demand Effect

Figure 8.1 Export Price Instability for a Developing Nation

Not only do changes in demand induce wide fluctuations in price when supply is inelastic, but changes in supply induce wide fluctuations in price when demand is inelastic. The latter situation is illustrated in Figure 8.1(b). Suppose that favorable growing conditions cause a rightward shift in the market supply curve of coffee to S_1. The result is a substantial drop in price from \$4.50 to

$2 per pound and producer revenues fall to $14 million ($2 * 7 million pounds = $14 million). We see that prices and revenues can be volatile when demand conditions are inelastic.

When the supply of a commodity is highly price-inelastic, decreases (or increases) in demand will generate wide variations in price. When the demand for a commodity is highly price-inelastic, increases (or decreases) in supply will generate wide variations in price.

8.2.3 Falling Commodity Prices Threaten Growth of Exporting Nations

During the first decade of the 2000s, increasing commodity prices and favorable growing conditions benefitted producers and governments in many developing nations. Higher prices resulted in rising profits and increasing tax revenues that were used by governments to pay off some of their debts and spend more on social programs. In Latin America, stronger commodity markets contributed to economic growth that averaged 5 percent per year during 2003—2008 as compared to 3.5 percent per year during the previous three decades.

However, that upward cycle took a sharp hit when many advanced economies plunged into recession in 2008 and 2009. As these economies shrank, so did their demand for commodities. Lower demand resulted in a dramatic tumbling in the prices of copper, tin, iron ore, soybeans, oil and the like. As export revenues declined, commodity producing nations such as Peru and Bolivia had to put on the shelf natural resource investments such as iron ore extraction.

8.2.3 商品价格下跌威胁到出口国的增长

然而，当许多发达经济体在2008年和2009年陷入衰退时，这种上行周期受到了严重冲击。随着这些经济体的萎缩，他们对大宗商品的需求也在下降。需求下降导致铜、锡、铁矿石、大豆、石油等商品价格大幅下跌。由于出口收入下降，秘鲁和玻利维亚等大宗商品生产国不得不搁置铁矿石开采等自然资源投资。

Brazil paid a steep price for relying on primary products, such as soybeans and iron ore, for 40 percent of its exports. The price of soybeans decreased from $600 per ton to $365 per ton during 2008—2009. As Brazil's export prices declined, so did its once sizable trade surplus. Brazil's corporations such as mining giant Cia. Vale do Rio Doce, had to cut back production and lay off workers. Also, the region's big gas and oil producers, including Bolivia, Ecuador, and Venezuela, were hit hard by the global economic downturn.

延伸思考 8.3

The economies of many developing nations are tied to primary products and a majority of their exports go to advanced nations. When advanced nations encounter economic downturns, they can be quickly transmitted to their developing country trading partners as seen in the global economic downturn of 2008—2009.

8.2.4 Worsening Terms of Trade

8.2.4 贸易条件恶化

How the gains from international trade are distributed among trading partners has been controversial, especially among developing nations whose exports are concentrated in primary products. These nations generally maintain that the benefits of international trade accrue disproportionately to the advanced nations.

延伸思考 8.4

Developing nations complain that their commodity terms of trade have deteriorated in the past century or so, suggesting that the prices of their exports relative to their imports have fallen. Worsening terms of trade have been used to justify the refusal of many developing nations to participate in trade liberalization negotiations. It also has underlain developing nations' demands for preferential treatment in trade relations with advanced nations.

Observers maintain that the monopoly power of manufacturers in the advanced nations results in higher prices. Gains in productivity accrue to manufacturers in the form of higher earnings rather than price reductions. Observers further contend that the export prices of primary products of developing nations are determined in competitive markets. These prices fluctuate downward as well as upward. Gains in productivity are shared with foreign consumers in the form of lower prices. Developing nations maintain that market forces cause the prices they pay for imports to rise faster than the prices commanded by their exports, resulting in a deterioration in their commodity terms of trade. As income rises, people tend to spend more on manufactured goods than primary goods, thus contributing to a worsening in the developing nations' terms of trade.

The developing nations' assertion of worsening commodity terms of trade was supported by a United Nations (UN) study in 1949. The study concluded that from the period 1876—1880 to 1946—1947, the prices of primary products compared with those of manufactured goods fell by 32 percent. Because of inadequacies in data and the problems of constructing price indexes, the UN study was hardly conclusive. Other studies led to opposite conclusions about terms of trade movements.

In 2004, economists at the United Nations found that between 1961 and 2001, the average prices of agricultural commodities sold by developing nations fell by almost 70 percent relative to the prices of manufactured goods purchased from developed nations. Such terms of trade declines were especially harmful for the poorest nations of Sub-Saharan Africa. Also, the World Bank estimated that between 1970 and 1997 declining terms of trade cost non-oil exporting nations in Africa the equivalent of 119 percent of their combined annual gross domestic product in lost revenues. In theory, a decline in the terms of trade could be counteracted by increases in the quantity produced and exported so as to maintain or increase the value of export earnings. In practice, export quantities did not grow sufficiently in the nations of Africa to cover the loss.

Regarding other developing nations—such as China, India, and Russia—and other developing world oil exporters, the declining terms of trade argument appears to hold less well in recent years. Many of these nations have been able to realize economies of scale in the production of certain other primary products such as corn or cotton, and have diversified their economies away from exclusive reliance on raw material exports. It is difficult to conclude whether the developing nations as a whole have experienced a deterioration or an improvement in their terms of trade. Conclusions about terms of trade movements become clouded by the choice of the base year used in comparisons, the problem of making allowances for changes in technology and productivity as well as for new products and product qualities, and the methods used to value exports and imports and to weight the commodities used in the index.

8.2.5 Limited Market Access

8.2.5 市场准入限制

In the past two decades, developing nations as a whole have improved their penetration of world markets. Global protectionism has been a hindrance to their market access. This is especially true for agriculture and labor-intensive manufactured products such as clothing and textiles. These products are important to the world's poor because they represent more than half of low income nations' exports and about 70 percent of least developed nations' export revenues.

Tariffs imposed by the advanced nations on imports from developing nations tend to be higher than those they levy on other advanced nations. The differences in tariff averages reflect in part the presence of major trading blocs such as the European Union (EU) and the North American Free Trade Agreement (NAFTA), that have abolished tariffs for advanced nation trade partners. Also, because developing nations did not actively participate in multilateral trade liberalization agreements prior to the 1990s, their products tended to be omitted from the sharp reductions in tariffs made in those rounds. Average tariff rates in rich nations are low, but they maintain barriers in exactly the areas where developing nations have comparative advantage: agriculture and labor-intensive manufactured goods.

发达国家对从发展中国家进口的商品征收的关税往往高于对其他发达国家征收的关税。

Developing nations also are plagued by tariff escalation. In advanced nations, tariffs escalate steeply, especially on agricultural products. Tariff escalation has the potential of decreasing demand for processed imports from developing nations, restricting their diversification into higher value added exports. Though less prevalent, tariff escalation also affects imports of industrial products, especially at the semi-processed stage. Examples of such products, in which many developing nations have a comparative advantage, include textiles and clothing, leather and leather products, wood, paper, furniture, metals, and rubber products.

Moreover, protectionist barriers have caused developing country producers of textiles and clothing to forego sizable export earnings. For decades, advanced nations imposed quotas on imports of these products. Although the Uruguay Round Agreement on Textiles and Clothing resulted in the abolishment of the quotas in 2005, market access in textiles and clothing will remain restricted because tariff barriers are high.

Anti-dumping and countervailing duties have become popular substitutes for traditional trade barriers that are gradually being reduced in the course of regional and multilateral trade liberalization.

在区域和多边贸易自由化过程中，反倾销和反补贴关税已成为传统贸易壁垒的流行替代品。

Developing nations have argued that advanced nations such as the United States have limited access to their markets through aggressive use of ant-idumping and countervailing duties. Such policies have resulted insignificant reductions in export volumes and market shares, according to the developing nations.

延伸思考 8.5

Indeed, poor nations have leaned on the United States and Europe to reduce trade barriers. Rich nations note that poor nations need to reduce their own tariffs that are often higher than those of their rich counterparts, as seen in Table 8.3. Tariff escalation is also widely practiced by developing nations; their average tariff for fully processed agricultural and manufactured products is higher than on unprocessed products. Although trade among developing nations is a much smaller share of total trade, average tariffs in manufactured goods are about three times higher for trade among developing nations than for exports to advanced nations. Critics note that developing nations are part of their own problem and they should liberalize trade.

Table 8.3 Tariffs of Selected Developing Nations and Advanced Nations, All Products, 2012

Countries	Average Applied Tariff Rate* /%
Bahamas	35.9
Maldives	20.5
Zimbabwe	19.5
Brazil	13.7
India	13.0
Republic of Korea	12.1
Russian Federation	9.5
European Union	5.1
Japan	4.4
Canada	3.7
United States	3.5

* Average applied tariff rates are duties that are actually charged on imports. These can be below the bound rates which are commitments to increase a rate of duty beyond an agreed level. Once a rate of duty is bound, it may not be raised without compensating the affected parties.

Source: the World Trade Organization, World Tariff Profiles, 2012.

However, this argument does not sit well with many poor nations. They contend that quickly reducing tariffs could throw their already fragile economies into an even worse state. Justas is the case in rich nations that reduce tariffs, some workers will inevitably lose jobs as businesses switch to the lowest cost centers. Unlike the United States and European nations, poor nations do not have a social safety net and reeducation programs to cushion the blow.

The message that the developing world receives is that it should do some market liberalization of its own. Nevertheless, it is paradoxical for advanced nations to want developing nations to lift their trade barriers, yet advanced nations like the United States and Canada benefitted from significant trade barriers during their developing stages.

8.3 Generalized System of Preferences

8.3 普惠制

Given inadequate access to markets of advanced nations, developing nations have pressed them to reduce their tariff walls. **To help developing nations strengthen their international competitiveness and expand their industrial base, many advanced nations have extended nonreciprocal tariff preferences to exports of developing nations. Under this generalized system of preferences (GSP), major advanced nations temporarily reduce tariffs on designated manufactured imports from developing nations below the levels applied to imports from other advanced nations. The GSP is not a uniform system because it consists of many individual schemes that differ in the types of products covered and the extent of tariff reduction.** The GSP attempts to promote economic development in developing nations through increased trade rather than foreign aid.

为了帮助发展中国家增强其国际竞争力并扩大其工业基础，许多发达国家向发展中国家提供了非互惠的关税优惠。在这种普惠制下（GSP），主要发达国家暂时将从发展中国家指定的制成品进口关税降至其从发达国家进口的关税水平以下。GSP并不是一个统一的体系，因为它包含了许多不同的方案，这些方案在所涉及的产品种类和关税削减的程度上存在差异。

Trade preferences granted by advanced nations are voluntary. They are not WTO obligations. Donor nations determine eligibility criteria, product coverage, the size of preference margins, and the duration of the preference. In practice, advanced country governments rarely grant deep preferences in sectors where developing nations have a large export potential. Thus, developing nations often obtain only limited preferences in sectors where they have a comparative advantage. The main reason for limited preferences is that in some sectors there is strong domestic opposition to liberalization in advanced nations.

延伸思考 8.6

Since its origin in 1976, the U.S. GSP program has extended duty-free treatment to about 3,000 items. Criteria for eligibility include not aiding international terrorists and complying with international environmental, labor, and intellectual property laws. The U.S. program grants complete tariff free and quota free access to eligible products from eligible nations. Beneficiaries of the U.S. program include 130 developing nations and their dependent territories. Like the GSP programs of other advanced nations, the U. S. program excludes certain import-sensitive products from preferential tariff treatment. Textiles and apparel, footwear, and some agricultural products are not eligible for the GSP. Also, a country's GSP eligibility for a given product may be removed if annual exports of that product reach $100 million or if there is significant damage to domestic industry. From time to time, as GSP participants have grown wealthier, they have been "graduated" out of the program. Among the alumni are Hong Kong of China, Taiwan of China, Malaysia, and Singapore.

Although the GSP program provides preferential access to advanced nations' markets, several factors erode its effectiveness in reducing trade barriers faced by poor nations. First, preferences mainly apply to products that already face relatively low tariffs. Second, tariff preferences can also be eroded by non-tariff measures, such as anti-dumping duties and safeguards. Products and nations have been removed from GSP eligibility because of lobbying by domestic interest groups in importing nations. Preferences do little to assist the majority of the world's poor. Most of those living on less than $1 per day live in nations like India and Pakistan that receive limited preferences in products in which they have a comparative advantage. As a result, developing nations and resions have been frustrated about limited access to the markets of advanced nations.

8.4 Stabilizing Primary Product Price

Although developing nations have shown some improvement in exports of manufactured goods, agriculture and natural resource products remain a main source of employment. As we have learned, the export prices and revenues for these products can be quite volatile.

In an attempt to stabilize export prices and revenues of primary products, developing nations have attempted to form international commodity agreements (ICAs). These agreements are between leading producing and consuming nations of commodities such as coffee, rubber and cocoa about matters such as stabilizing prices, assuring adequate supplies to consumers, and promoting the economic development of producers. To promote stability in commodity markets, ICAs have relied on production and export controls, buffer stocks, and multilateral contracts. We should note that these measures have generally had only limited (if any) success in improving the economic condition of developing nations, and that other methods of helping these nations are needed.

8.4.1 Production and Export Controls

If an ICA accounts for a large share of total world output (or exports) of a commodity, its members may agree on production and export controls to stabilize export revenues. **Production and export controls affect the price of commodities by influencing the world supply of the commodity.** The total quantity of production or exports allowed under a commodity agreement is based on the target price that is agreed to by member nations. If it is thought that the price of tin will decrease below the target price in the future, producing nations will be assigned a lower production level or export quota. By makingtin more scarce, its price will remain at the target level. Conversely, if it is anticipatedthat the price of tin will increase above the target price in the future, producing nations will be allowed to increase their levels of production and exports.

An obstacle in attempting to impose limits on production and

8.4 稳定初级产品价格

为了稳定初级产品的出口价格和收入，发展中国家试图建立国际商品协议（ICAs）。这些协议是一些大宗商品（比如咖啡、橡胶和可可等）的主要生产国和消费国之间达成的事项，如稳定价格、向消费者提供充足的供应、促进生产者的经济发展等。为了促进商品市场的稳定，ICAs 依赖于生产和出口控制、缓冲库存和多边合同。

8.4.1 生产和出口控制

生产和出口控制通过影响世界商品供给来影响商品价格。

exports is the distribution of the limits among producing nations. If a decline in the total quantity of coffee exports is needed to offset a falling price, how would that decline be allocated among individual producers? Small producers may be hesitant to decrease their levels of output when prices are declining. Another problem is the appearance of new producers of coffee that may be drawn into the market by artificially high prices. Producing nations just embarking on the production or export of coffee would likely be reluctant to reduce their levels of production or exports at that time. Producers have the incentive to cheat on output restrictions and enforcement is difficult.

8.4.2 Buffer Stocks

8.4.2 缓冲库存

另一种限制商品价格波动的技术是缓冲库存，在这种情况下，生产者联盟（或国际机构）准备大量买进和卖出一种商品。

Another technique for limiting commodity price swings is the buffer stock, in which a producers' association (or international agency) is prepared to buy and sell a commodity in large amounts. The buffer stock consists of supplies of a commodity financed and held by the producers' association. The buffer stock manager buys from the market when supplies are abundant and prices are falling below acceptable levels, and sells from the buffer stock when supplies are tight and prices are high.

Figure 8.2 illustrates the hypothetical price stabilization efforts of the International Tin Agreement. Assume that the association sets a price range with a floor of \$3.27 per pound and a ceiling of \$4.02 per pound to guide the stabilization operations of the buffer stock manager. Starting at equilibrium point A in Figure 8.2(a), suppose the buffer stock manager sees the demand for tin rising from D_0 to D_1. To defend the ceiling price of \$4.02, the manager must be prepared to sell 20,000 pounds of tin to offset the excess demand for tin at the ceiling price. Conversely, starting at equilibrium point E in Figure 8.2(b), suppose the supply of tin rises from S_0 to S_1. To defend the floor price of \$3.27, the buffer stock manager must purchase the 20,000-pound excess supply that exists at that price.

延伸思考 8.7

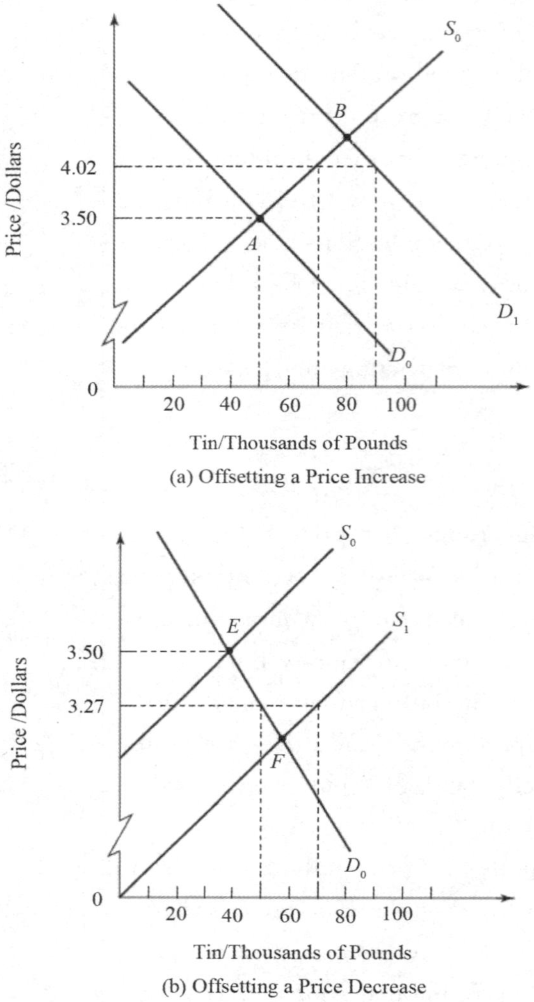

Figure 8.2　Buffer Stock: Price Ceiling and Price Support

During periods of rising tin demand, the buffer-stock manager sells tin to prevent the price from rising above the ceiling level. However, prolonged defense of the ceiling price may result in depletion of the tin stockpile that undermines the effectiveness of this price stabilization tool and lending to an upward revision of the ceiling price. During periods of abundant tin supplies, the manager purchases tin to prevent the price from falling below the floor level. Again, prolonged defense of the price floor may exhaust the funds to purchase excess supplies of tin at the floor price and may lead to a downward revision of the floor price.

Proponents of buffer stocks contend that the scheme offers the primary producing nations several advantages. A well run buffer stock can promote economic efficiency because primary producers can plan investment and expansion if they know that prices will not gyrate. It is also argued that soaring commodity prices invariably ratchet industrial prices upward, whereas commodity price decreases exert no comparable downward pressure. By stabilizing commodity prices, buffer stocks can moderate the price inflation of the advanced nations. Buffer stocks in this context are viewed as a means of providing primary producers more stability than is allowed by the free market.

Setting up and administering a buffer stock program is not without costs and problems. The basic difficulty in stabilizing prices with buffer stocks is agreeing on a target price that reflects long-term market trends. If the target price is set too low, the buffer stocks will become depleted as the stock manager sells the commodity on the open market in an attempt to hold market prices in line with the target price. If the target price is set too high, the stock manager must purchase large quantities of the commodity in an effort to support market prices. The costs of holding the stocks tend to be high because they include transportation expenses, insurance, and labor costs. In their choice of price targets, buffer stock officials have often made poor decisions. Rather than conduct massive stabilization operations, buffer stock officials will periodically revise target prices should they fall out of line with long-term price trends.

8.4.3 Multilateral Contracts

Multilateral contracts are another method of stabilizing commodity prices. **Such contracts generally stipulate a minimum price at which importers will purchase guaranteed quantities from the producing nations and a maximum price at which producing nations will sell guaranteed amounts to the importers. Such purchases and sales are designed to hold prices within a target range.** Trading under a multilateral contract has often occurred among several exporting and importing nations, as in the case of the International Sugar Agreement and the International Wheat Agreement.

One possible advantage of the multilateral contract as a price

8.4.3 多边合同

这样的合同一般规定了一个最低的价格，（如果低于此价格）进口商将从生产国家购买保证数量的产品；以及一个最大的价格，(如果高于此价格)生产国家将向进口商销售保证数量的产品。这样的购买和销售是为了把价格保持在一个目标范围内。

stabilization device is that, in comparison with bufferstocks or export controls, it results in less distortion of the marketmechanism and the allocation of resources. This result is because the typical multilateral contract does not involve output restraints and thus does not check the development of more efficient low-cost producers. If target prices are not set near the long-term equilibrium price, however, discrepancies will occur between supply and demand. Excess demand would indicate a ceiling too low, whereas excess supply would suggest a floor too high. Multilateral contracts also tend to furnish only limited market stability given the relative ease of withdrawal and entry by participating members.

8.4.4 Does the Fair Trade Movement Help Poor Coffee Farmers?

8.4.4 公平贸易运动能帮助贫穷的咖啡农民吗?

We have seen that low commodity prices are troublesome for producers in developing nations. Can consumers of commodities be of assistance to producers? Consider the case of coffee produced in Nicaragua.

Nicaraguan coffee farmer Santiago Rivera has traveled far beyond his mountain home to publicize what is known as the fair trade coffee movement. Have you heard of fair trade coffee? You soon may. Started in Europe in the early 1990s, the objective of the fair trade coffee movement is to increase the income of poor farmers in developing nations by implementing a system where the farmers can sell their beans directly to roasters and retailers, bypassing the traditional practice of selling to middlemen in their own nations.

This arrangement permits farmers, who farm mainly in the mountainous regions of Latin America and other tropical regions where high flavor, high priced beans sold to gourmet stores are grown, to earn as much as \$1.26 per pound for their beans, compared with the \$0.40 per pound they were getting from middlemen.

Under the fair trade system, farmers organize in cooperatives of as many as 2,500 members that set prices and arrange for export directly to brokerage firms and other distributors. Middlemen—known as "coyotes" in Nicaragua—previously handled this role. So far, 500,000 of the developing world's 4 million coffee farmers have joined the fair trade movement. The movement has led to incidents of violence in some places in Latin America, mostly involving the middlemen who are being bypassed.

The fair trade coffee movement is the latest example of how social activists are using free market economics to foster social change. Organizers of the movement say they have signed up eight gourmet roasters and about 120 stores, including big chains like Safeway, Inc. Fair trade coffee carries a logo identifying it as such.

Fair trade achieved great success in Europe, where fair trade coffee sells in 35,000 stores and has sales of \$250 million a year. In some nations like the Netherlands and Switzerland, fair trade coffee accounts for as much as five percent of total coffee sales. Based on those achievements, organizers in Europe are expanding their fair trade efforts to include other commodity items, including sugar, tea, chocolate, and bananas. Fair-trade activists admit that selling Americans on the idea of buying coffee with a social theme will be more challenging than it was in Europe. Americans, they note, tend to be less aware of social problems in the developing world than Europeans. The fair trade movement has yet to get the support of major U.S. coffee houses such as Maxwell and Folgers. Nevertheless, organizers are trying to nudge Seattle's two coffee giants, Starbuck's Coffee Co. and the Seattle Coffee Co., into agreeing to purchase some of the fair trade coffee. However, critics question the extent to which "fair traded" coffee actually helps. They note that the biggest winners are not the farmers, but rather the retailers that sometimes charge huge markups on fair traded coffee while promoting themselves as corporate citizens. They can get away with it because consumers generally are given little or no information about how much of a product's price goes to farmers.

8.5 Economics Growth Strategies

8.5 经济增长战略

Besides seeking economic assistance from advanced nations, developing nations have pursued two competing strategies for industrialization: **an inward-looking strategy (import substitution) in which industries are established largely to supply the domestic**

一种是内向型战略(进口替代):建立工业主要是为了供应国内市场,而对

market, and foreign trade is assigned negligible importance; and an outward-looking strategy (export-led growth) of encouraging the development of industries in which the country enjoys comparative advantage, with heavy reliance on foreign nations as purchasers of the increased production of exportable goods.

外贸易不重要；另一种是外向型战略（出口导向增长）：鼓励发展本国具有比较优势的产业，依靠外国购买其生产的出口品。

8.5.1 Import Substitution

8.5.1 进口替代

During the 1950s and 1960s, the industrialization strategy of import substitution became popular in developing nations such as Argentina, Brazil, and Mexico; some nations still use it today. Import substitution involves extensive use of trade barriers to protect domestic industries from import competition. The strategy is inward-oriented in that trade and industrial incentives favor production for the domestic market over the export market. If fertilizer imports occur, import substitution calls for establishment of a domestic fertilizer industry to produce replacements for fertilizer imports. In the extreme, import substitution policies could lead to complete self sufficiency.

The rationale for import substitution arises from the developing nations' perspective on trade. Many developing nations feel that they cannot export manufactured goods because they cannot compete with established firms of the advanced nations, especially in view of the high trade barriers maintained by advanced nations. Given the need for economic growth and development, developing nations have no choice but to manufacture for themselves some of the goods they now import. The use of trade restrictions block imports and the domestic market is reserved for domestic manufacturers. This rationale is often combined with the infant-industry argument: protecting start-up industries will allow them to grow to a size where they can compete with the industries of advanced nations.

In one respect, import substitution appears logical: if a good is demanded and imported, why not produce it domestically? The economist's answer is that it may be more costly to produce it domestically and cheaper to import it; comparative advantage should decide which goods are imported and which are exported.

Encouraging economic development via import substitution has

通过进口替代来促进经济发展有以下几个优点：

- 建立国内产业以取代进口的风险很低，因为制成品的国内市场已经存在。
- 发展中国家保护本国制造商不受外国竞争对手的影响，比迫使发达国家减少对发展中国家出口产品的贸易限制要容易得多。
- 为了避免发展中国家的进口关税壁垒，外国人有动机在发展中国家建厂，为当地工人提供就业机会。

相比这些优点，有

several advantages as follows:

- **The risks of establishing a home industry to replace imports are low because the home market for the manufactured good already exists.**
- **It is easier for a developing nation to protect its manufacturers against foreign competitors than to force advanced nations to reduce their trade restrictions on products exported by developing nations.**
- **To avoid the import tariff walls of the developing country, foreigners have an incentive to locate manufacturing plants in the country, providing jobs for local workers.**

In contrast to these advantages, there are several disadvantages as follows:

- **Because trade restrictions shelter domestic industries from international competition, they have no incentive to increase their efficiency.**
- **Given the small size of the domestic market in many developing nations, manufacturers cannot take advantage of economies of scale and thus have high unit costs.**
- **Because the resources employed in the protected industry would otherwise have been employed elsewhere; protection of import-competing producers automatically discriminates against all other industries, including potential exporting ones.**
- **Once investment is sunk in activities that were profitable only because of tariffs and quotas, any attempt to remove those restrictions is generally strongly resisted.**
- **Import substitution also breeds corruption. The more protected the economy, the greater the gains to be had from illicit activity such as smuggling.**

During the 1970s, criticisms of import substitution industrialization became increasingly common. Empirical studies appeared to suggest that developing countries that adopted freer trade policies tended to grow faster than those that adopted protectionist policies. Therefore, many developing countries removed quotas and decreased tariffs by the mid 1980s.

以下几个缺点：
- 贸易限制为国内产业提供免于国际竞争的庇护，因此它们没有动力提高效率。
- 鉴于许多发展中国家的国内市场规模较小，制造商无法利用规模经济，因此拥有较高的单位成本。
- 因为在受保护的行业中使用的资源本可以在其他地方使用；对进口竞争的生产者的保护会自动地对所有其他行业产生歧视，包括潜在的出口企业。
- 一旦投资因关税和配额而有利可图，任何试图取消这些限制的尝试通常都会遭到强烈抵制。
- 进口替代也会滋生腐败。经济越受保护，走私等非法活动获得的收益就越大。

8.5.2 Export-led Growth

8.2.5 出口导向增长

Another development strategy is export-led growth, or **export-oriented policy**. This strategy is outward oriented because it links the domestic economy to the world economy. Instead of pursuing growth through the protection of domestic industries suffering comparative

出口导向政策

disadvantage, the strategy involves promoting growth through the export of manufactured goods. Trade controls are either nonexistent or low, in the sense that any disincentives to export resulting from import barriers are counterbalanced by export subsidies. Industrialization is viewed as a natural outcome of development instead of being an objective pursued at the expense of the economy's efficiency. By the mid-1980s, many developing nations were abandoning their import substitution strategies and shifting their emphasis to export led growth.

Export-oriented policies have three advantages: they encourage industries in which developing nations are likely to have a comparative advantage, such as labor-intensive manufactured goods; by providing a larger market in which to sell, they allow domestic manufacturers greater scope for exploiting economies of scale; by maintaining low restrictions on imported goods, they impose a competitive discipline on domestic firms that forces them to increase efficiency.

出口导向政策有三个优势：它们鼓励发展中国家具有潜在比较优势的产业，比如劳动密集型的制成品；通过提供一个更大的销售市场，他们允许国内制造商扩大规模经济的范围；通过保持对进口商品的低限制，他们对国内企业施加了竞争的压力，迫使他们提高效率。

Economists at the World Bank have investigated the relation between openness to international trade and economic growth for developing nations. They divided a sample of 72 nations into "globalizers" and "non-globalizers". The globalizers are defined as the 24 nations that achieved the largest increases in their ratio of trade to gross domestic product from 1975 to 1995. During the 1960s and 1970s, the non-globalizers experienced somewhat faster growth of real income per capita on average than the globalizers. However, during the 1980s, globalizers experienced much higher growth rates; real income per capita grew an average of 3.5 percent a year in these nations, compared with 0.8 percent for the non-globalizers. These findings support the concept that the economic performance of nations implementing export-led growth policies has been superior to that of nations using import substitution policies.

8.5.3 Is Economic Growth Good for the Poor?

8.5.3 经济增长对穷人有好处吗？

Although the evidence strongly suggests that trade is good for growth, is growth good for poor workers in developing nations? Critics argue that growth tends to be bad for the poor if the growth in question has been promoted by trade or foreign investment. Investment inflows, they say, make economies less stable, exposing workers to the risk of financial crisis and to the attentions of advanced nation banks. Moreover, they contend that growth driven by trade provides Western multinational corporations a dominant role in third-world development. That is bad, because Western multinationals are not interested in development at all, only in making larger profits by ensuring that the poor stay poor. The proof of this, say critics, lies in the evidence that economic inequality increases even as developing nations, and advanced nations, increase their national income, and in the multinationals' use of sweatshops when producing goods. So if workers' welfare is your primary concern, the fact that trade promotes growth, even if true, misses the point.

There is strong evidence that growth aids the poor. Developing nations that have achieved continuing growth, as in East Asia, have made significant progress in decreasing poverty. The nations where widespread poverty persists, or is worsening, are those where growth is weakest, notably in Africa. Although economic policy can affect the extent of poverty, in the long run growth is much more important.

There is intense debate over the extent to which the poor benefit from economic growth. Critics argue that the potential benefits of economic growth for the poor are undermined or even offset entirely by sharp increases in inequality that accompany growth. On the other hand, proponents contend that liberal economic policies such as open markets and monetary and fiscal stability raise the incomes of the poor and everyone else in society proportionately.

Suppose it were true that income inequality is increasing between the advanced and developing nations. Would this be a terrible indictment of globalization? Perhaps not. It would be disturbing if inequality throughout the world were increasing because incomes of the poorest were decreasing in absolute terms, instead of in relative terms. However, this is rare. **Even in Africa that is behaving poorly in relative terms, incomes have been increasing and broader indicators of development have been improving. Perhaps it is too little, but something is better than nothing.**

即使在非洲，相对而言是贫穷的，但其收入也增加了，许多发展指标也得到了改善。或许改善太少，但聊总胜于无。

8.5.4 Can All Developing Nations Achieve Export-led Growth?

8.5.4 所有的发展中国家都能实现出口导向的增长吗?

Although exporting can promote growth for developing economies, it depends on the willingness and ability of advanced nations to go on absorbing large amounts of goods from developing nations. Pessimists argue that this process involves a fallacy of composition. If all developing nations tried to export simultaneously, the price of their exports would be driven down on world markets. Moreover, advanced nations may become apprehensive of foreign competition, especially during eras of high unemployment, and impose tariffs to reduce competition from imports. Will liberalizing trade be self-defeating if too many developing nations try to export simultaneously?

Although developing nations as a group are enormous in terms of geography and population, in economic terms they are small. Taken together, the exports of all the world's poor and middle-income nations equal only five percent of world output. This is an amount approximately equivalent to the national output of the United Kingdom. Even if growth in the global demand for imports were somehow capped, a concerted export drive by those parts of the developing world not already engaged in the effort would put no great strain on the global trading system.

尽管发展中国家在地理和人口方面是巨大的，但从经济角度来看，它们是很小的。总的来说，世界上所有的贫穷和中等收入国家的出口仅占世界产出的5%。这一数字大约相当于英国的国民产出。即使全球进口需求的增长受到某种程度上的限制，但发展中国家中那些尚未参与出口的国家即使参与出口，也不会对全球贸易体系造成巨大压力。

Pessimists also tend to underestimate the scope for intra-industry specialization in trade, that gives developing nations a further set of new trade opportunities. The same goes for new trade among developing nations, as opposed to trade with the advanced nations. **Often, as developing nations grow, they move away from labor-intensive manufactures to more sophisticated kinds of production. This movement makes room in the markets they previously served for goods from nations that are not yet so advanced.** In the 1970s, Japan withdrew from labor-intensive manufacturing, making way for exports from the Republic of Korea, and Singapore. In the 1980s and 1990s, the Republic of Korea, and Singapore did the same, as China began moving into those markets. As developing nations grow through exporting, their own demand for imports rises.

通常，随着发展中国家的发展，它们会从劳动密集型制造业转向更为复杂的生产。这一过程为那些他们曾为之提供产品的发展程度较差的国家提供了机会。

☞ Key Terms

advanced nations, developing nations, unstable export markets, worsening terms of trade, limited access to the markets of advanced nations, generalized system of preferences, international commodity agreements (ICAs), production and export controls, buffer stocks, multilateral contracts, import substitution, export-led growth

☞ 关键术语

发达国家、发展中国家、不稳定的出口市场、贸易条件恶化、进入发达国家的市场有限、普遍优惠制、国际商品协定、生产和出口管制、缓冲库存、多边合约、进口替代、出口导向增长

☞ Questions

☞ 本章习题

1. What are the major reasons for the skepticism of many developing nations regarding the comparative-advantage principle and free trade?

2. Stabilizing commodity prices has been a major objective of many primary product nations. What are the major methods used to achieve price stabilization?

3. What are some examples of international commodity agreements? Why have many of them broken down over time?

4. Why are the developing nations concerned with commodity price stabilization?

5. The generalized system of preferences is intended to help developing nations gain access to world markets. Explain.

6. How are import substitution and export promotion policies used to aid in the industrialization of developing nations?

7. How has China achieved the status of a high-performing Asian economy? Why has China's normal trade relation status been a source of controversy in the United States?

Chapter 9

Trade Policies for Developed Nations

第九章 发达国家的贸易政策

In the last chapter we mentioned that, depending on income, we can divide the world into developed and developing countries. These two countries have very different positions and situations in the world economy and trade. Their attitude towards international trade and their policies in industry and trade also have many differences. In this chapter, we introduce common trade policy in developed countries (of course, these policies will also appear in some developing countries), and focus on two typical developed countries: the United States and Japan's industrial policy.

9.1 Strategic Trade Policy

9.1 战略性贸易政策

Beginning in the 1980s, a new argument for industrial policy gained prominence. **The theory behind strategic trade policy is that government can assist domestic companies in capturing economic profits from foreign competitors.**[①] **Such assistance entails government support for certain "strategic" industries (such as high technology) that are important to future domestic economic growth and provide widespread benefits (externalities) to society.**

战略贸易政策背后的理论是，政府可以通过对国内企业实施援助以从外国竞争者手中获取经济利润。这些援助包括政府对某些"战略性"产业(如高科技)的支持，这些产业对未来的国内经济增长至关重要，并为社会提供广泛的福利(外部效应)。

The essential notion underlying strategic trade policy is imperfect competition. Many industries participating in trade, the argument goes, are dominated by a small number of large

① The argument for strategic trade policy was first presented in J. Brander and B. Spencer, "International R&D Rivalry and Industrial Strategy", *Review of Economic Studies 50* (1983), pp. 707-722. See also P. Krugman, ed., *Strategic Trade Policy and the New International Economics* (Cambridge, MA, MIT Press, 1986) and P. Krugman, "Is Free Trade Passe?", *Economic Perspectives*, Fall 1987, pp. 131-144.

companies—large enough for each company to significantly influence market price. Such market power gives these companies the potential to attain long-run economic profits. **According to the strategic trade policy argument, government policy can alter the terms of competition to favor domestic companies over foreign companies and shift economic profits in imperfectly competitive markets from foreign to domestic companies.**

根据战略贸易政策的观点，政府政策可以改变竞争条件，使国内企业在和外国企业竞争中受益，并在不完全竞争的市场中将经济利润从外国公司转移到国内企业。

A standard example is the aircraft industry.[①] With the high fixed costs of introducing a new aircraft and a significant learning curve in production that leads to decreasing unit production costs, this industry can support only a small number of manufacturers. The aircraft industry is also an industry that typically is closely associated with national prestige.

Assume that two competing manufacturers, Boeing (representing the United States) and Airbus (a consortium owned jointly by four European governments) are considering whether to construct a new aircraft. If either firm manufactures the aircraft by itself, it will attain profits of \$100 million. If both firms manufacture the aircraft, they will each suffer a loss of \$5 million.

Now assume the European governments decide to subsidize Airbus production in the amount of \$10 million. Even if both companies manufacture the new aircraft, Airbus is now certain of making a \$5 million profit. The point is this: Boeing will cancel its new aircraft project. The European subsidy ensures not only that Airbus will manufacture the new aircraft but also that Boeing will suffer a loss if it joins in. The result is that Airbus achieves a profit of \$110 million and can easily repay its subsidy to the European governments. If we assume that the two manufacturers produce entirely for export, the subsidy of \$10 million results in a transfer of \$100 million in profits from the United States to Europe. Figure 9.1 summarizes these results. The welfare effects of strategic trade policy can be found at www.cengage.com/economics/Carbaugh. According to the theory of strategic trade policy, government subsidies can assist domestic firms in capturing economic profits from foreign competitors.

---

① This is an example from Paul Krugman, "Is Free Trade Passe?", *Economic Perspectives*, Fall 1987, pp. 131-144.

Without Subsidy

		Airbus: Produces	Airbus: Does Not Produce
Boeing	Produces	Airbus −5 Boeing −5	Airbus 0 Boeing 100
Boeing	Does Not Produce	Airbus 100 Boeing 0	Airbus 0 Boeing 0

With European Subsidy

		Airbus: Produces	Airbus: Does Not Produce
Boeing	Produces	Airbus −5 Boeing −5	Airbus 0 Boeing 100
Boeing	Does Not Produce	Airbus 100 Boeing 0	Airbus 0 Boeing 0

Figure 9.1 Effects of a European Subsidy Granted to Airbus

Consider another example. Suppose the electronics industry has just two companies, one in Japan and one in the United States. In this industry, learning by doing reduces unit production costs indefinitely with the expansion of output. Assume the Japanese government considers its electronics industry to be "strategic" and imposes trade barriers that close its domestic market to the U.S. competitor; consider that the United States keeps its electronics market open. The Japanese manufacturer can expand its output and reduce its unit cost. Over a period of time, this competitive advantage permits it to drive the U. S. manufacturer out of business. The profits the U.S. company had extracted from U.S. buyers are transferred to the Japanese.

Advocates of strategic trade policy recognize that the classical argument for free trade considered externalities at length. The difference, they maintain, is that the classical theory was based on perfect competition and does not appreciate the most likely source of the externality, whereas modern theories based on imperfect competition does. The externality in question is the ability of companies to capture the fruits of expensive innovation. Classical theory based on perfect competition neglected this factor because large fixed costs are involved in innovation and research and development, and such costs ensure the number of competitors in an industry will be small.

The strategic trade policy concept has been criticized on several grounds. From a political perspective, special interest groups may dictate who will receive government support. Also, if a worldwide cycle of activist trade policy retaliation and counter retaliation were to occur, all nations would be worse off. Governments lack the information to intervene intelligently in the marketplace. In the Boeing-Airbus example, the activist government must know how much profit would be achieved as a result of proceeding with the new aircraft, both with and without foreign competition. Minor miscalculations could result in an intervention that makes the home economy worse off instead of better. Finally, the mere existence of imperfect competition does not guarantee that there is a strategic opportunity to be pursued, even by an omniscient government. There must also be a continuing source of economic profits with no potential competition to erase them. But continuing economic profits are probably less common than governments think.

The case of the European subsidization of aircraft during the 1970s provides an example of the benefits and costs encountered when applying the strategic trade policy concept. During the 1970s, Airbus received a government subsidy of $1.5 billion. The subsidy was intended to help Airbus offset the 20 percent cost disadvantage it faced on the production of its A300 aircraft compared to that of its main competitor, the Boeing 767.

Did the subsidy help the European nations involved in the Airbus consortium? Evidence suggests it did not. Airbus itself lost money on its A300 plane and continued to face cost disadvantages relative to Boeing. European airlines and passengers did benefit because the subsidy kept Airbus prices lower; however, the amount of Airbus's losses roughly matched this gain. Because the costs of the subsidy had to be financed by higher taxes, Europe was probably worse off with the subsidy. The United States also lost, because Boeing's profits were smaller and not fully offset by lower prices accruing to U.S. aircraft users; but the European subsidy did not drive Boeing out of the market. The only obvious gainers were other nations, whose airlines and passengers enjoyed benefits from lower Airbus prices at no cost to themselves.

9.2 Economic Sanctions

9.2 经济制裁

Instead of promoting trade, governments may restrict trade for domestic and foreign policy objectives. **Economic sanctions are government mandated limitations placed on customary trade or financial relations among nations.** They have been used to protect

经济制裁是政府规定的对国家间的贸易或金融关系的限制。

the domestic economy, reduce nuclear proliferation, set compensation for property expropriated by foreign governments, combat international terrorism, preserve national security, and protect human rights. **The nation initiating the economic sanctions, the imposing nation, hopes to impair the economic capabilities of the target nation to such an extent that the target nation will succumb to its objectives.**

发起经济制裁的国家，即实施国，希望削弱目标国家的经济能力，使目标国家屈服于它的目标。

The imposing nation can levy several types of economic sanctions. **Trade sanctions involve boycotts on imposing-nation exports.** The United States has used its role as a major producer of grain, military hardware, and high technology goods as a lever to win overseas compliance with its foreign policy objectives. **Trade sanctions may alsoinclude quotas on imposing-nation imports from the target nation. Financial sanctions can entail limitations on official lending or aid.** During the late 1970s, the U.S. policy of freezing the financial assets of Iran was seen as a factor in the freeing of the U. S. hostages. Table 9. 1 provides examples of economic sanctions levied by the United States for foreign policy objectives.

贸易制裁包括对实施国出口的抵制。

贸易制裁可能还包括实施国从目标国进口的配额。金融制裁可对官方贷款或援助进行限制。

Table 9.1 Selected Economic Sanctions of the United States

Year	Target Country	Objectives
2014	Russia	Discourage annexation of Crimea.
2010	Iran	Discourage nuclear proliferation.
1998	Pakistan & India	Discourage nuclear proliferation.
1993	Haiti	Improve human rights.
1992	Serbia	Terminate civil war in Bosnia-Herzegovina.
1990	Iraq	Terminate Iraq's military takeover of Kuwait.
1985	South Africa	Improve human rights.
1981	Soviet Union	Terminate martial law in Poland.
1979	Iran	Release U. S. hostages; settle expropriation claims.
1961	Cuba	Improve national security.

Figure 9. 2 can be used to illustrate the goal of economic sanctions levied against a target country, say, Iraq. The figure shows the hypothetical production possibilities curve of Iraq for machines and oil. Prior to the imposition of sanctions, suppose that

延伸思考 9.1

Iraq can operate at maximum efficiency as shown by point A along production possibilities curve PPC_0.

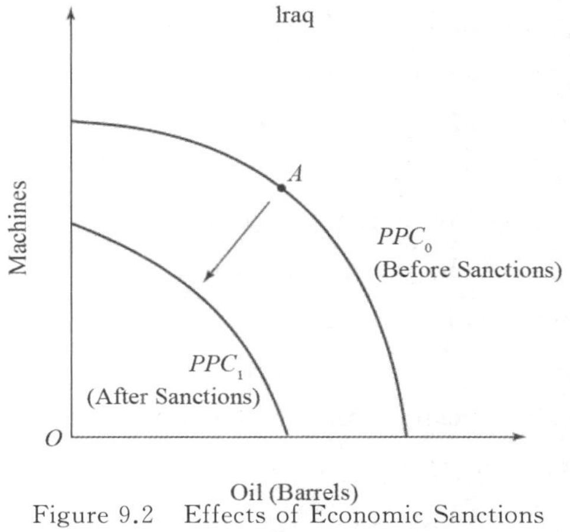

Figure 9.2 Effects of Economic Sanctions

Under the sanctions program, a refusal of the imposing nations to purchase Iraqi oil leads to idle wells, refineries, and workers in Iraq.

Unused production capacity forces Iraq to move inside PP C_0. If imposing nations also impose export sanctions on productive inputs, and curtail equipment sales to Iraq, the output potential of Iraq would decrease. This is shown by an inward shift of Iraq's production possibilities curve to PPC_1. Economic inefficiencies and reduced production possibilities caused by economic sanctions are intended to inflict hardship on the people and government of Iraq. Over time, sanctions may cause a reduced growth rate for Iraq. Even if short run welfare losses from sanctions are not large, they can appear in inefficiencies in the usage of labor and capital, deteriorating domestic expectations and reductions in savings, investment, and employment. Sanctions do reduce Iraq's output potential.

9.2.1 Factors Influencing the Success of Sanctions

9.2.1 影响制裁成功的因素

影响经济制裁成功的因素中最重要的有：(1)实施制裁的国家数量；(2)目标国与实施国之间经济的和政治的关系程度；(3)目标国

The historical record of economic sanctions provides some insight into the factors that govern their effectiveness. **Among the most important determinants of the success of economic sanctions are: (1) the number of nations imposing sanctions, (2) the degree to which the target nation has economic and political ties to the imposing nation(s), (3) the extent of political opposition in the target nation,**

and (4) cultural factors in the target nation.

的政治反对程度；(4)目标国的文化因素。

Although unilateral sanctions may have some success in achieving intended results, it helps if sanctions are imposed by a large number of nations. Multilateral sanctions generally result in greater economic pressure on the target nation than do unilateral measures. Multilateral measures also increase the probability of success by demonstrating that more than one nation disagrees with the target nation's behavior and enhances the political legitimacy of the effort. International ostracism can have a significant psychological impact on the people of a target nation. Failure to generate strong multilateral cooperation can result in sanctions' becoming counterproductive; disputes among the imposing nations over sanctions can be interpreted by the target nation as a sign of disarray and weakness.

Sanctions tend to be more effective if the target nation had substantial economic and political relationships with the imposing nation(s) before the sanctions are imposed. Then the potential costs to the target nation are high if it does not comply with the wishes of the imposing nation(s). Western sanctions against South Africa during the 1980s helped convince the government to reform its apartheid system, in part because South Africa conducted four-fifths of its trade with six Western industrial nations and obtained almost all of its capital from the West.

Strength of political opposition within the target nation also affects the success of sanctions. When the target government faces substantial domestic opposition, economic sanctions can lead powerful business interests (such as companies with international ties) to pressure the government to conform to the imposing nation's wishes. Selected, moderate sanctions with the threat of more severe measures to follow, inflict economic hardship on domestic residents while providing an incentive for them to lobby for compliance to forestall more severe sanctions; the political advantage of levying graduated sanctions may outweigh the disadvantage of giving the target nation time to adjust its economy. If harsh, comprehensive sanctions are imposed immediately, domestic business interests have little incentive to pressure the target government to modify its policy; the economic damage has already been done.

When the people of the target nation have strong cultural ties to the imposing nation(s), they are likely to identify with the imposing nation's objectives that enhances the effectiveness of sanctions. South African whites have generally thought of themselves as part of the Western community. When economic sanctions were imposed onSouth Africa in the 1980s because of its apartheid practices, many liberal whites felt isolated and morally ostracized by the Western world; this encouraged them to lobby the South African government for political reforms.

9.2.2 Economic Sanctions and Weapons of Mass Destruction: Democratic People's Republic of Korea (DPRK) and Iran

9.2.2 经济制裁和大规模杀伤性武器：朝鲜和伊朗

For decades the United States and the United Nations have imposed economic sanctions against countries that have been implicated in the use of terrorism and the development of chemical, biological, and nuclear weapons. Are economic sanctions useful in discouraging this behavior? Let us consider the cases of Iran and DPRK proliferation of weapons of mass destruction such as nuclear bombs and missiles.

延伸思考 9.2

Among the sanctions that have been used against DPRK are bans on trade and the entry of DPRK's ships and people into other countries. The United States has applied financial sanctions to banks that conduct business with DPRK. Once a bank is targeted, it is effectively terminated from the U. S. financial system. The bank cannot clear U.S. dollars and it cannot have transactions with other U.S. banks and financial institutions.

In 2005, the United States blacklisted a bank in Macao, called Banco Delta Asia, that provided illicit financial services to the government of DPRK: it helped the people of DPRK feed counterfeit U.S. $100 bills into circulation, laundered money from drug deals, and financed cigarette smuggling. Because this bank was a main conduit for DPRK to the international financial system, the sanctions had a chilling effect on DPRK's trade and finance. Nevertheless, the sanctions were unable to halt DPRK from testing a nuclear weapon.

One reason why sanctions have not been able to pressure

DPRK into changing its behavior is because DPRK's trade and financial relations with the rest of the world are limited. These limited relations restrict the scope of sanctions and their leverage on DPRK. Another problem is that China and ROK, the main economic lifelines of DPRK, have refrained from implementing substantial sanctions against their neighbor for fear of possible turmoil in the region. To date, it appears that the government of DPRK considers nuclear weapons as vital to its political survival. It will be difficult for sanctions to fulfill their goal of stopping DPRK from developing nuclear weapons.

The case of Iran also demonstrates the limitations of sanctions as a deterrent to the development of nuclear weapons. Since 1987, the United States has implemented numerous sanctions against Iran, such as trade and financial sanctions. These sanctions were intensified in 2006 when Iran openly pursued the development of a nuclear reactor. Iran insisted that it was merely fostering nuclear energy, but other countries have been suspicious that this technology can be shifted to the development of nuclear bombs. In 2011, the United States implemented sanctions targeting Iran's central bank and oil exports. A year later, the United States blacklisted Iran's shipping, shipbuilding and energy sectors. The result was a sharp drop in the value of Iran's currency, the rial, an increase in the rate of inflation to over 50 percent, a dramatic decline in Iran's gross domestic product, and an unemployment rate of 20 percent. Iran's oil exports that fund nearly half of Iran's government spending, fell by about half, from 2.5 million barrels a day to about 1.25 million barrels. The drop was driven by an EU embargo and U.S. pressure on Iranian oil customers.

Proponents of sanctions have maintained that Iran's economy is vulnerable to outside economic pressure. Iran relies on foreign capital and investment to develop its untapped oil fields and fledgling nuclear energy sector. Iran's sizeable role in oil production makes it difficult for oil dependent countries such as the United States to impose severe sanctions against Iran. As U.S. trade with Iran has decreased in the past two decades, Iran's trade with the rest of the world has increased, reducing the leverage that the United States has against Iran. Iran continues to export oil to

China, India, ROK, and Japan, the main sources of its oil revenues.

With the pressure of the sanctions mounting, in 2013 the government ofIran indicated that it was ready to resolve the nation's nuclear standoff with the West. This resulted in an interim agreement between Iran and the West: some of the sanctions against Iran were eased in exchange for Iran promising to temporarily curb part of its nuclear program. The hope was that the interim agreement would eventually lead to a permanent nuclear agreement. At the writing of this text, it remains to be seen how negotiations will play out.

9.3 Protection of Intellectual Property Rights

9.3 知识产权保护

In the 1800s, Charles Dickens criticized U.S. publishers for printing unauthorized versions of his works without paying him one penny. U.S. copyright protection did not apply to foreign (British) authors, so Dickens's popular fiction could be pirated without punishment. In recent years, it is U.S. companies whose profit expectations have been frustrated. Publishers in ROK run off copies of bootlegged U.S. textbooks without providing royalty payments. American research laboratories find certain industries and products are well-known targets of pirates, counterfeiters, and other infringers of **intellectual property rights** (IPRs). Counterfeiting is common in industries such as automobile parts, jewelry, sporting goods, and watches. Piracy of audio and videotapes, computer software, themselves in legal tangles with Japanese electronics manufacturers concerning patent infringement.

知识产权

And printed materials is widespread throughout the world. Industries in which product life cycles are shorter than the time necessary to obtain and enforce a patent are also subject to thievery; examples are photographic equipment and telecommunications. Table 9.2 provides examples of IPR violations in China.

Table 9.2 Examples of Intellectual Property Right Violations in China

Affected Firms	Violation in China
Epson	Copying machines and ink cartridges are counterfeited.
Microsoft	Counterfeiting of Windows and Windows NT, with packaging virtually indistinguishable from the real product and sold in authorized outlets.
Yamaha	5 of every 6 JYM150-A motorcycles and ZY125 scooters bearing Yamaha's name are fake in China. Some state-owned factories manufacture copies four months following the introduction of a new model.
Gillette	Up to one-fourth of its Parker pens, Duracell batteries, and Gillette razors sold in China are pirated.
Anheuser-Busch	Some 640 million bottles of fake Budweiser beer are sold annually in China.
Bestfoods	Bogus versions of Knorr bouillon and Skippy Peanut Butter lead to tens of millions of dollars in forgone sales each year.

Source: U.S. Trade Representative. National Trade Estimate Report on Foreign Trade Barriers, various issues. http://www.ustr.gov.

Intellectual property is an invention, idea, product, or process that has been registered with the government and awards the inventor (or author) exclusive rights to use the invention for a given time period. Governments use several techniques to protect intellectual property. **Copyrights are awarded to protect works of original authorship (music compositions and textbooks); most nations issue copyright protection for the remainder of the author's life plus 50 years. Trademarks are awarded to manufacturers and provide exclusive rights to a distinguishing name or symbol (Coca-Cola). Patents secure to an inventor for a term, usually** 15 **years or more, the exclusive right to make, use, or sell the invention.**

知识产权是一项已在政府注册的发明、理念、产品或过程，政府授予发明人（或作者）在特定时间内使用该发明的专有权利。版权用于保护原作者的作品（音乐作品和教科书），大多数国家都对作者给予余生加上50年的版权保护。商标被授予制造商，以对其使用具有辨识度的名称或标志提供专有权利（如可口可乐）。专利对发明人进行一段时期的保护，通常是15年或更久，赋予其制造、使用或出售该发明的权利。

In spite of efforts to protect IPRs, competing firms sometimes infringe on the rights of others by making a cheaper imitation of the original product. In 1986, the courts ruled that Kodak had infringed on Polaroid's patents for instant cameras and awarded Polaroid more than $900 million in damages. Another infringement would occur if a company manufactured an instant camera similar to Polaroid's and labeled and marketed it as a Polaroid camera; this is an example of a counterfeit product.

延伸思考 9. 3

The lack of effective international procedures for protecting IPRs becomes a problem when the expense of copying an innovation (including the cost of penalties if caught) is less than the cost of purchasing or leasing the technology. Suppose that Warner-Lambert Drug Co. develops a product that cures the common cold, called "Cold-Free", and the firm plans to export it to Japan. If Cold-Free is not protected, Japan either because, Japan does not recognize IPRs or Warner-Lambert has not filed for protection, cheaper copies of Cold-Free could legally be developed and marketed. If Warner-Lambert's trademark is not protected, counterfeit cold remedies that are indistinguishable from Cold-Free could be legally sold in Japan. These copies would result in reduced sales and profits for Warner-Lambert. If "Cold-Free" is a trademark that consumers strongly associate with Warner-Lambert, a counterfeit product of noticeably inferior quality could adversely affect Warner-Lambert's reputation and detract from the sales of both Cold-Free and other Warner-Lambert products.

Although most nations have regulations protecting IPRs, many problems have been associated with trade in products affected by IPRs. One problem is differing IPR regulations across nations. The United States uses a first-to-invent rule when determining patent eligibility, whereas most other nations employ a first-to-file rule. Another problem is lack of enforcement of international IPR agreements. These problems stem largely from differing incentives to protect intellectual property, especially between nations that are innovating, technological exporters and those that are aren't technological importers. Developing nations lacking in research and development and patent innovation, sometimes pirate foreign technology and use it to produce goods at costs lower than could be achieved in the innovating nation. Poorer developing nations often find it difficult to pay the higher prices that would prevail if innovated products (such as medical supplies) were provided patent protection. They have little incentive to provide patent protection to the products they need.

As long as the cost of pirating technology, including the probability and costs of being caught, is less than the profits captured by the firm doing the pirating, technology pirating tends to continue. However, pirating reduces the rate of profitability earned by firms in the innovating nations that in turn deters them from investing in research and development. Over time, this lack of investment leads to fewer products and welfare losses for the people of both nations.

The United States has faced many obstacles in trying to protect its intellectual property. Dozens of nations lack adequate legal structures to protect the patents of foreign firms.

Others have consciously excluded certain products (such as chemicals) from protection to support their industries. Even in developed countries where legal safeguards exist, the fast pace of technological innovation often outruns the protection provided by the legal system.

Microsoft Scorns China's Piracy of Software

微软排斥中国的盗版软件

延伸思考 9. 4

China's rapid economic transformation has presented both opportunities and challenges to many U. S. businesses. Although firms such as Boeing and General Electric have realized success in the China market, U. S. firms have reported losses associated with IPR infringement in China, including losses in sales, profits, license and royalty fees, as well as damage to brand names and product reputation. Analysts have estimated that U. S. firms' reported losses from IPR infringement in China amounted to about $48 billion in 2009, as seen in Table 9. 3.

Consider the case of Microsoft Corp., the maker of computer software. Microsoft is among the firms whose sales have suffered because of Chinese piracy. In 2011, Microsoft's revenue in China was only about 5 percent of what it received in the United States, even though personal computer sales in the two countries were about the same. In China, illegal copies of Microsoft's Office and Windows programs were sold on street corners for $2 to $3 each, a fraction of their retail price, despite attempts by the company to discourage illegal counterfeiting. Also, Microsoft's software revenue per personal computer sold in China was only about a sixth of the amount it earned in India. Microsoft's total revenue in China, with a population 1. 3 billion, was less than what it received in the Netherlands in 2011, a country of fewer than 17 million.

Table 9. 3 Reported Losses* from Intellectual Property Right Infringement in China on U. S. Businesses, 2009

Sectors	Losses / billion dollars
Information and Other Services	26. 7
High-tech and Heavy Manufacturing	18. 5
Chemical Manufacturing	2. 0
Consumer Goods Manufacturing	0. 8
Transportation Manufacturing	0. 2
Subtotal	48. 2
Copyright Infringement	23. 7
Trademark Infringement	6. 1
Patent Infringement	1. 3
Misappropriation of Trade Secrets	1. 1
Other	16. 0
Subtotal	48. 2

* In response to a U. S. International Trade Commission survey.

Source: U. S. International Trade Commission. China: Effects of Intellectual Property Infringement and Indigenous Innovation Policies on the U. S. Economy, May 2011.

Microsoft has rejected the argument widespread in China, that many Chinese consumers use pirated software because authentic versions are too expensive. Although Microsoft recognizes that not everyone in China can afford a personal computer, the firm maintains that if you can afford a PC, you can afford the software that accompanies it. Despite having frustrations about piracy, Microsoft has continued to invest in China that will soon be the world's largest PC market.

The company has historically attempted a cooperative strategy with Chinese officials, reaching deals to require Chinese PC makers to ship their products with legitinmate copies of Office and Windows from their factories. The government of China has admitted counterfeiting problems but contends that it is making efforts to improve the situation. The government of China has ordered all state institutions to buy authentic software.

Nevertheless, analysts have estimated that about 78 percent of the PC software installed in China in 2011 was pirated. Indeed, China's counterfeit and piracy market is the biggest in the world and copyright infringement in the country has long been a sticking point in U. S. -Chinese relations.

9.4 Industrial Policies of United States

9.4 美国的产业政策

Besides enacting regulations intended to produce a fair trading environment for all parties engaging in international business, **the United States has implemented industrial policies to enhance the competitiveness of domestic producers. Such policies involve government channeling of resources into specific, targeted industries that it views as important for future economic growth. Among the methods used to channel resources are tax incentives, loan guarantees, and low interest loans.**

美国还实施了旨在提高国内生产商竞争力的产业政策。这些政策包括政府将资源引导到特定的、有针对性的行业，这些行业被认为对未来的经济增长至关重要。用于引导资源的方法包括税收激励、贷款担保和低利率贷款。

What has been the U.S. approach to industrial policy? The U.S. government has attempted to provide a favorable climate for business given the social, environmental, and safety constraints imposed by modern society. Rather than formulating a coordinated industrial policy to affect particular industries, the U. S. government has generally emphasized macroeconomic policies (fiscal and monetary policies) aimed at objectives as economic stability, growth, and the broad allocation of the gross domestic product.

However, there is no doubt that the U.S. government uses a number of measures to shape the structure of the economy that would be called "industrial policies" in other nations. **The most notable of these measures is agricultural policy.** In agriculture, a farmer who initiates a major innovation can be imitated by many other farmers who capture the benefits without sharing the risks. To rectify this problem, the U. S. government is involved in research in agricultural techniques and in the dissemination of this information to farmers through its agricultural extension service, as well as the fostering of large scale projects such as irrigation facilities. **The U.S. government has also provided support for the shipping, aerospace, shipbuilding, energy, and defense industries, primarily on the grounds of national security.**

（美国）最著名的“产业政策”是农业政策。

美国政府还为航运、航空航天、造船、能源和国防工业提供了支持，主要是基于国家安全的考虑。

Another element of U.S. industrial policy is export promotion. The U. S. government furnishes exporters with marketing information and technical assistance, in addition to trade missions that help expose new exporters to foreign customers. The government also promotes exports by sponsoring exhibits of U.S. goods at international trade fairs and establishing overseas trade centers that enable U.S. businesses to exhibit and sell machinery and equipment. The United States also encourages exports by allowing its manufacturers to form export trade associations to facilitate the marketing of U.S. products abroad.

美国产业政策的另一部分是出口促进。

The United States provides export subsidies to its producers to promote international sales. The U. S. Export-Import Bank (Eximbank) is the official export credit agency of the U. S. government. Founded in 1934, its purpose is to provide cheap credit for foreign customers who purchase American made products. Such credit is provided through a variety of loan, loan guarantee, and insurance programs. These programs are available to any American export firm regardless of size. The Eximbank does not compete with private sector lenders, but rather provides financing for transactions that would otherwise not occur because commercial lenders are either unable or unwilling to accept the risks inherent in the deal. Table 9.4 provides examples of direct loans and loan guarantees made by Eximbank. Major beneficiaries of Eximbank credit have included aircraft, telecommunications, power generating equipment, and energy developments. Firms such as Boeing, General Electric, Caterpillar, and Westinghouse have enjoyed substantial benefits from these programs as well as many small and medium size firms. Because of the fees and interest it charges borrowers, the Eximbank is self sustaining.

美国向生产商提供出口补贴以促进其国际销售。美国进出口银行（Eximbank）是美国政府的官方出口信贷机构。

Table 9.4 Examples of Loans Provided by Eximbank of the United States

Foreign Borrower/U.S. Exporter	Purpose
Banco Santander Noroeste of Brazil/General Electric	Locomotives
Government of Bulgaria/Westinghouse	Instruments
Air China/Boeing	Aircraft
Government of Croatia/Bechtel International	Highway construction
Government of Ghana/Wanan International	Electrical equipment
Government of Indonesia/IBM	Computer hardware
Japan Airlines/Boeing	Aircraft
Fevisa Industrial of Mexico/	
Pennsylvania Crusher Inc.	Glass manufacturing equipment
Delta Communications of Mexico/Motorola	Communications equipment

Source: Export-Import Bank of the United States. Annual Report, various issues. http://www.exim.gov.

延伸思考 9.5

Proponents of the Eximbank contend that American companies that use its financing compete in a global marketplace in which foreign companies and their governments systematically use export credit financing. A Chinese locomotive company can offer government export financing to international buyers that makes their trains less expensive in foreign markets such as India. When an American company such as General Electric is competing for that locomotive sale, it ought to be able to provide comparable financing for its locomotives. Such policies ensure a level playing field for American companies in a competitive global marketplace.

In offering cheap credit in financing exports, Eximbank has sometimes been criticized because some of its funds are borrowed from the U.S. Treasury. Critics question whether U.S. tax revenues should subsidize exports to foreign countries at interest rates lower than could be obtained from private institutions. To this extent, it is true that tax funds distort trade and redistribute income toward exporters.

Officially supported lending for U.S. exports is also provided by the Commodity Credit Corporation (CCC), a government owned corporation administered by the U. S. Department of Agriculture. The CCC makes available export credit financing for eligible agricultural commodities. The interest rates charged by the CCC are usually slightly below the prevailing rates charged by private financial institutions. We will next consider two cases of industrial policy.

9.4.1 U. S. Airlines and Boeing Spar over Export-Import Bank Credit

9.4.1 美国航空公司和波音公司因进出口银行信贷而争吵

In 2010, major airlines in the United States joined to oppose billions of dollars in subsidies for jetliners bought by their foreign rivals from Boeing Co. What they opposed was the export-financing practices of the U. S. Eximbank that provides cheap credit to foreign countries and companies that purchase American made products. Such credit is extended to foreign customers at below-market interest rates that do not qualify for loans from commercial lenders. In 2010, about 35 percent of Boeing's sales was supported by credit provided by the U.S. Eximbank.

Carriers such as Delta Airlines and Southwest Airlines contended that because they are American companies, they cannot receive these export subsidies that can greatly increase an airline's access to funding and cut its cost of borrowing while their foreign rivals can benefit from such subsidies. Delta maintained that its interest rate on jetliner purchases from Boeing was 4.5 percentage points higher than the rate paid by carriers in the United Arab Emirates. These international rivals obtained longer term financing and were able to finance a higher percentage of the purchase price than Delta. Delta maintained that giving foreign rivals access to cheap financing puts it at a cost disadvantage and floods the world airline market with uneconomic capacity.

Export subsidies are large because bankers generally dislike lending directly to airlines other than a handful of those with strong credit ratings. Rather than assuming the risk of default when making loans to airlines, bankers want the loans to be guaranteed by the government. Some bankers who are willing to accept more risk and thus charge higher interest rates on loans have maintained that the practices of the U.S. Eximbank squeeze them out of the market.

The dispute amounted to a conflict over which contributes more to the U.S. economy—airlines or plane manufacturers, and how the government can support them without distorting markets. According to Delta, the U.S. government must realize that export credit does more than help Boeing; it also has negative consequences for the American airline industry. Boeing criticized Delta's position by noting that curtailing export credit would jeopardize U. S. aerospace competitiveness as governments in Canada, Brazil, and Europe have ramped up access to export credit.

For the U.S. economy as a whole, the subsidy conflict revealed a tradeoff. Economic gains accrued to Boeing in the form of increased sales, profits, more jobs, and higher earnings for its workers. Increased jetliner exports by Boeing also strengthened the U. S. balance of trade. The cost disadvantage placed on American airlines by the export subsidy led to decreasing sales and profits, losses in jobs and earnings for their workers, and a weakening of the U.S. trade balance as American airlines lost market share to foreign airlines. It remains to be seen how this conflict will be resolved.

对美国整体经济而言，补贴冲突暴露了一个权衡取舍的问题。波音公司从增加的销售额、利润、更多的就业机会和工人更高的收入中获得了经济收益。波音公司飞机出口的增加也加强了美国的贸易平衡。出口补贴给美国航空公司带来的成本劣势导致了销售和利润的下降，工人的失业和收入的减少，以及美国航空公司失去了对外国航空公司的市场份额导致美国的贸易平衡被削弱。

9.4.2 U.S. Solar Industry Dims as China's Industrial Policy Lights Up

9.4.2 美国太阳能产业随着中国产业政策的发展而出现问题

Solar energy has been harnessed by humans since ancient times using a range of ever evolving technologies. Although there is no denying solar energy's promise and potential, debate remains about how the industry should develop. Should the market be relied on to determine winners and losers or should industrial policy carry out the task, whereby governments subsidize their producers to enhance their competitiveness?

The bankruptcy of three American solar power companies in 2011 left China's industry with a dominant sales position; about two-thirds of the market. Another major producer of solar energy, Germany, was also retrenching in that year. **Although some American, Japanese, and European solar companies had a technological edge over their Chinese rivals, they maintained that they could not beat the Chinese rivals when it came to cost. They noted that**

尽管一些美国、日本和欧洲的太阳能公司对中国的竞争对手有技术优势，但他们坚持认为，在成本问题上，他们无法击败中国。

the government of China has been particularly effective in developing an industrial policy that provides Chinese manufacturers with a number of advantages in the global solar industry, including access to lower cost capital, subsidized electricity rates, free access to land, and much a shortened permitting process for factories. China's solar energy producers have realized huge economies of scale that result in decreasing production cost and increased competitiveness. China is not alone in using industrial policy to promote clean energy. The EU and the United States provide governmental support for solar energy, including tax credits for buyers and low interest rate loans and loan guarantees for solar companies.

他们指出，中国政府在制定一项产业政策方面特别有效，这一政策为中国制造商在全球太阳能产业提供了许多优势，包括降低成本资本、补贴电价、免费获得土地，以及缩短审批过程。

At the heart of the solar industry's problems in 2011 were sharply decreasing prices for solar panels and their components—wafers, cells, polysilicon, and the modules themselves. The reason was obvious: there were simply too many manufacturers trying to sell their products. The glut of manufacturers was because of factors including efforts by the U.S. government to promote clean technology, venture capitalists pouring into the sector, investors purchasing stock issues of solar companies during an upswing in oil prices, and an increased sense of urgency for climate change. European governments offered substantial subsidies for solar installation, stimulating demand in the market. The abundant production of solar panels resulted in cutthroat price competition. In 2010, solar panels sold for \$1.60 per watt, on average. By 2011, the going price was between \$.90 per watt and \$1.05 per watt. Despite the buyers' market, customers were not purchasing solar panels fast enough to match the increase in supply. The result was the bankruptcy of numerous producers.

延伸思考 9.6

The bankruptcy of Solyndra Inc. in 2011, a California company making solar panels, received much publicity. In 2010, President Barack Obama visited Solyndra and touted it as a leading company in a growing industry. The company found that it could not compete with cheaper Chinese manufactured solar panels, so it defaulted on its government guaranteed loan of \$535 million. This resulted in attacks by critics of Obama who tried to make the failed solar panel company both a symbol of the failure of industrial policy in solar energy and a club with which to beat alternative renewable energy of all kinds.

9.5 Industrial Policies of Japan

9.5 日本的产业政策

Although the United States has generally not used explicit industrial policies to support specific industries, such policies have been used elsewhere. Consider the case of Japan.

Japan has become a technological leader in the post-World War II era. During the 1950s, Japan's exports consisted primarily of textiles and other low-tech products. By the 1960s and 1970s, its exports emphasized capital-intensive products such as autos, steel, and ships. By the 1980s and 1990s, Japan had become a major world competitor in high tech goods such as optical fibers and semiconductors. **Advocates of industrial policy assert that government assistance for emerging industries has helped transform the Japanese economy from low tech to heavy industry to high tech. They claim that protection from imports, R&D subsidies and the like fostered the development of Japanese industry.** Clearly, the Japanese government provided assistance to shipbuilding and steel during the 1950s, to autos and machine tools during the 1960s, and to high tech industries beginning in the early 1970s. Since the mid-1970s, the government's industrial policy has been more modest and subtle.

支持产业政策的人士声称，政府对新兴产业的扶持，帮助日本经济从低技术产业向重工业转变，向高科技产业转型。他们声称，限制进口、研发补贴等措施促进了日本工业的发展。

To implement its industrial policies in manufacturing, the Japanese government has created the Ministry of Economy, Trade and Industry (METI). This ministry attempts to facilitate the shifting of resources into high tech industries by targeting specific industries for support. With the assistance of consultants from leading corporations, trade unions, banks, and universities, METI forms a consensus on the best policies to pursue. The next step of industrial policy is to increase domestic R&D, investment, and production. Targeted industries have received support in the form of trade protection, allocations of foreign exchange, R&D subsidies, loans at below market interest rates, loans that must be repaid if a firm becomes profitable, favorable tax treatment, and joint government-industry research projects intended to develop promising technologies.

为了实施制造业的产业政策，日本政府成立了经济贸易产业省（METI）。这一部门试图通过针对特定行业的支持来促进资源向高科技产业转移。

然而，并不是所有的日本产业政策都取得了成功，正如计算机、铝和石化产品的例子所示。即使是日本在造船和

Without government support, it is improbable that Japanese semiconductor, telecommunications equipment, fiber optics, and machine tool industries would be as competitive as they are. **Not all Japanese industrial policies have been successful, however, as seen in the cases of computers, aluminum, and petrochemicals. Even industries in which Japan is competitive in world markets such as shipbuilding and steel have witnessed prolonged periods of excess capacity. Some of Japan's biggest success stories (TVs, stereos, and VCRs) were not the industries' most heavily targeted by the Japanese government. Although Japan has the most visible industrial policy of the industrialized nations, the importance of that policy to Japan's success should not be exaggerated.**

钢铁等世界市场上上具有竞争力的行业，也经历了长期的产能过剩。日本一些最大的成功故事（电视、音响和录像机）并不是日本政府最主要的目标。尽管日本拥有工业化国家最明显的产业政策，但这一政策对日本成功的重要性不应被夸大。

☞ Key Terms

strategic trade policy; imperfect competition; economic sanctions; financial sanctions; intellectual property rights (IPRs); industrial policies; Export-Import Bank; Ministry of Economy, Trade and Industry (METI)

☞ 关键术语

战略性贸易政策、不完全竞争、经济制裁、金融制裁、知识产权、产业政策、进出口银行、日本经济贸易产业省

☞ Questions

☞ 本章习题

1. What is the purpose of strategic trade policy?

2. Assume that the nation of Spain is "small" and unable to influence the Brazilian (world) price of steel. Spain's supply and demand schedules are illustrated in Table 9.5. Assume that Brazil's price is $400 per ton of steel. Using graph paper, plot the demand and supply schedules of Spain and Brazil on the same graph.

(1) With free trade, how many tons of steel will be produced, purchased, and imported by Spain? Calculate the dollar value of Spanish producer and consumer surpluses.

(2) Suppose the Brazilian government grants its steel firms a production subsidy of $200 per ton. Plot Brazil's subsidy adjusted supply schedule on your graph.

① What is the new market price of steel? At this price, how much steel will Spain produce, purchase, and import?

② The subsidy helps/hurts Spanish firms because their producer surplus rises/falls by \$ ____ ; Spanish steel users realize a rise/fall in the consumer surplus of \$ ____. The Spanish economy as a whole benefits/suffers from the subsidy by an amount totaling \$ ____.

Table 9.5 Steel Supply and Demand for Spain

Price/dollars	Quantity Supplied/million tons	Quantity Demanded/million tons
0	0	12
200	2	10
400	4	8
600	6	6
800	8	4
1,000	10	2
1,200	12	0

3. What is the purpose of economic sanctions? What problems do they pose for the nation initiating the sanctions? When are sanctions most successful in achieving their goals?

4. What is intellectual property? Why has intellectual property become a major issue in recent rounds of international trade negotiations?

5. Describe the industrial policies adopted by the U. S. government. How have these policies differed from those adopted by Japan?

6. If the United States is a net importer of a product that is being subsidized or dumped by Japan, not only do U.S. consumers gain, but they also gain more than U.S. producers lose from the Japanese subsidies or dumping. Explain why this is true.

Chapter 10

Regional Trade Agreements

Since World War Ⅱ, advanced nations have significantly lowered their trade restrictions. Such trade liberalization has been achieved from two approaches. The first occurs when a small group of nations, typically on regional basis, forms a regional trade agreement by discriminatively eliminating trade barriers through negotiation only among the nations joining together. The second is a reciprocal reduction of trade barriers on a nondiscriminatory basis. Under the GATT and its successor, the World Trade Organization, member nations acknowledge that trade-barrier reduction agreed by any two nations will be extended to all other members. Regional trade agreements have been an **exception** to the principle of nondiscrimination embodied in the GATT and WTO. Because of setback in the multinational negotiation, the regional agreements have been flourishing. This chapter will explore not only types and effects of regional trade agreements but also the development of GATT and the prospect of WTO.

第十章

区域贸易协定

第二次世界大战以来，发达国家的贸易壁垒通过两种途径已经显著降低。第一是区域贸易协定，歧视性地在小范围内削减关税与非关税壁垒；第二是全球性地非歧视地实现贸易自由化。

10.1 Types of Regional Trade Agreements

The degree of trading integration ranges from preferential trade agreements to free trade areas, customs unions, common markets, and economic unions.

Preferential trade agreements provide lower barriers on trade among participating nations than on trade with non-member nations. This is the loosest form of economic integration. The best example of a preferential trade agreement is the British Commonwealth Preference Scheme, established in 1932 by the United Kingdom with members and some former members of the

10.1 区域贸易协定的类型

根据一体化程度的不同可以分为优惠贸易安排、自由贸易区、关税同盟、共同市场与经济联盟。

优惠贸易协定

British Empire as a response to the Great Depression.

A **free trade area** is the form of economic integration wherein all barriers are removed on trade among members, but each nation retains its own barriers to trade with non-members. The best example is the North American Free Trade Agreement (NAFTA) formed by the United States, Canada and Mexico in 1993. We will discuss NAFTA further in next section.

自由贸易区

A **customs union** allows no tariffs or other barriers on trade among members as in a free trade area, and in addition it harmonizes trade policies, such as the setting of common tariff rates, towards the rest of the world. The most famous example is the European Union (EU), or European Common Market, formed in 1957. Another example is the Zollverein established in 1834 by a large number of sovereign German states, which proved significant in Bismarck's unification of Germany in 1870.

关税同盟

A **common market** goes beyond a customs union by also allowing the free movement of labor and capital among member nations. The EU achieved the status of a common market at the end of 1992.

共同市场

An **economic union** goes still further by harmonizing or even unifying the monetary and fiscal policies of member states. This is the most advanced type of economic integration. The creation of an economic union is more ambitious than achieving the other forms of integration, because an economic union requires an agreement to transfer economic sovereignty to a supranational authority. The economic union would thus include the dimension of a monetary union. Belgium and Luxembourg formed an economic union during 1920s. The United States serves as another example of monetary union.

经济同盟

10.2 Effects of Customs Union

10.2 关税同盟的效应

How good or how bad is all these trade agreements? The discussion in this chapter is generally in terms of customs union, especially in this section, we will examine effects of customs union. First are the static effects of economic integration on productive efficiency and consumer welfare. Second are the dynamic effects of economic integration, which relate to member nations' long run rates of growth. The static effects and dynamic effects determine the overall welfare gains or losses associated with the formation of a regional trade agreement.

10.2.1 Static Effects

10.2.1 静态效应

静态效应是关税同盟理论的局部均衡分析，包括贸易创造与贸易转移。

The static, partial equilibrium effects of forming a customs union are measured in terms of trade creation and trade diversion. Trade creation occurs when some domestic production in a nation that is a member of the customs union is replaced by lower-cost imports from another member nation. Trade diversion occurs when lower-cost imports from outside the customs union are replaced by higher cost imports from a union member. The effects of trade-creating and trade-diverting are illustrated in Figure 10.1.

Viner, who pioneered the development of the theory of customs unions in 1950, concentrated on the production effect of trade creation and ignored the consumption effect. Meade extended the theory of customs union in 1955 and was the first to consider the consumption effect. Johnson then added the two triangles to obtain the total welfare gain of a customs union.

Assume a world composed of three nations, including British, Japan and Germany. Suppose all economic resources are fully employed before and after formation of the customs union in the three nations and the British is an importing nation. Before formation of customs union, the British imposed a uniform tariff, GBP 1,000 per car. With no trade, the British could buy Japanese cars at GBP 5,000 and the next cheapest alternative is to buy German cars delivered at GBP 5,500. So Britain would import only Japanese cars and none from Germany as shown by Figure 10.1A. With identical tariff, Japanese cars continue to take price advantage over Germany cars and trade direction stays the same.

Now let Britain and Germany establish a customs union, removing all tariffs on goods between the two nations while leaving the same tariffs on goods from outside the union. German cars now cost only GBP 5,500 in Britain, while the price of Japanese cars in Britain remains GBP 6,000 because they still incur the tariff. After formation of the customs union, Trade direction divert from Britain with Japan to Britain with Germany. The trading price decreases from GBP 6,000 to GBP 5,500 as shown by Figure 10.1B.

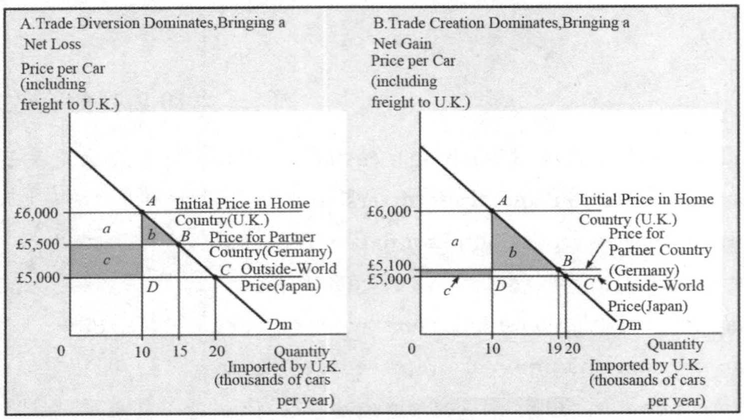

Figure 10.1 Trade Creation and Trade Diversion in Joining a Trade Agreement

Britain ends up with two effects on its well-being.

First is **a gain from trade creation.** Trade creation is the net volume of new trade created by forming the trade agreement. It increases the welfare of the country because it shifts productions from less efficient domestic producers to the more efficient producers inside union. Area b represents gains in the British economy which stem from the expansion of domestic consumption and the replacement of higher-cost British production by lower-cost partner production. Second is **a loss from trade diversion.** Trade diversion is the volume of trade diverted from low-cost outside exporters to higher-cost arranged-partner exporters and reduces the welfare of the country, worsens the international allocation of resources and shifts production away from comparative advantage, which is shown as area c.

贸易创造的福利利得

贸易转移的福利损失

At the same time, the British government loses all its previous tariff revenue, the area a+c.

The net effect on well-being, the trade-creation gain minus the trade-diversion loss, could be positive or negative. Several factors could contribute to the success of a customs union. One factor is the kinds of nations that tend to benefit from a customs union. Nations whose pre-union economies are quite competitive are likely to benefit from trade creation because the formation of the union

关税同盟的静态效应是贸易转移与贸易创造的福利加总。

offers greater opportunity for specialization in production. Another factor is the size and number of nations in the union. The larger the size and the greater the number, the greater gains are likely to be, because there is a greater possibility that the world's low-lost producers will be union members. In the extreme case in which the union consists of the entire world, there can be only trade creation, no trade diversion. In addition, the scope for trade diversion is smaller when the customs union's common external tariff is lower rather than higher. Because a lower tariff allows greater trade to take place with non-member nations, there will be less replacement of cheaper imports from non-member nations by relatively high-cost imports from partner nations. To the extent that a customs union does not increase trade barriers against the rest of the world, the elimination of trade barriers among union members represents a movement toward freer trade.

There are other static welfare effects resulting from the formation of a customs union. One is the **administrative saving** from the elimination of customs officers, border patrols and so on, for trade among member nations. Second, any customs union, by acting as a single unit in international trade negotiations, is likely to have much more **bargaining power** than all of its member separately. Finally, trade diversion effect reduces imports from the rest of the world and will lead to an **improvement in the collective terms** of trade of the customs union.

其他的关税同盟静态福利效应包括管理成本的节约、讨价还价能力的提高，以及贸易条件的改善。

10.2.2 Dynamic Effects

10.2.2 动态效应

Besides the static welfare effects discussed earlier, the nations forming a customs union are likely to receive several important dynamic effects. These are due to increased competition, economies of scale, stimulus to investment, and better utilization of economic resources.

The greatest dynamic effect from the formation of a customs union is the increased competition that is likely to result. In the absence of a customs union, producers, especially those in monopolistic and oligopolistic markets, are likely to grow sluggish and complacent behind trade barriers. But when a customs union is formed and trade barriers among member nations are eliminated,

关税同盟的形成所产生的最大动态效应是可能导致竞争加剧。

producers in each nation must become more efficient to meet the competition of other producers within the union, or they would go out of business. The increased level of competition is also likely to stimulate the development and utilization of new technology.

A second possible effect from the formation of a customs union is that economies of scale are likely to result from the enlarged market. Significant economies were achieved after formation of the EU by reducing the range of differentiated products manufactured in each plant and increasing production runs.

关税同盟形成的第二个可能的影响是市场扩大可产生规模经济。

Another possible effect is the stimulus to investment to take advantage of the enlarged market and to meet the increased competition. Furthermore, the formation of a customs union is likely to spur outsiders to set up production facilities within the customs union to avoid the discriminatory trade barriers imposed on non-union products. These are the so-called tariff factories. The massive investment that the United States firms made in Europe after 1955 and again after 1986 can be explained by their desire not to be excluded from this rapidly growing market.

另一个可能的影响是促进投资，以满足更大的市场需求和应对竞争。

Finally, in a customs union that is also a common market, the free community-wide movement of labor and capital is likely to result in better utilization of the economic resources of the entire community.

最后，在关税同盟这一共同市场中的，自由流动有助于劳动力和资本的整个社会资源的充分利用。

These dynamic gains resulting from the formation of a customs union are presumed to be much greater than the static gains discussed earlier and to be very significant. Indeed, the United Kingdom joined the EU in 1973 primarily because of them.

To be pointed out is that joining a customs union because of static and dynamic gains that it provides is only a second-best solution. Not all of these effects occur for every product or member nation when a trade agreement is signed, but they do occur for some products and some members. The optimal solution may be for a nation to unilaterally eliminate all trade barriers. But it is not realistic.

需要指出的是，加入关税同盟后的静态利得与动态利得都是次优选择。

10.3 Practices of Regional Integration

10.3 区域贸易安排的示例

In this section, we briefly survey some practices of regional integration with the formation of the EU, the North American Free Trade Area, and Association of Southeast Asian Nations.

10.3.1 European Union

10.3.1 欧盟

Europe has been the locus of the longest and deepest regional integration. The highlights of the chronology of European Union are illustrated as follows.

欧盟是一体化时间最长、程度最深的区域贸易安排。

The European Union is set up with the aim of ending the frequent and bloody wars between neighbors, which culminated in the Second World War. As of 1950, the European Coal and Steel Community began to unite European countries economically and politically in order to secure lasting peace. The six founding countries are Belgium, France, Germany, Italy, Luxembourg, and the Netherlands.

The 1950s are dominated by a Cold War between East and West. Protests in Hungary against the Communist regime are put down by Soviet tanks in 1956. In 1957, the Treaty of Rome creates the European Economic Community (EEC), or "Common Market".

The 1960s is a good period for the economy, helped by the fact that EU countries stopped charging custom duties when they traded with each other. They also agreed joint control over food production, so that everybody now has enough to eat and soon there was even surplus in agricultural production.

Denmark, Ireland, and the United Kingdom joined the European Union on 1 January 1973, raising the number of member states to nine. Studies in the 1960s and 1970s tended to conclude that the net gains from forming the EU were small but positive.

In the 1980s the EU moved beyond being a customs union and toward a single common market. With the collapse of communism across Central and Eastern Europe, Europeans become closer neighbors. In 1993 the single market is completed with the "four freedoms" of: movement of goods, services, people, and money. The Single European Act, which took full effect at the end of 1992, forced many changes. First, it neutralized separate national product standards that had often been thinly disguised devices for protecting higher-cost domestic producers against competition from firms in other member nations. Second, capital controls on the flows of financial investments were removed. Third, restrictions on people working in other member countries were generally removed, although there are still some limits on licensed professionals such as lawyers.

In 2004, 10 additional countries, including 8 former socialism countries in Central and Eastern Europe, joined the EU, and in 2007, 2 more former socialism countries joined. These new members are relatively poor, so they add about 27 percent to the EU's total population but less than 6 percent to its total GDP. In 2013, Croatia joined EU.

欧盟东扩：2004年，另外10个国家包括8个中东欧的前社会主义国家加入欧盟。2007年，又有2个社会主义国家加入。

The basicr equirements to join the EU are that the country has a functioning democracy, a commitment to respecting human rights, a market economy, and the capacity and willingness to adopt and to implement EU rules and standards. EU standards cover over 31 major areas, and the documents listing them are 80, 000 pages long. Integration of the new members has been generally smooth. Still, some features of EU policies were phased in slowly for them. The EU is not only faced with the dilemma of how to take care of them, but also finds itself the target of several terrorist attacks.

In 2016, the United Kingdom voted to exit EU, which is a big frustration to the development of EU. The outlook for future expansion is less clear.

2016年英国退出欧盟，是欧盟发展的一个打击。欧盟的前途未卜。

10.3.2 The North American Free Trade Area

10.3.2 北美自由贸易区

The North American Free Trade Area started from scratch in a few years during the late 1980s and early 1990s. **The first step was the Canada-U.S. Free Trade Area.** As late as 1986, when the two countries had a minor trade war over lumber and corn plus another tiff over Arctic navigational rights, there seemed to be little chance of forming a trade agreement. Yet the mood swung quickly, and negotiations that began in 1986 led to a free-trade area that came into force on January 1, 1989.

第一步，1989年美国和加拿大的自由贸易区生效。

The second step was bringing Mexico into the picture. Mexico's tariffs had been high and were raised even higher after the 1982 debt crisis which forced Mexico to tighten its belt. Starting in

第二步，将墨西哥纳入谈判。

1985, the Mexican government became increasingly determined to break down its own barriers to a free, more privatized, more efficient Mexican economy. A series of reforms deregulated business and reduced barriers to imports of goods. By 1992, Mexico had slashed its tariffs to an average of only 10%. In 1990 the U.S. government and the Mexican government began negotiations on a trade agreement, and Canada joined the talks in 1991. The agreement was completed in 1991, and NAFTA, which replaced CUSFTA, came into existence on January 1, 1994. Now, NAFTA is the world's largest free trade agreement. In 2017, U.S. president Trump claimed that the NAFTA was outdated and proposed a negotiation. If Canada and Mexico refused to negotiation, the U.S. government will withdraw from NAFTA.

Provisions 条款

The goal of NAFTA was to **eliminate barriers** to trade and investment between the U. S., Canada, and Mexico. The implementation of NAFTA on January 1, 1994 brought the immediate elimination of tariffs on more than one-half of Mexico's exports to the U.S. and more than one-third of U.S. exports to Mexico. Within 10 years of the implementation of the agreement, all U.S.-Mexico tariffs were to be eliminated except for some U.S. agricultural exports to Mexico to be phased out within 15 years. Most U. S.-Canada trade was already duty-free. NAFTA also sought to eliminate non-tariff trade barriers and to **protect the intellectual property** rights on traded products. NAFTA has its own set of procedure for **the resolution of disputes.** The roster of NAFTA adjudicators includes many retired judges. NAFTA does not call for free labor migration between these countries, nor does it denationalize Pemex, Mexico's huge government oil monopoly.

削减贸易壁垒

知识产权保护

贸易争端解决

Controversies 争议

NAFTA links 450 million people and its member economies generate $20.8 trillion in 2016. At the same time, it is so highly controversial. Most economic analyses indicate that NAFTA has been beneficial to the North American economies and the average citizen, but harmed to a small minority of workers in industries exposed to trade competition.

Pros

赞同的观点

First, it quadrupled trade between Canada, Mexico, and the United States. That is because the agreement eliminated tariffs. Trade increased to $1.14 trillion in 2015. During 1993—2015, the United States increased its exports of goods from $142 billion to $517 billion. That's a third of its total exports. Canada ($280 billion) and Mexico ($236 billion) were the top two U.S. export markets in 2015. Imports from Canada ($295.2 billion) and Mexico ($294.7 billion) increased from $151 billion in 1993 to $590 billion. That's 26 percent of total U.S. goods imports. That boosted economic growth, profits, and jobs for all three countries.

Second, lower tariffs lowered prices and also lessened the risk of inflation and allowed the Federal Reserve to keep interest rates low. That's especially important for oil prices since America's largest import is oil. The U.S. imported $144.2 billion oil from Mexico and Canada. NAFTA reduced U.S. reliance on oil imports from the Middle East and Venezuela. It was especially important when the U.S. banned oil imports from Iran. Mexico and Canada are friendly countries. Other oil exporters, such as Venezuela and Iran, use oil as a political chess piece. NAFTA lowered food prices in much the same way. It lowered the prices of fresh vegetables, chocolate, fruit (except bananas), and beef.

Third, NAFTA increased economic growth. NAFTA boosted U.S. economic growth by as much as 0.5 percent a year. The sectors that benefited the most were agriculture, automobiles, and services.

Fourth, NAFTA created jobs. NAFTA exports created five million new U.S. jobs. That's because manufacturers exported $487 billion in 2014. It generated $40,000 in export revenue for each factory worker. Even imports from NAFTA partners created jobs. That's because nearly 40 percent of U.S. imports from Mexico originated with American companies. They designed the products domestically, and then outsourced some portion of the process in Mexico. Without NAFTA, they would have gone to China. They may not have been created at all.

Fifth, foreign investment is more than tripled. U.S. businesses invested \$452 billion in Mexico and Canada. Companies in those two countries invested \$240.2 billion in the United States.

Sixth, NAFTA reduced government spending. That's because each nation's government contracts became available to suppliers in all three member countries.

Cons

反对的观点

First, it led to the loss of 500,000—750,000 U.S. jobs. Most were in the manufacturing industry in California, New York, Michigan, and Texas. Companies in some industries moved to Mexico because labor was cheap. These industries were automotive, textile, computer, and electrical appliance.

Second, job migration suppressed wages. Sixty-five percent of companies in the affected industries threatened to move to Mexico. The U.S. workers remaining in those industries could not bargain for higher wages.

Third, NAFTA put Mexican farmers out of business. It allowed government-subsidized U.S. farm products into Mexico. Local farmers could not compete with the artificially low prices.

Fourth, as Mexicans lost their farms, they went to work in sub-standard conditions in the maquiladora where United States-owned companies employ Mexican workers near the border. They assemble products for export back into the United States with very low wages. The program grew to employ 30 percent of Mexico's labor force.

Fifth, U.S. companies degraded the Mexican environment to keep costs low. In response to NAFTA's competitive pressure, Mexico agribusiness used more fertilizers and other chemicals, costing \$36 billion per year in pollution. Rural farmers expanded into marginal land, resulting in deforestation at a rate of 630,000 hectares per year.

Sixth, NAFTA allowed Mexican trucks' access into the United States. Mexican trucks are not held to the same safety standards as American trucks. Therefore, Congress prohibited this provision.

10.3.3 Association of Southeast Asian Nations

In the 1960s and 1970s, a different idea of gains from a trade agreement have become a common sense. The infant industry argument held sway. It was easy to imagine that formation a customs union or free-trade area among developing countries would give the bloc a market large enough to support a large-scale producer in each modern manufacturing sector without letting in manufacturers from the industrialized countries. However, the life expectancy of this type of trade agreement was mostly short. This section takes ASEAN as an example to discuss.

ASEAN is short for the Association of South East Asian Nations. It promotes the economic growth of 10 countries located south of China. Its combined economies grew 4.4% in 2016. ASEAN's total economic output, as measured by gross domestic product, was $6.9 trillion. That makes it the 7th largest market in the world.

ASEAN was created on August 8, 1967, in Bangkok, Thailand. The original member nations include Indonesia, Malaysia, Philippines Singapore, and Thailand. After several years' expansion, ASEAN was founded by Indonesia, Malaysia, Philippines, Singapore, and Thailand. On December 15, 2008, ASEAN approved a new charter, giving the organization status as a legal entity. All member countries must ratify it.

ASEAN's purpose is to form a European Union type of common market. The ASEAN Economic Community was established in 2015. It is working toward free movement of goods and services, investment, and capital, as well as skilled labor. It will also create common standards in agriculture and financial services, intellectual property rights, and consumer protection. These are all necessary to attract foreign direct investment and promote growth. AEC has identified 611 measures it must implement to achieve its goals. As of October 31, 2015, nearly 80% of these measures have been completed. ASEAN is lowering trade tariffs on 99% of its products to 0.5%. Rice is not included since it is so important to local economies. ASEAN is working to make regulations and product standards uniform among the nations.

China is ASEAN's largest trading partner, with $367 billion traded in 2014. ASEAN exported $150 billion and imported $216

10.3.3 东南亚联盟

20世纪六七十年代，从贸易协定当中获益已成共识。新兴产业的争论占据了主导地位。很容易想象，在发展中国家建立关税同盟或自由贸易区将为这个集团提供一个足够大的市场以支持每个发展中国家的现代制造业的大规模生产商，而且可以不让工业化国家的制造商进入。但是这种类型的贸易协定多半存活时间短。

东盟的目标是形成如同欧盟一样的共同市场。

中国是东盟的最大贸易伙伴。

billion from China during that time. ASEAN is China's third-largest trading partner, after the United States and the European Union. However, the nations are also wary of China's ability to dominate the area. They don't want cooperation to lead to absorption by their neighbor.

东盟与澳大利亚、中国、印度、日本、韩国和新西兰正在进行区域全面经济伙伴关系的谈判。

ASEAN is negotiating the regional Comprehensive Economic Partnership with Australia, China, India, Japan, Republic of Korea, and New Zealand. It is an economic cooperation and trade agreement that began in May 2013.

"10＋3"是东盟与中国、日本和韩国之间进行的贸易协定谈判。

ASEAN＋3 are the term that refers to the countries of ASEAN plus China, Japan, and Republic of Korea. It was formed in the aftermath of the 1997 Asian financial crisis. The East Asia Vision Group was formed to create a vision for cooperation among all 13 countries to prevent another crisis from happening again.

10.3.4 GATT and WTO

10.3.4 关贸总协定与世界贸易组织

Partly in response to trade disruptions during the Great Depression, the United States and some of its allies sought to impose order on trade flows after World War Ⅱ. The first major postwar step toward liberalization of world trade was the General Agreement on Tariffs and Trade signed in 1947. GATT was crafted as an agreement among contracting parties, the member nations on an equal footing in trading relationships. In 1995, GATT was transformed into World Trade Organization. The WTO embodies the main provisions of GATT, but its role was expanded to include a mechanism intended to improve GATT's process for resolving trade disputes among member nations. Let us first discuss the operation of the original GATT system.

Multilateral Trade Negotiations

多边贸易谈判

During 1947—1994, GATT has sponsored a series of negotiations, or rounds, to reduce tariffs and non-tariff trade barriers, as summarized in Table 10.1.

Table 10.1 GATT Negotiating Rounds

Negotiating Round and Coverage	Dates	Number of Participants	Tariff Cut Achieved
Addressed Tariffs			
Geneva	1947	23	21
Annecy	1949	13	2
Torquay	1951	38	3
Geneva	1956	26	4
Dillon Round	1960—1961	26	2
Kennedy Round	1964—1967	62	35
Addressed Tariff and Non-tariff Barriers			
Tokyo Round	1973—1979	99	33
Uruguay Round	1986—1993	125	34
Doha Round	2002—	142	

The GATT rounds from the 1940s to the 1960s focused almost entirely on tariff reduction. As average tariff rates in industrial nations decreased during the postwar period, the importance of non-tariff barriers increased. In response to these changes, negotiations shifted emphasis to the issue of non-tariff distortions in international trade.

During the Tokyo Round of 1973 to 1979, signatory nations agreed to tariff cuts that took the across-the-board form initiated in the Kennedy Round. After the Tokyo Round, tariffs were so low that they were not a significant barrier to trade in industrial countries. A second accomplishment of the Tokyo Round was to remove or lessen many non-tariff barriers. Codes of conduct were established in six areas: customs valuation, import licensing, government procurement, technical barriers to trade, anti-dumping procedures, and countervailing duties.

During the Uruguay Round from 1986 to 1993, many nations agreed for the first time to bind a significant portion of their tariffs, giving up the possibility of future rate increases above the bound levels. Significant progress was also made by the Uruguay Round in decreasing or eliminating non-tariff barriers. **Moreover, the Uruguay Round called for the transformation of the GATT into a**

此外，乌拉圭回合呼吁将关贸总协定转变为一个常设国际机构，即世贸组

permanent international institution, the WTO, responsible for governing the conduct of trade relations among its members.

织,负责管理其成员之间的贸易关系。

WTO

世界贸易组织

On January 1, 1995, the day on which the Uruguay Round took effect, GATT was transformed into the World Trade Organization. This transformation turned GATT from a trade accord into a membership organization, responsible for governing the conduct of trade relations among its member. GATT obligations remain at the core of the WTO. However, the WTO agreement requires that its members adhere not only to GATT rules, but also to the broad range of trade pacts that have been negotiated under GATT auspices in recent decades. This undertaking ends the free ride of many GATT members that benefited from, but refused to join, new agreements negotiated in GATT since the 1970s.

1995 年 1 月 1 日,乌拉圭回会正式生效,世界贸易组织取代关贸总协定。

Comparing with GATT, the WTO is a full-fledged international organization, has a far wider scope than the old GATT, bringing into the multilateral trading system, for the first time, trade in services, intellectual property, and investment. The WTO administers a unified package of agreements to which all members are committed through various councils and committees. It is also a watchdog of international trade, regularly examining the trade regimes of individual members. At the same time, a major objective of the WTO was strengthening the GATT mechanism for settling trade disputes.

相对于关贸总协定,世界贸易组织是一个成熟的国际组织,其涵盖的范围更广泛,首次将服务贸易、知识产权贸易和投资加入多边贸易体系。

A New Round of Trade Negotiations for the WTO

新一轮回合的谈判:多哈回合

The Doha Round of trade talks was an attempted multilateral trade agreement. It was launched at the Doha, Qatar, WTO meeting in November 2001. Its goal was to finish up by January 2005, but the deadline was then pushed back to 2006. The talks were finally suspended in June 2006. That's because the United States and the European Union refused to reduce agricultural subsidies.

The Doha Round was ambitious. First, all WTO members (almost every country in the world) participated. Second, decisions must be settled by consensus, as opposed to majority rule. That means every country must sign off. Third, there are no piecemeal

多哈回合谈判的目标雄心勃勃。

sub-agreements. That means there is either an entire agreement or none at all. In other words, unless every country agrees with the whole deal, it's off.

When the Doha Round was launched, ministers placed development at its center. "We seek to place developing countries' needs and interests at the heart of the Work Programme adopted in this Declaration," they said. "... We shall continue to make positive efforts designed to ensure that developing countries, and especially the least-developed among them, secure a share in the growth of world trade commensurate with the needs of their economic development. In this context, enhanced market access, balanced rules, and well targeted, sustainably financed technical assistance and capacity-building programmes have important roles to play." The agreement's purpose was to boost the economic growth of developing countries. It centered on reducing subsidies for developed countries' agriculture. That would allow developing countries to export food, something they were already good at producing. In return, the developing countries would open up their market to services, particularly banking. That would provide new markets to the developed countries' service industries. It would also modernize these markets for the developing countries.

If successful, the Doha Round would have improved the economic vitality of developing countries. It would have reduced government spending on subsidies in developed countries, but boosted financial companies.

多哈回合如果成功将极大利于发展中国家的经济发展。

Unfortunately, agribusiness lobbyists in the United States and the European Union put political pressure on their legislators which almost ended the Doha Round of negotiations. As a result, bilateral agreements have increased because they are easier to negotiate.

不幸的是美国和欧盟的农业企业游说者向立法者施加了政治压力，几乎终止了多哈回合的谈判。

Subsequent ministerial meetings took place in Cancún, Mexico (2003), and Hong Kong, China (2005). Related negotiations took place in Paris, France (2005), Potsdam, Germany (2007), Geneva, Switzerland (2004, 2006, 2008), Bali(2013), and Nairobi (2015).

On December 7, 2013, WTO negotiators concluded a four-day meeting in Bali, Indonesia. They agreed to streamline customs for all members. The Bali package has been inserted into the WTO

2013 年 12 月 7 日，世贸组织谈判代表在印度尼西亚巴厘岛结束了为期

Membership Protocol. More than 50 members have ratified it.

On December 19, 2015, the WTO took steps to help its poorest members. Members agreed to end agricultural export subsidies. Developed countries will do so immediately, emerging markets will do so by 2018, and poor nations have much longer. Countries that subsidize their farming industries undercut local farmers in underdeveloped countries. It also contains a series of six Ministerial Decisions on agriculture, cotton, and issues related to least-developed countries (LDCs). A Ministerial Declaration outlining the Package and the future work of the WTO was adopted at the end of the five-day Conference.

四天的会议。他们同意为所有成员简化海关手续。巴厘岛一揽子计划被纳入世贸组织成员议定书。

The 10 to 13 December Ministerial Conference held in 2017 brought together nearly 4,000 ministers, senior trade officials and other delegates from the WTO's 164 members and observers as well as representatives from civil society, business, and the global media. Members agreed to continue to engage constructively in the fisheries subsidies negotiations with a view to adopting an agreement by the next Ministerial Conference in 2019 on comprehensive and effective disciplines that prohibit certain forms of fisheries subsidies that contribute to overcapacity and overfishing, and eliminate subsidies that contribute to illegal, unreported, and unregulated (IUU) fishing.

However, the future of the Doha Round remains uncertain even after a series of development.

☞ Summary

☞ 本章小结

1. Trade liberalization has assumed two main forms. One involves the reciprocal reduction of trade barriers on a nondiscriminatory basis.

2. The term economic integration refers to the process of eliminating restrictions on international trade, payments, and factor mobility. The stages of economic integration are preferential trade agreement, free-trade area, customs union, common market, and economic union.

3. The welfare implications of economic integration can be analyzed from two perspectives. First are the static welfare effects, resulting from trade creation and trade diversion. Second are the dynamic welfare effects that stem from greater competition,

economies of scale, and the stimulus to investment spending that economic integration makes possible.

4. From a static perspective, the formation of a customs union yields net welfare gains if the consumption and production benefits of trade creation more than offset the loss on world efficiency owing to trade diversion.

5. The first major postwar step toward liberalization of world trade was the General Agreement on Tariffs and Trade signed in 1947. GATT was crafted as an agreement among contracting parties, the member nations on an equal footing in trading relationships. In 1995, GATT was transformed into World Trade Organization.

6. Comparing with GATT, the WTO is a full-fledged international organization, has a far wider scope than the old GATT, bringing into the multilateral trading system, for the first time, trade in services, intellectual property, and investment. The WTO administers a unified package of agreements to which all members are committed through various councils and committees. It is also a watchdog of international trade, regularly examining the trade regimes of individual members. At the same time, a major objective of the WTO was strengthening the GATT mechanism for settling trade disputes.

☞ Questions

☞ 本章习题

1. How can trade liberalization exist on a nondiscriminatory basis versus a discriminatory basis? What are some actual examples of each?

2. What is meant by the term economic integration? What are the various stages that economic integration can take?

3. How do static welfare effects of trade creation and trade diversion relate to a nation's decision to form a customs union?

4. Why has the so-called common agricultural policy been a controversial issue for the European Union?

5. Describe the development of WTO.

Chapter 11
Balance of Payments

第十一章
国际收支

Previous chapters have been concerned primarily with the problem of making the best use of the world's scarce productive resources at a single point in time. The branch of economics called **microeconomics** studies this problem from the perspective of individual firms and consumers. Microeconomics works "from the bottom up" to show how individual economic actors, by pursuing their own interests, collectively determine how resources are used. In our study of international microeconomics, we have learned how individual production and consumption decisions produce patterns of international trade and specialization. We have also seen that while free trade usually encourages efficient resource use, government intervention or market failures can cause waste even when all factors of production are fully employed.

微观经济学

Within this chapter we shift our focus and ask: How can economic policies ensure that factors of production are fully employed? And what determines how an economy's capacity to produce goods and services change over time? To answer these questions, we must understand **macroeconomics**, the branch of economics that studies how economies' overall levels of employment, production, and growth are determined. Like microeconomics, macroeconomics is concerned with the effective use of scarce resources. But while microeconomics focuses on the economic decisions of individuals, macroeconomics analyzes the behavior of an economy as a whole. In our study of international macroeconomics, we will learn how the interactions of national economies influence the worldwide pattern of macroeconomic activity.

宏观经济学

This chapter takes the first step in our study of international macroeconomics by explaining the accounting concepts economists use to describe a country's level of production and its international transactions. To get a complete picture of the macroeconomic linkages among economies that engage in international trade, we have to master two related and essential tools. The first of these tools, national income accounting, records all the expenditures that contribute to a country's income and output. The second tool, balance of payments accounting, helps us keep track of both changes in a country's indebtedness to foreigners and the fortunes of its export and import-competing industries. The balance of payments accounts also show the connection between foreign transactions and national money supplies.

11.1 The National Income Accounts

11.1 国民收入账户

Of central concern to macroeconomic analysis is a country's gross national product (GNP), the value of all final goods and services produced by the country's factors of production and sold on the market in a given time period. GNP, which is the basic measure of a country's output studied by macroeconomists, is calculated by adding up the market value of all expenditures on final output. GNP therefore includes the value of goods like bread sold in a supermarket and textbooks sold in a bookstore, as well as the value of services provided by stock brokers and plumbers. Because output cannot be produced without the aid of factor inputs, the expenditures that make up GNP are closely linked to the employment of labor, capital, and other factors of production.

To distinguish among the different types of expenditure that make up a country's GNP, government economists and statisticians who compile national income accounts divide GNP among the four possible uses for which a country's final output is purchased: consumption (the amount consumed by private domestic residents), investment (the amount put aside by private firms to build new plant and equipment for future production), government purchases (the amount used by the government), and the current account balance (the amount of net exports of goods and services to foreigners). The term national income accounts, rather than national output accounts, is used to describe this fourfold classification because a country's income in fact equals its output. Thus, the national income accounts can be thought of as classifying each transaction that contributes to national income according to the type of expenditure that gives rise to it.

Why is it useful to divide GNP into consumption, investment, government purchases, and the current account? One major reason is that we cannot hope to understand the cause of a particular recession or boom without knowing how the main categories of spending have changed. And without such an understanding, we cannot recommend a sound policy response. In addition, the national income accounts provide information essential for studying why some countries are rich—that is, have a high level of GNP relative to population size—while some are poor.

11.1.1 National Product and National Income

11.1.1 生产产品和国民收入

Our first task in understanding how economists analyze GNP is to explain in greater detail why the GNP a country generates over some time period must equal its national income, the income earned in that period by its factors of production.

The reason for this equality is that every dollar used to purchase goods or services automatically ends up in somebody's pocket. A visit to the doctor provides a simple example of how an increase in national output raises national income by the same amount. The $75 you pay the doctor represents the market value of the services he or she provides for you, so your visit raises GNP by $75. But the $75 you pay the doctor also raises his or her income. So national income rises by $75.

The principle that output and income are the same also applies to goods, even goods that are produced with the help of many factors of production. Consider the example of an economics textbook. When you purchase a new book from the publisher, the value of your purchase enters GNP. But your payment enters the income of the productive factors that cooperated in producing the book, because the publisher must pay for their services with the proceeds of sales. First, there are the authors, editors, artists, and compositors who provide the labor inputs necessary for the book's production. Second, there are the publishing company's shareholders, who receive dividends for having financed acquisition of the capital used in production. Finally, there are the suppliers of paper and ink, who provide the intermediate materials used in producing the book.

The paper and ink purchased by the publishing company to produce the book are not counted separately in GNP because their contribution to the value of national output is already included in the book's price. It is to avoid such double counting that we allow only the sale of final goods and services to enter the definition of GNP. Sales of intermediate goods, such as paper and ink purchased by a publisher, are not counted. Also notice that the sale of a used textbook does not enter GNP. Our definition counts only final goods and services that are produced, and a used textbook does not qualify: It was counted in GNP at the time it was first sold. Equivalently, the sale of a used textbook does not generate income for any factor of production.

11.1.2 Capital Depreciation and International Transfers

11.1.2 资本贬值和跨国转移

Because we have defined GNP and national income so that they are necessarily equal, their equality is really an identity. Two adjustments to the definition of GNP must be made, however, before the identification of GNP and national income is entirely correct in practice.

1. GNP does not take into account the economic loss due to the tendency of machinery and structures to wear out as they are used. This loss, called depreciation, reduces the income of capital owners. To calculate national income over a given period, we must therefore subtract from GNP the depreciation of capital over the period. GNP less depreciation is called net national product (NNP).

2. A country's income may include gifts from residents of foreign countries, called unilateral transfers. Examples of unilateral transfers of income are pension payments to retired citizens living abroad, reparation payments, and foreign aid such as relief funds donated to drought-stricken nations. For the United States in 2009, the balance of such payments amounted to around －$130.2 billion, representing a 0.9 percent of GNP net transfer to

foreigners. Net unilateral transfers are part of a country's income but are not part of its product, and they must be added to NNP in calculations of national income.

National income equals GNP less depreciation plus net unilateral transfers. The difference between GNP and national income is by no means an insignificant amount, but macroeconomics has little to say about it, and it is of little importance for macroeconomic analysis. Therefore, for the purposes of this text, we usually use the terms GNP and national income interchangeably, emphasizing the distinction between the two only when it is essential.

11.1.3 Gross Domestic Product

11.1.3 国内生产总值

Most countries other than the United States have long reported gross domestic product (GDP) rather than GNP as their primary measure of national economic activity. In 1991 the United States began to follow this practice as well. GDP is supposed to measure the volume of production within a country's borders, whereas GNP equals GDP plus net receipts of factor income from the rest of the world. For the Unifed States, these net receipts are primarily the income domestic residents earn on wealth they hold in other countries less the payments domestic residents make to foreign owners of wealth that is located in the domestic country.

GDP does not correct, as GNP does, for the portion of countries' production carried out using services provided by foreign-owned capital and labor. Consider an example: the earnings of a Spanish factory with British owners are counted in Spain's GDP but are part of Britain's GNP. The services British capital provides in Spain are a service export from Britain, therefore they are added to British GDP in calculating British GNP. At the same time, to figure Spain's GNP, we must subtract from its GDP the corresponding service import from Britain. As a practical matter, movements in GDP and GNP usually do not differ greatly. We will focus on GNP in this book, however, because GNP tracks national income more closely than GDP does, and national welfare depends more directly on national income than on domestic product.

11.1.4 National Income Accounting for an Open Economy

11.1.4 开放经济的国民收入账户

In this section we extend to the case of an open economy from the closed economy national income accounting framework you may have seen in earlier economics courses. We begin with a discussion of the national income accounts because they highlight the key role of international trade in open economy macroeconomic theory. Since a closed economy's residents cannot purchase foreign output or sell their own to foreigners, all of national income must be allocated to domestic consumption, investment, or government purchases. In an economy open to international trade, however, the closed economy version of national income accounting must be modified because some domestic output is exported to foreigners while some domestic income is spent on imported foreign products.

The main lesson of this section is the relationship among national saving, investment, and trade imbalances. We will see that in open economy, saving and investment are not necessarily equal, as they are in a closed economy. This occurs because countries can save in the form of foreign wealth by exporting more than they import, and they can dissave—that is, reduce their foreign wealth—by exporting less than they import.

11.1.5 Consumption

11.1.5 消费

The portion of GNP purchased by private households to fulfill current wants is called consumption. Purchases of movie tickets, food, dental work, and washing machines all fall into this category. Consumption expenditure is the largest component of GNP in most economies. In the United States, for example, the fraction of GNP devoted to consumption has been fluctuating in the range of about 62 to 70 percent over the past 60 years.

11.1.6 Investment

11.1.6 投资

The part of output used by private firms to produce future output is called investment. Investment spending may be viewed as the portion of GNP used to increase the nation's stock of capital. Steel and bricks used to build a factory are part of investment spending, as are services provided by a technician who helps build business computers. Firms' purchases of inventories are also counted in investment spending because carrying inventories is just another way for firms to transfer output from current use to future use.

Investment is usually more variable than consumption. In the United States, (gross) investment has fluctuated between 11 and 22 percent of GNP in recent years. We often use the word investment to describe individual households' purchases of stocks, bonds, or real estate, but you should be careful not to confuse this every meaning of the word with the economic definition of investment as a part of GNP. When you buy a share of Microsoft stock, you are buying neither a good nor a service, so your purchase does not show up in GNP.

11.1.7 Government Purchases

11.1.7 政府购买

Any goods and services purchased by federal, state, or local governments are classified as government purchases in the national income accounts. Included in government purchases are federal military spending, government support of cancer research, and government funds spent on highway repair and education. Government purchases include investment as well as consumption purchases. Government transfer payments such as social security and unemployment benefits do not require the recipient to give the government any goods or services in return. Thus, transfer payments are not included in government purchases.

Government purchases currently take up about 20 percent of U.S. GNP, and this share has not changed much since the late 1950s. (The corresponding figure for 1959, for example, was around 20 percent.) In 1929, however, government purchases accounted for only 8.5 percent of U.S. GNP.

11.1.8 The National Income Identity for an Open Economy

11.1.8 开放经济的国民收入恒等式

In a closed economy, any final good or service that is not purchased by households or the government must be used by firms to produce new plant, equipment, and inventories. If consumption goods are not sold immediately to consumers or the government, firms (perhaps reluctantly) add them to existing inventories, thereby increasing their investment.

This information leads to a fundamental identity for closed economies. Let Y stand for GNP, C for consumption, I for investment, and G for government purchases. Since all of a closed economy's output must be consumed, invested, or bought by the government, we can write $Y=C+I+G$.

We derived the national income identity for a closed economy by assuming that all output is consumed or invested by the country's citizens or purchased by its government. When foreign trade is possible, however, some output is purchased by foreigners while some domestic spending goes to purchase goods and services produced abroad. The GNP identity for open economy shows how the national income a country earns by selling its goods and services is divided between sales to domestic residents and sales to foreign residents.

Since residents of an open economy may spend some of their income on imports, that is, goods and services purchased from abroad, only the portion of their spending that is not devoted to imports is part of domestic GNP. The value of imports, denoted by IM, must be subtracted from total domestic spending, $Y=C+I+G$, to find the portion of domestic spending that generates domestic national income. Imports from abroad add to foreign countries' GNPs but do not add directly to domestic GNP.

Similarly, the goods and services sold to foreigners make up a country's exports. Exports, denoted by EX, are the amount foreign residents' purchases add to the national income of the domestic economy.

The national income of an open economy is therefore the sum of domestic and foreign expenditures on the goods and services produced by domestic factors of production. Thus, the national income identity for an open economy is $Y=C+I+G+EX-IM$.

The Current Account and Foreign Indebtedness

经常项目和外债

In reality, a country's foreign trade is exactly balanced only rarely. The difference between exports of goods and services and imports of goods and services is known as the current account balance (or current account). If we denote the current account by

CA, we can express this definition in symbols as $CA = EX - IM$.

When a country's imports exceed its exports, we say the country has a current account deficit. A country has a current account surplus when its exports exceed its imports. The GNP identity, $Y = C + I + G + EX - IM$, shows one reason why the current account is important in international macroeconomics. Since the right-hand side of GNP identity gives total expenditures on domestic output, changes in the current account can be associated with changes in output and, thus, employment.

The current account is also important because it measures the size and direction of international borrowing. When a country imports more than it exports, it is buying more from foreigners than it sells to them and must somehow finance this current account deficit. How does it pay for additional imports once it has spent its export earnings? Since the country as a whole can import more than it exports only if it can borrow the difference from foreigners, a country with a current account deficit must be increasing its net foreign debts by the amount of the deficit. This is currently the position of the United States, which has a significant current account deficit.

Similarly, a country with a current account surplus is earning more from its exports than it spends on imports. This country finances the current account deficit of its trading partners by lending to them. The foreign wealth of a surplus country rises because foreigners pay for any imports not covered by their exports by issuing IOUs that they will eventually have to redeem. The preceding reasoning shows that a country's current account balance equals the change in its net foreign wealth.

We have defined the current account as the difference between exports and imports. Equation GNP identity says that the current account is also equal to the difference between national income and domestic residents' total spending $C+I+G$: $Y-(C+I+G)=CA$.

It is only by borrowing abroad that a country can have a current account deficit and use more output than it is currently producing. If it uses less than its output, it has a current account surplus and is lending the surplus to foreigners. International borrowing and lending were identified with **intertemporal trade** in

Chapter 6. A country with a current account deficit is importing present consumption and exporting future consumption. A country with a current account surplus is exporting present consumption and importing future consumption.

11.1.9 Saving and the Current Account

11.1.9 储蓄和经常项目

Simple as it is, the GNP identity has many illuminating implications. To explain the most important of these implications, we define the concept of **national saving**, that is, the portion of output, Y, that is not devoted to household consumption, C, or government purchases, G. **In a closed economy, national saving always equals investment.** This tells us that the closed economy as a whole can increase its wealth only by accumulating new capital. Let S stand for national saving. Our definition of S tells us that $S = Y - C - G$.

国民收入

在封闭经济中，国民储蓄总是等于投资。

Since the closed economy GNP identity, $Y = C + I + G$, may also be written as $I = Y - C - G$, then $S = I$, and national saving must equal investment in a closed economy. Whereas in a closed economy, saving and investment must always be equal, in an open economy they can differ. Remembering that national saving, S, equals $Y - C - G$ and that $CA = EX - IM$, we can rewrite the GNP identity as $S = I + CA$.

The equation highlights an important difference between open and closed economies: An open economy can save either by building up its capital stock or by acquiring foreign wealth, but a closed economy can save only by building up its capital stock.

Unlike a closed economy, an open economy with profitable investment opportunities does not have to increase its saving in order to exploit them. The preceding expression shows that it is possible simultaneously to raise investment and foreign borrowing without changing saving. For example, if New Zealand decides to build a new hydroelectric plant, it can import the materials it needs from the United States and borrow the United States funds to pay for them. This transaction raises New Zealand's domestic investment because the imported materials contribute to expanding the country's capital stock. The transaction also raises New Zealand's current account deficit by an amount equal to the increase in investment. New Zealand's saving does not have to change, even though investment rises. For this to be possible, however, the United States residents must be willing to save more so that the resources needed to build the plant are freed for New Zealand's use. The result is another example of intertemporal trade, in which New Zealand imports present consumption (when it borrows from the United States) and exports future consumption (when it pays off the loan).

Because one country's savings can be borrowed by a second country in order to increase the second country's stock of capital, a country's current account surplus is often referred to as its **net foreign investment**. Of course, when one country lends to another to finance investment, part of the income generated by the investment in future years must be used to pay back the lender. Domestic investment and foreign investment are two different ways in which a country can use current savings to increase its future income.

国外净投资

11.1.10 Private and Government Saving

11.1.10 个人和政府储蓄

So far our discussion of saving has not stressed the distinction between saving decisions made by the private sector and saving decisions made by the government. Unlike private saving decisions, however, government saving decisions are often made with an eye toward their effect on output and employment. The national income identity can help us to analyze the channels through which government saving decisions influence macroeconomic conditions. To use the national income identity in this way, we first have to divide national saving into its private and government components.

Private saving is defined as the part of disposable income that is saved rather than consumed. Disposable income is national income, Y, less the net taxes collected from households and firms by the government, T. Private saving, denoted S^p, can therefore be expressed as $S^p = Y - T - C$.

个人储蓄

Government saving is defined similarly to private saving. The government's "income" is its net tax revenue, T, while its "consumption" is government purchases, G. If we let S^g stand for government saving, then $S^g = T - G$

政府储蓄

The two types of saving we have defined, private and

government, add up to national saving. To see why, recall the definition of national saving, S, as $Y-C-G$. Then $S=Y-C-G=(Y-T-C)+(T-G)=S^p+S^g$.

We can use the definitions of private and government saving to rewrite the national income identity in a form that is useful for analyzing the effects of government saving decisions on open economy. Because $S=S^p+S^g=I+CA$, $S^p=I+CA-S^g=I+CA-(T-G)=I+CA+(G-T)$.

This equation relates private saving to domestic investment, the current account surplus, and government saving. To interpret the equation, we define the **government budget deficit** as government saving preceded by a minus sign. The government budget deficit measures the extent to which the government is borrowing to finance its expenditures. Equation then states that a country's private saving can take three forms: investment in domestic capital (I), purchases of wealth from foreigners, and purchases of the domestic government's newly issued debt.

政府预算赤字

11.1.11 The Balance of Payments Accounts

11.1.11 收支账户的均衡

In addition to national income accounts, government economists and statisticians also keep balance of payments accounts, a detailed record of the composition of the current account balance and of the many transactions that finance it. Balance of payments figures are of great interest to the general public, as indicated by the attention that various news media pay to them. But press reports sometimes confuse different measures of international payments flows. Should we be alarmed or cheered by a *Wall Street Journal* headline proclaiming, "U. S. Chalks Up Record Balance of Payments Deficit"? A thorough understanding of balance of payments accounting will help us evaluate the implications of a country's international transactions.

A country's balance of payments accounts keep track of both its payments to and its receipts from foreigners. Any transaction resulting in a receipt from foreigners is entered in the balance of payments accounts as a **credit**. Any transaction resulting in a payment to foreigners is entered as a **debit**. Three types of international transaction are recorded in the balance of payments.

贷方
借方

1. Transactions that arise from the export or import of goods or services and therefore enter directly into the current account. When a French consumer imports American blue jeans, for example, the transaction enters the U. S. balance of payments accounts as a credit on the current account.

2. Transactions that arise from the purchase or sale of financial assets. An **asset** is any one of the forms in which wealth can be held, such as money, stocks, factories, or government debt. The **financial account** of the balance of payments records all international purchases or sales of financial assets. When an American company buys a French factory, the transaction enters the U.S. balance of payments as a debit in the financial account. It enters as a debit because the transaction requires a payment from the United States to foreigners. Correspondingly, a U. S. sale of assets to foreigners enters the U. S. financial account as a credit. The difference between a country's purchases and sales of foreign assets is called its **financial account balance**, or its **net financial flows.**

资产

金融账户

金融项目差额、净资金流

3. Certain other activities resulting in transfers of wealth between countries are recorded in the **capital account.** These international asset movements—which are generally very small for the United States—differ from those recorded in the financial account. For the most part they result from non-market activities or represent the acquisition or disposal of non-produced, non-financial, and possibly intangible assets (such as copyrights and trademarks). For example, if the U. S. government forgives \$1 billion in debt owed to it by the government of Pakistan, the U.S. wealth declines by \$1 billion and a \$1 billion debit is recorded in the U.S. capital account.

资本账户

You will find the complexities of the balance of payments accounts less confusing if you keep in mind the following simple rule of double-entry bookkeeping: **every international transaction automatically enters the balance of payments twice, once as a credit and once as a debit.** This principle of balance of payments accounting holds true because every transaction has two sides: If you buy something from a foreigner, you must pay him in some way, and the foreigner must then somehow spend or store your payment.

每一笔国际交易都会自动计入国际收支平衡表两次，一次为贷方，一次为借方。

11.1.12 Examples of Paired Transactions

11.1.12 案例分析

1. Imagine you buy an ink-jet fax machine from the Italian company Olivetti and pay for your purchase with a \$1,000 check. Your payment to buy a goods (the fax machine) from a foreign resident enters the U.S. current account as a debit. But where is the offsetting balance of payments credit? Olivetti's U.S. salesperson must do something with your check—let's say he deposits it in Olivetti's account at Citibank in New York. In this case, Olivetti has purchased, and Citibank has sold, a U.S. asset—a bank deposit worth \$1,000—and the transaction shows up as a \$1,000 credit in the U.S. financial account. The transaction creates the following two offsetting bookkeeping entries in the U.S. balance of payments (see Figure 11.1).

	Credit	Debit
Fax Machine Purchase (current account, U.S. goods import)		\$1,000
Sale of Bank Deposit by Citibank (financial account, U.S. asset sale)	\$1,000	

Figure 11.1 Two Offsetting Bookkeeping

2. As another example, suppose that during your travel in France, you pay \$200 for a fine dinner at the Restaurant de l'Escargot d'Or. Lacking cash, you place the charge on your Visa credit card. Your payment, which is a tourist expenditure, will be counted as a service import for the U.S., and therefore as a current account debit. Where is the offsetting credit? Your signature on the Visa slip entitles the restaurant to receive \$200 (actually, its local currency equivalent) from First Card, the company that issued your Visa card. It is therefore an asset, a claim on a future payment from First Card. So when you pay for your meal abroad with your credit card, you are selling an asset to France and generating a \$200 credit in the U.S. financial account. The pattern of offsetting debits and credits in this case is(see Figure 11.2):

	Credit	Debit
Meal Purchase (current account, U.S. service import)		\$200
Sale of Claim on First Card (financial account, U.S. asset sale)	\$200	

Figure 11.2 The Pattern of Offsetting Debits

3. Imagine next that your Uncle Sid fromLos Angeles buys a newly issued share of stock in the U.K. oil giant British Petroleum (BP). He places his order with his stockbroker, Go-for-Broke, Inc., paying $95 with a check drawn on his Go-for-Broke money market account. BP, in turn, deposits the $95 Sid has paid into its own U.S. bank account at Second Bank of Chicago. Uncle Sid's acquisition of the stock creates a $95 debit in the U.S. financial account (he has purchased an asset from a foreign resident, BP), while BP's $95 deposit at its Chicago bank is the offsetting financial account credit (BP has expanded its U.S. asset holdings). The mirror-image effects on the U.S. balance of payments therefore both appear in the financial account (Figure 11.3).

	Credit	Debit
Uncle Sid's Purchase of a Share of BP (financial account, U.S. asset purchase)		$95
BP's Deposit of Uncle Sid's Payment at Second Bank of Chicago (financial account, U.S. asset sale)	$95	

Figure 11.3 The Mirror-image Effects on the U.S. Balance of Payments

4. Finally, let's consider how the U.S. balance of payments accounts are affected when U.S. banks forgive (that is, announce that they will simply forget about) $5,000 in debt owed to them by the government of the imaginary country of Bosnia. In this case, the United States makes a $5,000 capital transfer to Bosnia, which appears as a $5,000 debit entry in the capital account. The associated credit is in the financial account, in the form of a $5,000 reduction in U.S. assets held abroad (a negative "acquisition" of foreign assets, and therefore a balance of payments credit). See Figure 11.4.

	Credit	Debit
U.S. Banks' Debt Forgiveness (capital account, U.S. transfer payment)		$5,000
Reduction in Banks' Claims on Bosnia (financial account, U.S. asset sale)	$5,000	

Figure 11.4 The U.S. Capital Account and Financial Account

These examples show that many circumstances can affect the way a transaction generates its offsetting balance of payments entry. We can never predict with certainty where the flip side of a particular transaction will show up, but we can be sure that it will show up somewhere.

11.2 The Fundamental Balance of Payments Identity

11.2 国际收支恒等式

Because any international transaction automatically gives rise to offsetting credit and debit entries in the balance of payments, the sum of the current account balance and the capital account balance automatically equals the financial account balance:

current account + capital account = financial account.

In examples 1, 2, and 4 above, current or capital account entries have offsetting counterparts in the financial account, while in example 3, two financial account entries offset each other. You can understand this identity another way. Recall the relationship linking the current account to international lending and borrowing. Because the sum of the current and capital accounts is the total change in a country's net foreign assets (including, through the capital account, non-market asset transfers), that sum necessarily equals the difference between a country's purchases of assets from foreigners and its sales of assets to them—that is, the financial account balance (also called net financial flows).

11.2.1 The Current Account, Once Again

11.2.1 经常项目

As you have learned, the current account balance measures a country's net exports of goods and services. Table 11.1 shows that U.S. exports (on the credit side) were ＄2,159.0 billion, while U.S. imports (on the debit side) were ＄2,412.5 billion.

The balance of payments accounts divide exports and imports into three finer categories. The first is goods trade, that is, exports or imports of merchandise. The second category, services, includes items such as payments for legal assistance, tourists' expenditures, and shipping fees. The final category, income, is made up mostly of international interest and dividend payments and the earnings of domestically owned firms operating abroad. If you own a share of a German firm's stock and receive a dividend payment of ＄5, that payment shows up in the accounts as a U.S. investment income receipt of ＄5. Wages that workers earn abroad can also enter the income account.

Table 11.1 The U.S. Current Account, Capital Accout, and Finacial Account

Current Account	
(1) Exports	**2,159.0**
Of which:	
Goods	1,068.5
Services	502.3
Income receipts(primary income)	588.2
(2) Imports	**2,412.5**
Of which:	
Goods	1,575.4
Services	370.3
Income payments(primary income)	466.8
(3) Net unilateral transfers(secondary income)	−124.9
Balance on current account [(1) + (2) + (3)]	**−378.4**
Capital Account	
(4)	**−0.1**
Financial Account	
(5) Net U.S. acquisition of financial assets,excluding financial derivatives	**140.5**
Of which:	
Official reserve assets	52.3
Other assets	88.2
(6) Net U.S. incurrence of liabilities,excluding financial derivatives	**305.7**
Of which:	
Official reserve assets	450.0
Other assets	−144.3
(7) Financial derivatives, net	−50.8
Net financial flows [(5) − (6) + (7)]	**−216.0**
Net errors and omissions [Net financial flows less sum of current and capital accounts]	162.5

Source: U.S. Department of Commerce, Bureau of Economic Analysis, June 17, 2010, release. Totals may differ from suma because of rounding.

We include income on foreign investments in the current account because that income really is compensation for the services provided by foreign investments. This idea, as we saw earlier, is behind the distinction between GNP and GDP. When a U. S. corporation builds a plant in Canada, for instance, the productive services the plant generates are viewed as a service export from the U. S. to Canada equal in value to the profits the plant yields for its American owner. To be consistent, we must be sure to include these profits in American GNP and not in Canadian GNP. Remember, the definition of GNP refers to goods and services generated by a country's factors of production, but it does not specify that those factors must work within the borders of the country that owns them.

Before calculating the current account, we must include one additional type of international transaction that we have largely ignored until now. In discussing the relationship between GNP and national income, we defined unilateral transfers between countries as international gifts, that is, payments that do not correspond to the purchase of any good, service, or asset. Net unilateral transfers are considered part of the current account as well as a part of national income, and the identity $Y=C+I+G+CA$ holds exactly if Y is interpreted as GNP plus net transfers. The U.S. balance of unilateral transfers was －＄124.9billion.

The table shows a current account balance of ＄2,159.0 billion －＄2,412.5 billion －＄124.9 billion ＝ －＄378.4 billion, a deficit. The negative sign means that current payment to foreigners exceeded current receipts and that U.S. residents used more output than they produced. Since these current account transactions were paid for in some way, we know that this ＄378.4 billion net debit entry must be offset by a net ＄378.4 billion credit elsewhere in the balance of payments.

11.2.2 The Capital Account

11.2.2 资本项目

The capital account entry in Table 11.1 shows that, the United States paid out net capital asset transfers of roughly ＄0.1 billion. These payments by the United States are a net balance of payments debit. After we add them to the payments deficit implied by the current account, we find that the United States' need to cover its excess payments to foreigners is raised very slightly, from ＄378.4 billion to ＄378.5 billion. Because an excess of national spending over income must be covered by net borrowing from foreigners, this negative current plus capital account balance must be matched by an equal negative balance of net financial flows, representing the net liabilities the United States incurred to foreigners in order to fund its deficit.

11.2.3 The Financial Account

11.2.3 金融项目

While the current account is the difference between sales of goods and services to foreigners and purchases of goods and services from them, the financial account measures the difference between acquisitions of assets from foreigners and the buildup of liabilities to them. When the United States borrows ＄1 from foreigners, it is selling them an asset—a promise that they will be repaid ＄1, with interest, in the future. Likewise, when the United States lends abroad, it acquires an asset: the right to claim future repayment from foreigners.

To cover its current plus capital account deficit of $378.5 billion, the United States needed to borrow from foreigners (or otherwise sell assets to them) in the net amount of $378.5 billion. We can look again at Table 11.1 to see exactly how this net sale of assets to foreigners came about.

Table 11.1 records separately U.S. acquisitions of foreign financial assets (which are balance of payments debits, because the United States must pay foreigners for those assets) and increases in foreign claims on residents of the United States (which are balance of payments credits, because the United States receives payments when it sells assets overseas).

These data on increases in U.S. asset holdings abroad and foreign holdings of U.S. assets do not include holdings of financial derivatives, which are a class of assets that are more complicated than ordinary stocks and bonds, but have values that can depend on stock and bond values. The U.S. Department of Commerce was able to assemble data on net cross-border derivative flows for the United States (U.S. net purchases of foreign-issued derivatives less foreign net purchases of U.S.-issued derivatives). Derivatives transactions enter the balance of payments accounts in the same way as do other international asset transactions.

According to Table 11.1, U.S. owned assets abroad (other than derivatives) increased (on a net basis) by $140.5 billion in 2009. The figure is "on a net basis" because some U.S. residents bought foreign assets while others sold foreign assets they already owned, the difference between U.S. gross purchases and sales of foreign assets being $140.5 billion. In the same year (again on a net basis), the United States incurred new liabilities to foreigners equal to $305.7 billion. Some U.S. residents undoubtedly repaid foreign debts, but new borrowing from foreigners exceeded these repayments by $305.7 billion. The balance of U.S. sales and purchases of financial derivatives was −$50.8 billion: The United States sold more derivative claims to foreigners than it acquired. We calculate the balance on financial account (net financial flows) as $140.5 billion − $305.7 billion − $50.8 billion = −$216.0 billion. The negative value for net financial flows means that, the United States increased its net liability to foreigners (liabilities minus assets) by $216.0 billion.

11.2.4 Net Errors and Omissions

11.2.4 遗漏和错误

We come out with net financial flows smaller in absolute value than the amount that we'd expected. According to our data on trade and financial flows, the United States found less financing abroad than it needed to fund its current plus capital account deficit. If every balance of payments credit automatically generates an equal counterpart debit and vice versa, how is this difference possible? The reason is that information about the offsetting debit and credit items associated with a given transaction may be collected from different sources. For example, the import debit that a shipment of DVD players from Japan generates may come from a U.S. customs inspector's report and the corresponding financial account credit from a report by the U.S. bank in which the check paying for the DVD players is deposited. Because data from different sources may differ in coverage, accuracy, and timing, the balance of payments accounts seldom balance in practice as they must in theory. Account keepers force the two sides to balance by adding to the accounts a net errors and omissions item. For 2009, unrecorded (or mis-recorded) international transactions generated a balancing accounting credit of $162.5 billion—the difference between the recorded net financial flows and the sum of the recorded current and capital accounts.

We have no way of knowing exactly how to allocate this discrepancy among the current, capital, and financial accounts. (If we did, it wouldn't be a discrepancy!) The financial account is the most likely culprit, since it is notoriously difficult to keep track of the complicated financial trades between residents of different countries. But we cannot conclude that net financial flows were $162.5 billion lower than recorded, because the current account is also highly suspect. Balance of payments accountants consider merchandise trade data relatively reliable, but data on services are not. Service transactions such as sales of financial advice and computer programming assistance may escape detection. Accurate measurement of international interest and dividend receipts is particularly difficult.

11.2.5 Official Reserve Transactions

11.2.5 官方储备交易

Although there are many types of financial account transactions, one type is important enough to merit separate discussion. This type of transaction is the purchase or sale of official reserve assets by central banks. An economy's central bank is the institution responsible for managing the supply of money. In the United States, the central bank is the Federal Reserve System. Official international reserves are foreign assets held by central banks as a cushion against national economic misfortune. At one time, official reserves consisted largely of gold, but today, central banks' reserves include substantial foreign financial assets, particularly U.S. dollar assets such as treasury bills. The Federal Reserve itself holds only a small level of official reserve assets other than gold; its own holdings of U.S. dollar assets are not considered international reserves.

Central banks often buy or sell international reserves in private asset markets to affect macroeconomic conditions in their economies. Official transactions of this type are called official foreign exchange intervention. One reason why foreign exchange intervention can alter macroeconomic conditions is that it is a way for the central bank to inject money into the economy or withdraw it from circulation. We will have much more to say later about the causes and consequences of foreign exchange intervention.

Government agencies other than central banks may hold foreign reserves and intervene officially in exchange markets. The U.S. Treasury, for example, operates an Exchange Stabilization Fund that at times has played an active role in market trading. Because the operations of such agencies usually have no noticeable impact on the money supply, however, we will simplify our discussion by speaking (when it is not too misleading) as if the central bank alone holds foreign reserves and intervenes.

When a central bank purchases or sells a foreign asset, the transaction appears in its country's financial account just as if the same transaction had been carried out by a private citizen. A transaction in which the central bank of Japan (the Bank of Japan) acquires dollar assets might occur as follows: A U.S. auto dealer imports a Nissan sedan from Japan and pays the auto company with a check for \$20,000. Nissan does not want to invest the money in dollar assets, but it so happens that the Bank of Japan is willing to give Nissan Japanese money in exchange for the \$20,000 check. The Bank of Japan's international reserves rise by \$20,000 as a result of the deal. Because the Bank of Japan's dollar reserves are part of total Japanese assets held in the United States, the latter rise by \$20,000. This transaction therefore results in a \$20,000 credit in the U.S. financial account, the other side of the \$20,000 debit in the U.S. current account due to the import of the car.

Table 11.1 shows the size and direction of official reserve transactions involving the United States. U.S. official reserve assets—that is, international reserves held by the Federal Reserve—rose by \$52.3 billion. Foreign central banks purchased \$450.0 billion to add to their reserves. The net increase in U.S. official reserves less the increase in foreign official reserve claims on the United States is the level of net central bank financial flows, which stood at \$52.3 − \$450.0 billion = − \$397.7 billion.

You can think of this − \$397.7 billion net central bank financial flow as measuring the degree to which monetary authorities in the United States and abroad joined with other lenders to cover the U.S. current account deficit. In the example above, the Bank of Japan, by acquiring a \$20,000 U.S. bank deposit, indirectly finances an American import of a \$20,000 Japanese car. The level of net central bank financial flows is called the official settlements balance or (in less formal usage) the balance of payments. This balance is the sum of the current account and capital account balances, less the non-reserve portion of the financial account balance, and it indicates the payments gap that official reserve transactions need to cover. Thus the U.S. balance of payments was − \$397.7 billion.

The balance of payments played an important historical role as a measure of disequilibrium in international payments, and for many countries it still plays this role. A negative balance of payments (a deficit) may signal a crisis, for it means that a country is running down its international reserve assets or incurring debts to foreign monetary authorities. If a country faces the risk of being suddenly cut off from foreign loans, it will want to maintain a "war chest" of international reserves as a precaution. Developing countries, in particular, are in this position.

Like any summary measure, however, the balance of payments must be interpreted with caution. To return to our running example, the Bank of Japan's decision to expand its U.S. bank deposit holdings by $20,000 swells the measured U.S. balance of payments deficit by the same amount. Suppose the Bank of Japan instead places its $20,000 with Barclays Bank in London, which in turn deposits the money with Citibank in New York. The United States incurs an extra $20,000 in liabilities to private foreigners in this case, and the U.S. balance of payments deficit does not rise. But this "improvement" in the balance of payments is of little economic importance: It makes no real difference to the United States whether it borrows the Bank of Japan's money directly or through a London bank.

11.2.6 Case Study

11.2.6 案例分析

The Assets and Liabilities of the World's Biggest Debtor

We saw earlier that the current account balance measures the flow of new net claims on foreign wealth that a country acquires by exporting more goods and services than it imports. This flow is not, however, the only important factor that causes a country's net foreign wealth to change. In addition, changes in the market price of wealth previously acquired can alter a country's net foreign wealth. When Japan's stock market lost three quarters of its value over the 1990s, for example, American and European owners of Japanese shares saw the value of their claims on Japan plummet, and Japan's net foreign wealth increased as a result. Exchange rate changes have a similar effect. When the dollar depreciates against foreign currencies, for example, foreigners who hold dollar assets see their wealth fall when measured in their home currencies.

The Bureau of Economic Analysis (BEA) of the U.S. Department of Commerce, which oversees the vast job of data collection behind the U.S. national income and balance of payments statistics, reports annual estimates of the net "international investment position" of the United States—the country's foreign assets less its foreign liabilities. Because asset price and exchange rate changes alter the dollar values of foreign assets and liabilities alike, the BEA must adjust the values of existing claims to reflect such capital gains and losses in order to estimate U.S. net foreign wealth. These estimates show that at the end of 2009, the United States had a negative net foreign wealth position far greater than that of any other country.

Until 1991, foreign direct investments such as foreign factories owned by U.S. corporations were valued at their historical, that is, or iginal, purchase prices. Now the BEA uses two different methods to place current values on foreign direct investments: the current cost method, which values direct investments at the cost of buying them today, and the market value method, which is meant to measure the price at which the investments could be sold. These methods can lead to different valuations because the cost of replacing a particular direct investment and the price it would command if sold on the market may be hard to measure.

☞ Summary

☞ 本章小结

1. International macroeconomics is concerned with the full employment of scarce economic resources and price level stability throughout the world economy. Because they reflect national expenditure patterns and their international repercussions, the national income accounts and the balance of payments accounts are essential tools for studying the macroeconomics of open, interdependent economies.

2. A country's gross national product (GNP) is equal to the income received by its factors of production. The national income accounts divide national income according to the types of spending that generate it: consumption, investment, government purchases, and the current account balance. Gross domestic product (GDP), equal to GNP less net receipts of factor income from abroad, measures the output produced within a country's territorial borders.

3. In an economy closed to international trade, GNP must be consumed, invested, or purchased by the government. By using

current output to build plant, equipment, and inventories, investment transforms present output into future output. For a closed economy, investment is the only way to save in the aggregate, so the sum of the saving carried out by the private and public sectors, national saving, must equal investment.

4. In an open economy, GNP equals the sum of consumption, investment, government purchases, and net exports of goods and services. Trade does not have to be balanced if the economy can borrow from and lend to the rest of the world. The difference between the economy's exports and imports, the current account balance, equals the difference between the economy's output and its total use of goods and services.

5. The current account also equals the country's net lending to foreigners. Unlike a closed economy, an open economy can save by domestic and foreign investments. National saving therefore equals domestic investment plus the current account balance.

6. Balance of payments accounts provide a detailed picture of the composition and financing of the current account. All transactions between a country and the rest of the world are recorded in the country's balance of payments accounts. The accounts are based on the convention that any transaction resulting in a payment to foreigners is entered as a debit while any transaction resulting in a receipt from foreigners is entered as a credit.

7. Transactions involving goods and services appear in the current account of the balance of payments, while international sales or purchases of assets appear in the financial account. The capital account records mainly non-market asset transfers and tends to be small for the United States. The sum of the current and capital account balances must equal the financial account balance (net financial flows). This feature of the accounts reflects the fact that discrepancies between export earnings and import expenditures must be matched by a promise to repay the difference, usually with interest, in the future.

8. International asset transactions carried out by central banks are included in the financial account. Any central bank transaction in private markets for foreign currency assets is called official foreign exchange intervention. One reason intervention is important

is that central banks use it as a way to change the amount of money in circulation. A country has a deficit in its balance of payments when it is running down its official international reserves or borrowing from foreign central banks; it has a surplus in the opposite case.

☞ Key Terms

☞ 关键术语

asset, balance of payments, accounting, capital account, central bank, consumption, current account balance, financial account, government budget deficit, government purchases, gross domestic product (GDP), gross national product (GNP), investment, macroeconomics, microeconomics, national income, national income accounting, national saving, official settlements balance(or balance of payments), private saving

资产、国际收支、会计、资本账户、中央银行、消费、经常账户差额、金融账户、政府预算赤字、政府购买、国内生产总值、国民生产总值、投资、宏观经济学、微观经济学、国民收入、国民收入账户、国民储蓄、官方结算差额、个人储蓄

☞ Questions

☞ 本章习题

1. We stated in this chapter that GNP accounts avoid double counting by including only the value of final goods and services sold on the market. Should the measure of imports used in the GNP accounts therefore be defined to include only imports of final goods and services from abroad? What about exports?

2. A New Yorker travels to New Jersey to buy a \$100 telephone answering machine. The New Jersey company that sells the machine then deposits the \$100 check in its account at a New York bank. How would these transactions show up in the balance of payments accounts of New York and New Jersey? What if the New Yorker pays cash for the machine?

3. Can you think of reasons why a government might be concerned about a large current account deficit or surplus? Why might a government be concerned about its official settlements balance (that is, its balance of payments)?

4. Do data on the U.S. official settlements balance give an accurate picture of the extent to which foreign central banks buy and sell dollars in currency markets?

5. Is it possible for a country to have a current account deficit

at the same time it has a surplus in its balance of payments? Explain your answer, using hypothetical figures for the current and non-reserve financial accounts. Be sure to discuss the possible implications for official international reserve flows.

Chapter 12

Money, Interest Rates, and Exchange Rates

第十二章 货币、利率与汇率

The exchange rate between currencies depends on two factors, the interest that can be earned on deposits of those currencies and the expected future exchange rate. To understand fully the determination of exchange rates, however, we have to learn how interest rates themselves are determined and how expectations of future exchange rates are formed. In this chapter and the next chapter we examine these topics by building an economic model that links exchange rates, interest rates, and other important macroeconomic variables such as the inflation rate and output.

The first step in building the model is to explain the effects of a country's money supply and of the demand for its money on its interest rate and exchange rate. Because exchange rates are the relative prices of national monies, factors that affect a country's money supply or demand are among the most powerful determinants of its currency's exchange rate against foreign currencies. It is therefore natural to begin a deeper study of exchange rate determination with a discussion of money supply and money demand. Monetary developments influence the exchange rate by changing both interest rates and people's expectations about future exchange rates. Expectations about future exchange rates are closely connected with expectations about the future money prices of countries' products; these price movements, in turn, depend on changes in money supply and demand. In examining monetary influences on the exchange rate, we therefore look at how monetary factors influence output prices along with interest rates. Expectations of future exchange rates depend on many factors other than money, however, and these non-monetary factors are taken up in the next chapter.

Once the theories and determinants of money supply and

demand are laid out, we use them to examine how equilibrium interest rates are determined by the equality of money supply and money demand. Then we combine our model of interest rate determination with the interest parity condition to study the effects of monetary shifts on the exchange rate, given the prices of goods and services, the level of output, and market expectations about the future. Finally, we take a first look at the long-term effects of monetary changes on output prices and expected future exchange rates.

12.1 Money Defined: a Brief Review

12.1 货币的定义：简单回顾

We are so accustomed to using money that we seldom notice the roles it plays in almost all of our everyday transactions. As with many other modern conveniences, we take money for granted until something goes wrong with it! In fact, the easiest way to appreciate the importance of money is to imagine what economic life would be like without it.

In this section we do just that. Our purpose in carrying out this "thought experiment" is to distinguish money from other assets and to describe the characteristics of money that lead people to hold it. These characteristics are central to an analysis of the demand for money.

12.1.1 Money as a Medium of Exchange

12.1.1 作为交易媒介的货币

The most important function of money is to serve as a medium of exchange, a generally accepted means of payment. To see why a medium of exchange is necessary, imagine how time-consuming it would be for people to purchase goods and services in a world where the only type of trade possible is barter trade—the direct trade of goods or services for other goods or services. To have her car repaired, for example, your professor would have to find a mechanic in need of economics lessons!

Money eliminates the enormous search costs connected with a barter system because money is universally acceptable. It eliminates these search costs by enabling an individual to sell the goods and services she produces to people other than the producers of the goods and services she wishes to consume. A complex modern economy would cease functioning without some standardized and convenient means of payment.

12.1.2 Money as a Unit of Account

12.1.2 作为度量单位的货币

Money's second important role is to serve as a unit of account, that is, as a widely recognized measure of value. It is in this role that we encountered money: prices of goods, services, and assets are typically expressed in terms of money. Exchange rates allow us to translate different countries' money prices into comparable terms.

The convention of quoting prices in money terms simplifies economic calculations by making it easy to compare the prices of different commodities. The international price comparisons, which used exchange rates to compare the prices of different countries' outputs, are similar to the calculations you would have to do many times each day if different commodities' prices were not expressed in terms of a standardized unit of account. If the calculations in Chapter 14 gave you a headache, imagine what it would be like to have to calculate the relative prices of each good and service you consume in terms of several other goods and services—for example, the price of a slice of pizza in terms of bananas. This thought experiment should give you a keener appreciation of using money as a unit of account.

12.1.3 Money as a Store of Value

12.1.3 作为价值储存的货币

Because money can be used to transfer purchasing power from the present into the future, it is also an asset, or a store of value. This attribute is essential for any medium of exchange because no one would be willing to accept it in payment if its value in terms of goods and services evaporated immediately.

Money's usefulness as a medium of exchange, however, automatically makes it the most liquid of all assets. As you will recall from the last chapter, an asset is said to be liquid when it can be transformed into goods and services rapidly and without high transaction costs, such as brokers' fees. Since money is readily acceptable as a means of payment, money sets the standard against which the liquidity of other assets is judged.

12.1.4 What Is Money?

12.1.4 什么是货币?

Currency and bank deposits on which checks may be written certainly qualify as money. These are widely accepted means of payment that can be transferred between owners at low cost. Households and firms hold currency and checking deposits as a convenient way of financing routine transactions as they arise. Assets such as real estate do not qualify as money, because unlike currency and checking deposits, they lack the essential property of liquidity. When we speak in this book of the money supply, we are referring to the monetary aggregate the Federal Reserve calls M1, that is, the total amount of currency and checking deposits held by households and firms. The large deposits traded by participants in the foreign exchange market are not considered part of the money supply. These deposits are less liquid than money and are not used to finance routine transactions.

12.2 Money Supply and Money Demand

12.2 货币供求

12.2.1 How the Money Supply Is Determined?

12.2.1 货币供给如何决定?

An economy's money supply is controlled by its central bank. The central bank directly regulates the amount of currency in existence and also has indirect control over the amount of checking deposits issued by private banks. The procedures through which the central bank controls the money supply are complex, and we assume for now that the central bank simply sets the size of the money supply at the level it desires.

12.2.2 The Demand for Money by Individuals

12.2.2 个体的货币需求

Having discussed the functions of money and the definition of the money supply, we now examine the factors that determine the amount of money an individual desires to hold. The determinants of individual money demand can be derived from the theory of asset demand. We saw in the last chapter that individuals base their demand for an asset on three characteristics.

1. The expected return the asset offers compared with the returns offered by other assets.

2. The riskiness of the asset's expected return.

3. The asset's liquidity.

While liquidity plays no important role in determining the relative demands for assets traded in the foreign exchange market, households and firms hold money only because of its liquidity. To understand how the economy's households and firms decide the amount of money they wish to hold, we must look more closely at how the three considerations listed above influence money demand.

12.2.3 Expected Return

12.2.3 预期收益

Currency pays no interest. Checking deposits often do pay some interest, but they offer a rate of return that usually fails to keep pace with the higher returns offered by less liquid forms of wealth. When you hold money, you therefore sacrifice the higher interest rate you could earn by holding your wealth in a government bond, a large time deposit, or some other relatively illiquid asset such as vintage baseball cards or real estate. It is this last rate of interest we have in mind when we refer to "the" interest rate. Since the interest paid on currency is zero while that paid on "checkable" deposits tends to be relatively constant, the difference between the rate of return of money in general and that of less liquid alternative assets is reflected by the market interest rate: The higher the interest rate, the more you sacrifice by holding wealth in the form of money.

Suppose, for example, that the interest rate you could earn from a U.S. treasury bill is 10 percent per year. If you use $10,000 of your wealth to buy a treasury bill, you will be paid $11,000 by Uncle Sam at the end of a year, but if you choose instead to keep the $10,000 as cash in a safe-deposit box, you give up the $1,000 interest you could have earned by buying the treasury bill. You thus sacrifice a 10 percent rate of return by holding your $10,000 as money.

The theory of asset demand developed in the last chapter shows how changes in the rate of interest affect the demand for money. The theory states that, other things equal, people prefer assets offering higher expected returns. Because an increase in the interest rate is a rise in the rate of return on less liquid assets relative to the rate of return on money, individuals will want to hold more of their wealth in non-money assets that pay the market interest rate and less of their wealth in the form of money if the interest rate rises. We conclude that, all else equal, a rise in the interest rate causes the demand for money to fall.

We can also describe the influence of the interest rate on money demand in terms of the economic concept of opportunity cost—the amount you sacrifice by taking one course of action rather than another. The interest rate measures the opportunity cost of holding money rather than interest-bearing bonds. A rise in the interest rate therefore raises the cost of holding money and causes money demand to fall.

12.2.4 Risk

12.2.4 风险

Risk is not an important factor in money demand. It is risky to hold money because an unexpected increase in the prices of goods and services could reduce the value of your money in terms of the commodities you consume. Since interest-paying assets such as government bonds have face values fixed in terms of money, however, the same unexpected increase in prices would reduce the real value of those assets by the same percentage. Because any change in the riskiness of money causes an equal change in the riskiness of bonds, changes in the risk of holding money need not cause individuals to reduce their demand for money and increase their demand for interest-paying assets.

12.2.5 Liquidity

12.2.5 流动性

The main benefit of holding money comes from its liquidity. Households and firms hold money because it is the easiest way of financing their everyday purchases. Some large purchases can be financed through the sale of a substantial illiquid asset. An art collector, for example, could sell one of her Picassos to buy a house. To finance a continuing stream of smaller expenditures at various times and for various amounts, however, households and firms have to hold some money. An individual's need for liquidity rises when the average daily value of his transactions rises. A student who takes the bus every day, for example, does not need to hold as much cash as a business executive who takes taxis during rush hour. We conclude that a rise in the average value of transactions carried out by a household or firm causes its demand for money to rise.

12.2.6 Aggregate Money Demand

12.2.6 货币总需求

Our discussion of how individual households and firms determine their demands for money can now be applied to derive the determinants of aggregate money demand, the total demand for money by all households and firms in the economy. Aggregate money demand is just the sum of all the economy's individual money demands. Three main factors determine aggregate money demand.

1. The interest rate. A rise in the interest rate causes each individual in the economy to reduce her demand for money. All else equal, aggregate money demand therefore falls when the interest rate rises.

2. The price level. The economy's price level is the price of a broad reference basket of goods and services in terms of currency. Generally the reference basket includes the standard, everyday consumption items such as food, clothing, and housing, but also less routine purchases such as medical care and legal fees. If the price level rises, individual households and firms must spend more money than before to purchase their usual weekly baskets of goods and services. To maintain the same level of liquidity as before the price level increase, they will therefore have to hold more money.

3. Real national income. When real national income (GNP) rises, more goods and services are being sold in the economy. This increase in the real value of transactions raises the demand for money, given the price level.

If P is the price level, R is the interest rate, and Y is real GNP, the aggregate demand for money can be expressed as

$$M^d = P \times L(R, Y) \quad (12.1)$$

where the value of $L(R, Y)$ falls when R rises, and rises when Y rises. To see why we have specified that aggregate money demand is proportional to the price level, imagine that all prices doubled but the interest rate and everyone's real incomes remained unchanged. The money value of each individual's average daily transactions would then simply double, as would the amount of money each wished to hold. We usually write the aggregate money demand relation in the equivalent form

$$M^d/P = L(R, Y) \tag{12.2}$$

and call $L(R,Y)$ aggregate real money demand. This way of expressing money demand shows that the aggregate demand for liquidity, $L(R, Y)$, is not a demand for a certain number of currency units but is instead a demand to hold a certain amount of real purchasing power in liquid form. The ratio M_d/P —that is, desired money holdings measured in terms of a typical reference basket of commodities—equals the amount of real purchasing power people would like to hold in liquid form. For example, if people wished to hold \$1,000 in cash at a price level of \$100 per commodity basket, their real money holdings would be equivalent to \$1,000/ (\$100 per basket) = 10 baskets. If the price level doubled (to \$200 per basket), the purchasing power of their \$1,000 in cash would be halved, since it would now be worth only 5 baskets.

Figure 12. 1 shows how aggregate real money demand is affected by the interest rate for a fixed level of real income, Y. The aggregate real money demand schedule $L(R, Y)$ slopes downward because a fall in the interest rate raises the desired real money holdings of each household and firm in the economy. For a given level of real GNP, changes in the interest rate cause movements along the schedule. Changes in real GNP, however, cause the schedule itself to shift.

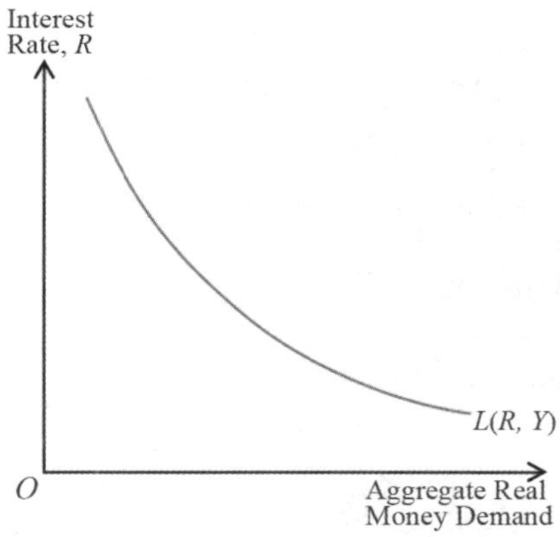

Figure 12.1 Aggregate Real Money Demand and the Interest Rate

Note: The downward-sloping shows that for a given real income level Y, real money demand rises as the interest rate falls.

Figure 12.2 shows how a rise in real GNP from Y_1 to Y_2 affects the position of the aggregate real money demand schedule. Because a rise in real GNP raises aggregate real money demand for a given interest rate, the schedule $L(R, Y_2)$ lies to the right of $L(R, Y_1)$ when Y_2 is greater than Y_1.

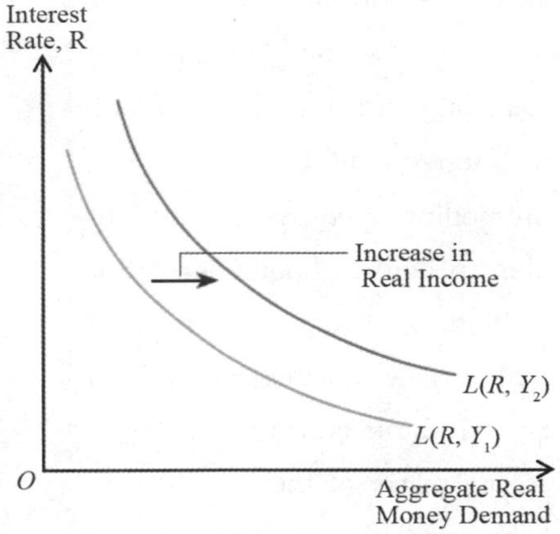

Figure 12.2 Effect on the Aggregate Real Money Demand Schedule of a Rise in Real Income

Note: An increase in real income from Y_1 to Y_2 raises the demand for real money balances at every level of the interest rate and causes the whole demand schedule to shift upward.

12.2.7 The Equilibrium Interest Rate: the Interaction of Money Supply and Demand

12.2.7 均衡利率：货币供给与货币需求

As you might expect from other economics courses you've taken, the money market is in equilibrium when the money supply set by the central bank equals aggregate money demand. In this section we see how the interest rate is determined by money market equilibrium, given the price level and output, both of which are temporarily assumed to be unaffected by monetary changes.

12.2.8 Equilibrium in the Money Market

12.2.8 货币市场的均衡

If M_s is the money supply, the condition for equilibrium in the money market is

$$M_s = M_d \tag{12.3}$$

After dividing both sides of this equality by the price level, we can express the money market equilibrium condition in terms of aggregate real money demand as

$$P_s/P = L(R, Y)$$

Given the price level P, and the level of output Y, the equilibrium interest rate is the one at which aggregate real money demand equals the real money supply. In Figure 12.3, the aggregate real money demand schedule intersects the real money supply schedule at point 1 to give an equilibrium interest rate of R_1. The money supply schedule is vertical at M_s/P because M^s is set by the central bank while P is taken as given. Let's see why the interest rate tends to settle at its equilibrium level by considering what happens if the market is initially at point 2, with an interest rate R_2, that is above R_1.

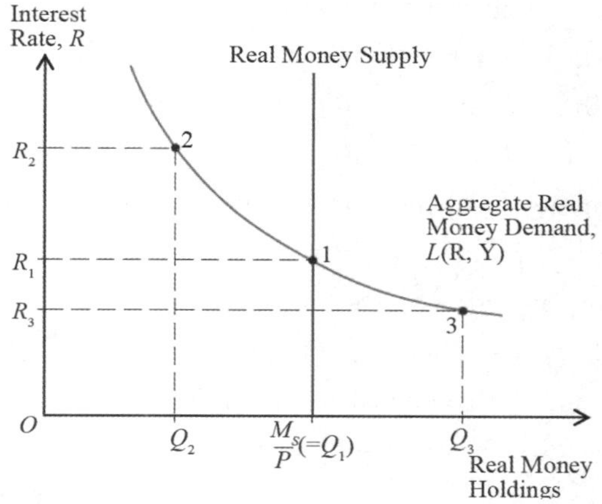

Figure 12.3 Determination of the Equilibrium Interest Rate

Note: With P and Y given and a real money supply of M_s/P, money market equilibrium is at point 1. At this point, aggregate real money demand and the real money supply are equal and the equilibrium interest rate is R_1.

At point 2 the demand for real money holdings falls short of the supply by $Q_1 - Q_2$, so there is an excess supply of money. If individuals are holding more money than they desire given the interest rate of R_2, they will attempt to reduce their liquidity by using some money to purchase interest-bearing assets. In other words, individuals will attempt to get rid of their excess money by lending it to others. Since there is an aggregate excess supply of money at R_2, however, not everyone can succeed in doing this: There are more people who would like to lend money to reduce their liquidity than there are people who would like to borrow money to increase theirs. Those who cannot unload their extra money try to tempt potential borrowers by lowering the interest rate they charge for loans below R_2. The downward pressure on the interest rate continues until the rate reaches R_1. At this interest rate, anyone wishing to lend money can do so because the aggregate excess supply of money has disappeared; that is, supply once again equals demand. Once the market reaches point 1, there is therefore no further tendency for the interest rate to drop.

Similarly, if the interest rate is initially at a level R_3 below R_1, it will tend to rise. As Figure 12.3 shows, there is excess demand for money equal to $Q_3 - Q_1$ at point 3. Individuals therefore attempt to sell interest-bearing assets such as bonds to increase their money holdings (that is, they sell bonds for cash). At point 3, however, not everyone can succeed in selling enough interest-bearing assets to satisfy his or her demand for money. Thus, people bid for money by offering to borrow at progressively higher interest rates and push the interest rate upward toward R_1. Only when the market has reached point 1 and the excess demand for money has been eliminated does the interest rate stop rising.

We can summarize our findings as follows: the market always moves toward an interest rate at which the real money supply equals aggregate real money demand. If there is initially an excess supply of money, the interest rate falls, and if there is initially an excess demand, it rises.

12.2.9 Interest Rates and the Money Supply

12.2.9 利率和货币供给

The effect of increasing the money supply at a given price level is illustrated in Figure 12.4. Initially the money market is in equilibrium at point 1, with a money supply M_1 and an interest rate R_1. Since we are holding P constant, a rise in the money supply to M_2 increases the real money supply from M_1/P to M_2/P. With a real money supply of M_2/P, point 2 is the new equilibrium and R_2 is the new, lower interest rate that induces people to hold the increased available real money supply.

The process through which the interest rate falls is by now familiar. After M_s is increased by the central bank, there is initially an excess real supply of money at the old equilibrium interest rate, R_1, which previously balanced the market. Since people are holding more money than they desire, they use their surplus funds to bid for assets that pay interest. The economy as a whole cannot reduce its money holdings, so interest rates are driven down as unwilling money holders compete to lend their excess cash balances. At point 2 in Figure 12.4, the interest rate has fallen sufficiently to induce an increase in real money demand equal to the increase in the real money supply.

By running the above policy experiment in reverse, we can see how a reduction of the money supply forces interest rates upward. A fall in M_s causes an excess demand for money at the interest rate that previously balanced supply and demand. People attempt to sell interest-bearing assets—that is, to borrow—to rebuild their depleted real money holdings. Since they cannot all be successful when there is excess money demand, the interest rate is pushed upward until everyone is content to hold the smaller real money stock.

We conclude that an increase in the money supply lowers the interest rate, while a fall in the money supply raises the interest rate, given the price level and output.

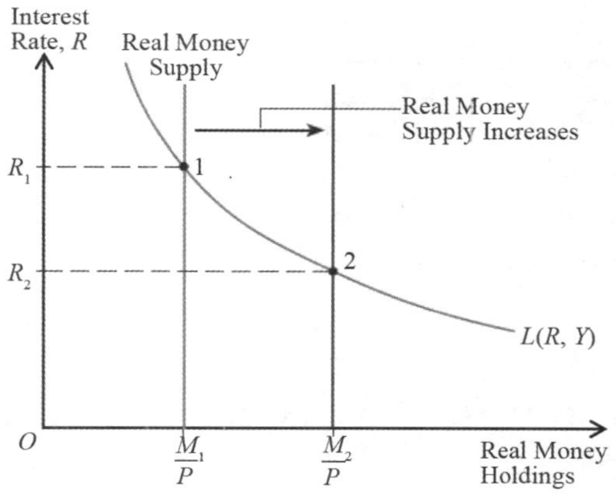

Figure 12.4 Effect of an Increase in the Money Supply on the Interest Rate

Note: For a given price level P, and real income level Y, and increase in the money supply from M_1 to M_2 reduces the interest rate from R_1 (point 1) to R_2 (point 2).

12.2.10 Output and the Interest Rate

12.2.10 产出和利率

Figure 12.5 shows the effect on the interest rate of a rise in the level of output from Y_1 to Y_2, given the money supply and the price level. As we saw earlier, an increase in output causes the entire aggregate real money demand schedule to shift to the right, moving the equilibrium away from point 1. At the old equilibrium interest rate R_1, there is an excess demand for money equal to $Q_2 - Q_1$ (point 1'). Since the real money supply is given, the interest rate is bid up until it reaches the higher, new equilibrium level R_2 (point 2). A fall in output has opposite effects, causing the aggregate real money demand schedule to shift to the left and therefore causing the equilibrium interest rate to fall.

We conclude that an increase in real output raises the interest rate, while a fall in real output lowers the interest rate, given the price level and the money supply.

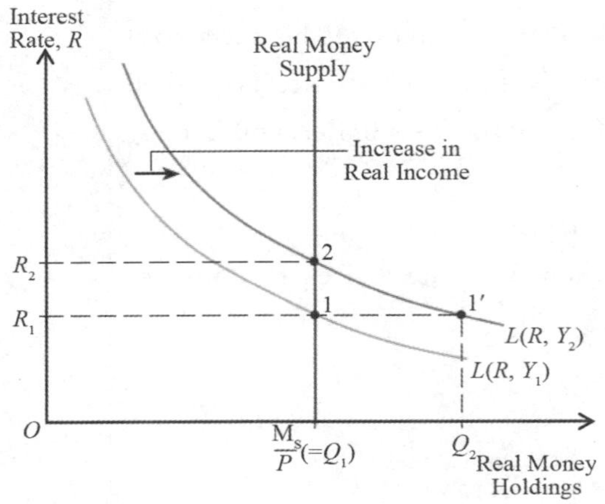

Figure 12.5 Effect on the Interest Rate of a Rise in Real Income

Note: Given the real money supply, $M_s/P(=Q_1)$, a rise In real Income from Y_1 to Y_2 raises the Interest rate from R_1 (point 1) to R_2 (point 2).

12.3 The Money Supply and the Exchange Rate in the Short Run

12.3 短期条件下的货币供给和汇率

We have learned about the interest parity condition, which predicts how interest rate movements influence the exchange rate, given expectations about the exchange rate's future level. Now that we know how shifts in a country's money supply affect the interest rate on non-money assets denominated in its currency, we can see how monetary changes affect the exchange rate. We will discover that an increase in a country's money supply causes its currency to depreciate in the foreign exchange market, while a reduction in the money supply causes its currency to appreciate.

In this section we continue to take the price level (along with real output) as given, and for that reason we label the analysis of this section short run. The long-run analysis of an economic event allows for the complete adjustment of the price level (which may take a long time) and for full employment of all factors of production. Later in this chapter we examine the long-run effects of money supply changes on the price level, the exchange rate, and other macroeconomic variables. Our long-run analysis will show how the money supply influences exchange rate expectations, which we also continue to take as given for now.

12.3.1 Linking Money, the Interest Rate, and the Exchange Rate

12.3.1 连接资金、利率和汇率

To analyze the relationship between money and the exchange rate in the short run in Figure 12.6, we combine two diagrams that we have already studied separately. Let's assume once again that we are looking at the dollar/euro exchange rate, that is, the price of euros in terms of dollars.

The first diagram shows equilibrium in the foreign exchange market and how it is determined given interest rates and expectations about future exchange rates. This diagram appears as the top part of Figure 12.6. The dollar interest rate, $R^1_\$$ which is determined in the money market, defines the vertical schedule.

The downward-sloping expected euro return schedule shows the expected return on euro deposits, measured in dollars. The schedule slopes downward because of the effect of current exchange rate changes on expectations of future depreciation: A strengthening of the dollar today (a fall in $E^1_{\$/€}$) relative to its given expected future level makes euro deposits more attractive by leading people to anticipate a sharper dollar depreciation in the future.

At the intersection of the two schedules (point 1'), the expected rates of return on dollar and euro deposits are equal, and therefore interest parity holds. $E^1_{\$/€}$ is the equilibrium exchange rate.

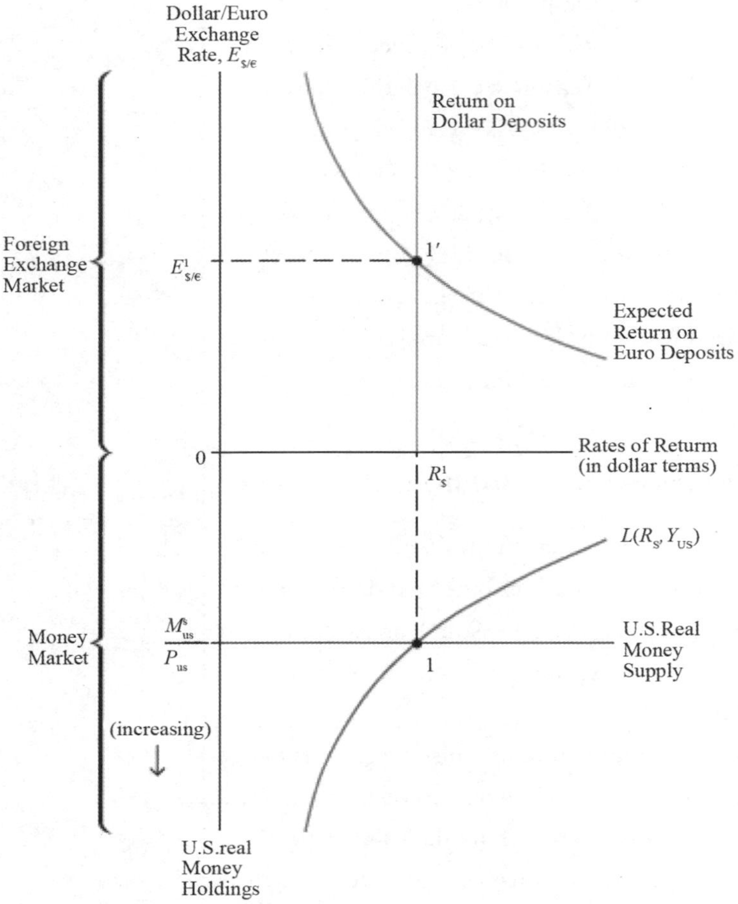

Figure 12.6 Simultaneous Equilibrium in the U.S. Money Market and the Foreign Exchange Market

Note: Both asset markets are in equilibrium at the interest rate $R^1_\$$ and exchange rate $E^1_{\$/€}$; at these values, money supply equals money demand (point 1) and the interest parity condition holds (point 1).

The second diagram we need to examine the relationship between money and the exchange rate was introduced as Figure 12.3. This figure shows how a country's equilibrium interest rate is determined in its money market, and it appears as the bottom part of Figure 12.6. For convenience, however, the figure has been rotated clockwise by 90 degrees so that dollar interest rates are measured from 0 on the horizontal axis and the U.S. real money supply is measured from 0 on the descending vertical axis. Money market equilibrium is shown at point 1, where the dollar interest rate $R^1_\$$ induces people to demand real balances equal to the U.S.

real money supply, M^s_{US}/P_{US}.

Figure 12.6 emphasizes the link between the U. S. money market (bottom) and the foreign exchange market (top)—the U.S. money market determines the dollar interest rate, which in turn affects the exchange rate that maintains interest parity. (Of course, there is a similar link between the European money market and the foreign exchange market that operates through changes in the euro interest rate.)

Figure 12.7 illustrates these linkages. The U. S. and European central banks, the Federal Reserve System and the European System of Central Banks (ESCB), respectively, determine the U.S. and European money supplies, M^s_{US} and M^s_E Given the price levels and national incomes of the two countries, equilibrium in national money markets leads to the dollar and euro interest rates $R_\$$ and $R_€$. These interest rates feed into the foreign exchange market, where, given expectations about the future dollar/euro exchange rate, the current rate $E_{\$/€}$ is determined by the interest parity condition.

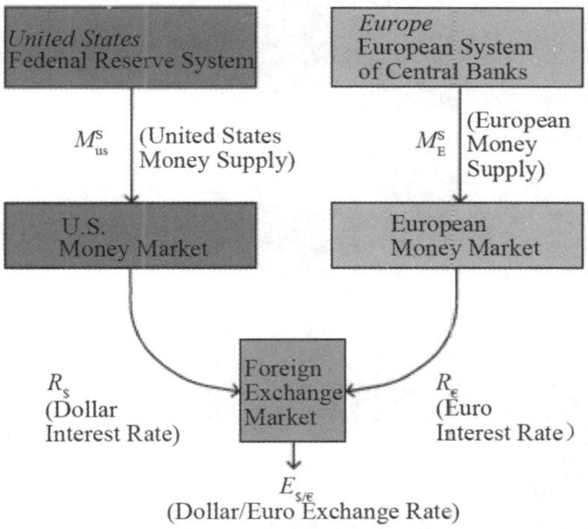

Figure 12.7 Money Market/Exchange Rate Linkages

Note: Monetary policy actions by the Fed affect the U.S. interest rate, changing the dollar/euro exchange rate that clears the foreign exchange market. The ESCB can affect the exchange rate by changing the European money supply and interest rate.

12.3.2 U.S. Money Supply and the Dollar/Euro Exchange Rate

12.3.2 美国货币供给和美元与欧元的汇率

We now use our model of asset market linkages (the links between the money and foreign exchange markets) to ask how the dollar/euro exchange rate changes when the Federal Reserve changes the U.S. money supply M^s_{US}. The effects of this change are summarized in Figure 12.8.

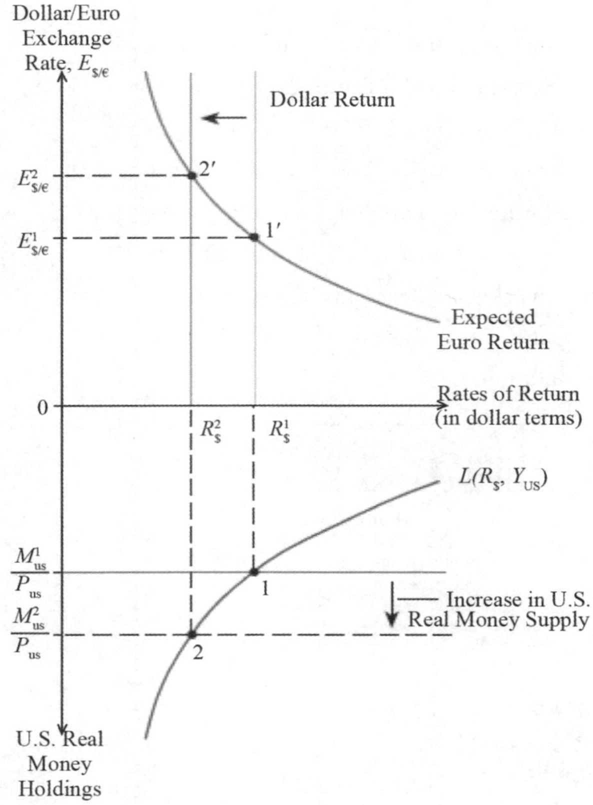

Figure 12.8 Effect on the Dollar/Euro Exchange Rate and Dollar Interest Rate of and Increase in the U.S. Money Supply

Note: Given P_{US} and Y_{US} when the money supply rises from M^1_{US} to M^2_{US} the dollar interest rate declines (as money market equilibrium is reestablished at point 2) and the dollar depreciates against the euro (as foreign exchange market equilibrium is reestablished at point 2).

At the initial money supply M^1_{US}, the money market is in equilibrium at point 1 with an interest rate $R^1_\$$. Given the euro interest rate and the expected future exchange rate, a dollar interest rate of $R^1_\$$ implies that foreign exchange market equilibrium occurs at point 1', with an exchange rate equal to $E^1_{\$/€}$.

What happens when the Federal Reserve, perhaps fearing the onset of a recession, raises the U.S. money supply to M^2_{US}? This increase sets in motion the following sequence of events. (1) At the initial interest rate $R^1_{\$}$, there is an excess supply of money in the U.S. money market, so the dollar interest rate falls to $R^2_{\$}$ as the money market reaches its new equilibrium position (point 2). (2) Given the initial exchange rate $E^1_{\$/€}$ and the new, lower interest rate on dollars, $R^2_{\$}$, the expected return on euro deposits is greater than that on dollar deposits. Holders of dollar deposits therefore try to sell them for euro deposits, which are momentarily more attractive. (3) The dollar depreciates to $E^2_{\$/€}$ as holders of dollar deposits bid for euro deposits. The foreign exchange market is once again in equilibrium at point 2' because the exchange rate's move to $E^2_{\$/€}$ causes a fall in the dollar's expected future depreciation rate sufficient to offset the fall in the dollar interest rate.

We conclude that an increase in a country's money supply causes its currency to depreciate in the foreign exchange market. By running Figure 12.8 in reverse, you can see that a reduction in a country's money supply causes its currency to appreciate in the foreign exchange market.

12.3.3 Europe's Money Supply and the Dollar/Euro Exchange Rate

12.3.3 欧洲货币供给和美元与欧元汇率

The conclusions we have reached also apply when the ESCB changes Europe's money supply. Suppose that the ESCB fears a recession in Europe and hopes to head it off through a looser monetary policy. An increase in M^s_E causes a depreciation of the euro(that is, an appreciation of the dollar, or a fall in $E_{\$/€}$), while a reduction in M^s_E causes an appreciation of the euro (that is, a depreciation of the dollar, or a rise in $E_{\$/€}$).

The mechanism at work, which runs from the European interest rate to the exchange rate, is the same as the one we just analyzed. It is a good exercise to verify these assertions by drawing figures similar to Figures 12.6 and 12.8 that illustrate the linkage between the European money market and the foreign exchange market.

Here we use a different approach to show how changes in Europe's money supply affect the dollar/euro exchange rate. We have learned that a fall in the euro interest rate, $R_€$ shifts the downward-sloping schedule in the upper part of Figure 12.6 to the left. The reason is that for any level of the exchange rate, a fall in $R_€$ lowers the expected rate of return on euro deposits. Since a rise in the European money supply M_E^s lowers $R_€$, we can see the effect on the exchange rate by shifting the expected euro return schedule in the top part of Figure 12.6 to the left.

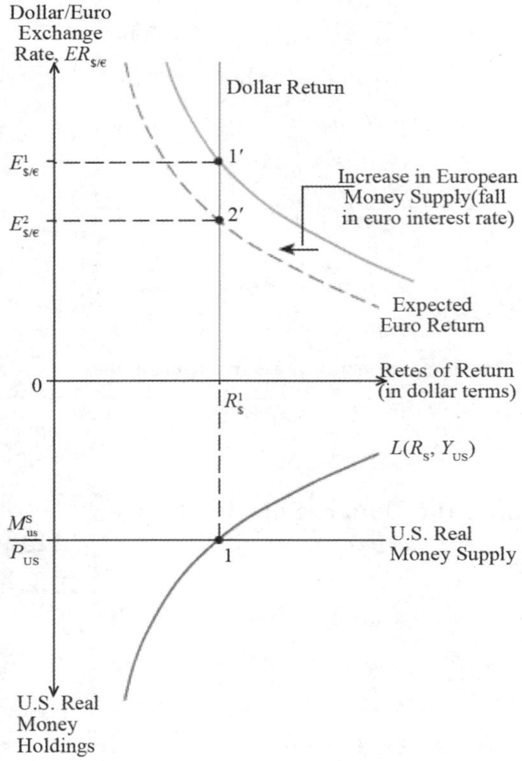

Figure 12.9 Effect of and Increase in the European Money Supply on the Dollar/Euro Exchange Rate

Note: By lowering the dollar return on euro deposits (shown as a leftward shift in the expected euro return curve), and increase in Europe's money supply causes the dollar to appreciate against the euro, equilibrium in the foreign exchange market shifts from point 1′ to point 2′, but equilibrium in the U.S. money market remains at point 1.

The result of an increase in the European money supply is shown in Figure 12. 9. Initially the U. S. money market is in equilibrium at point 1 and the foreign exchange market is in equilibrium at point1' with an exchange rate $E^1_{\$/€}$. An increase in Europe's money supply lowers $R_€$ and therefore shifts to the left the schedule linking the expected return on euro deposits to the exchange rate. Foreign exchange market equilibrium is restored at point with an exchange rate of $E^2_{\$/€}$. We see that the increase in European money causes the euro to depreciate against the dollar (that is, causes a fall in the dollar price of euros). Similarly, a fall in Europe's money supply would cause the euro to appreciate against the dollar (that is, $E_{\$/€}$ would rise). The change in the European money supply does not disturb the U.S. money market equilibrium, which remains at point 1.

12.4 Money, the Price Level, and the Exchange Rate in the Long Run

12.4 长期条件下的货币、价格水平和汇率

Our short-run analysis of the link between countries' money markets and the foreign exchange market rested on the simplifying assumption that price levels and exchange rate expectations were given. To extend our understanding of how money supply and money demand affect exchange rates, we must examine how monetary factors affect a country's price level in the long run.

An economy's long-run equilibrium is the position it would eventually reach if no new economic shocks occurred during the adjustment to full employment. You can think of long-run equilibrium as the equilibrium that would be maintained after all wages and prices had had enough time to adjust to their market-clearing levels. An equivalent way of thinking of it is as the equilibrium that would occur if prices were perfectly flexible and always adjusted immediately to preserve full employment.

In studying how monetary changes work themselves out over the long run, we will examine how such changes shift the economy's long-run equilibrium. Our main tool is once again the theory of aggregate money demand.

12.4.1 Money and Money Prices

12.4.1 货币和货币价格

If the price level and output are fixed in the short run, the condition (12.4) of money market equilibrium,

$$M^s/P = L(R, Y) \qquad (12.4)$$

determines the domestic interest rate, R. The money market always moves to equilibrium, however, even if we drop our "short-run" assumption and think of periods over which P and Y, as well as R, can vary. The above equilibrium condition can therefore be rearranged to give

$$P = M^s/L(R, Y) \qquad (12.5)$$

which shows how the price level depends on the interest rate, real output, and the domestic money supply.

The long-run equilibrium price level is just the value of P that satisfies condition (12.5) when the interest rate and output are at their long-run levels, that is, at levels consistent with full employment. When the money market is in equilibrium and all factors of production are fully employed, the price level will remain steady if the money supply, the aggregate money demand function, and the long-run values of R and Y remain steady.

One of the most important predictions of the above equation for P concerns the relationship between a country's price level and its money supply, M^s: all else equal, an increase in a country's money supply causes a proportional increase in its price level. If, for example, the money supply doubles (to $2M^s$) but output and the interest rate do not change, the price level must also double (to $2P$) to maintain equilibrium in the money market.

The economic reasoning behind this very precise prediction follows from our observation above that the demand for money is a demand for real money holdings: real money demand is not altered by an increase in M^s that leaves R and Y (and thus aggregate real money demand $L(R, Y)$) unchanged. If aggregate real money demand does not change, however, the money market will remain in equilibrium only if the real money supply also stays the same. To keep the real money supply M^s/P constant, P must rise in proportion to M^s.

12.4.2 The Long-run Effects of Money Supply Changes

12.4.2 货币供给变化的长期影响

Our theory of how the money supply affects the price level given the interest rate and output is not yet a theory of how money supply changes affect the price level in the long run. To develop such a theory, we still have to determine the long-run effects of a money supply change on the interest rate and output. This is easier than you might think. As we now argue, a change in the supply of money has no effect on the long-run values of the interest rate or real output.

The best way to understand the long-run effects of money supply on the interest rate and output is to think first about a currency reform, in which a country's government redefines the national currency unit. For example, the government of Turkey reformed its currency on January 1, 2005, simply by issuing "new" Turkish lira, each equal to 1 million "old" Turkish lira. The effect of this reform was to lower the number of currency units in circulation, and all lira prices, to 1/1,000,000 of their old lira values. But the redefinition of the monetary unit had no effect on real output, the interest rate, or the relative prices of goods: all that occurred was a one-time change in all values measured in lira. A decision to measure distance in half-miles rather than miles would have as little effect on real economic variables as the Turkish government's decision to chop six zeros off the end of every magnitude measured in terms of money.

An increase in the supply of a country's currency has the same effect in the long run as a currency reform. A doubling of the money supply, for example, has the same long-run effect as a currency reform in which each unit of currency is replaced by two units of "new" currency. If the economy is initially fully employed, every money price in the economy eventually doubles, but real GNP, the interest rate, and all relative prices return to their long-run or full-employment levels.

12.4.3 Empirical Evidence on Money Supplies and Price Levels

12.4.3 货币供给和价格水平的实证证据

In looking at actual data on money and prices, we should not expect to see an exactly proportional relationship over long periods, partly because output, the interest rate, and the aggregate real money demand function can shift for reasons that have nothing to do with the supply of money. Output changes as a result of capital accumulation and technological advance (for example, more powerful computers), and money demand behavior may change as a result of demographic trends or financial innovations such as electronic cash-transfer facilities. In addition, actual economies are rarely in positions of long-run equilibrium. Nonetheless, we should expect the data to show a clear-cut positive association between money supplies and price levels. If real-world data did not provide strong evidence that money supplies and price levels move together in the long run, the usefulness of the theory of money demand we have developed would be in severe doubt.

The wide swings in Latin American rates of price level increase in recent decades make the region an ideal case study of the relationship between money supplies and price levels. Price level inflation had been high and variable in Latin America for more than a decade, when efforts at macroeconomic reform began to bring inflation lower by the mid-1990s.

12.4.4 Money and the Exchange Rate in the Long Run

12.4.4 长期条件下的货币和汇率

The domestic currency price of foreign currency is one of the many prices in the economy that rise in the long run after a permanent increase in the money supply. If you think again about the effects of a currency reform, you will see how the exchange rate moves in the long run. Suppose, for example, that the U.S. government replaced every pair of "old" dollars with one "new" dollar. Then if the dollar/euro exchange rate had been 1.20 old dollars per euro before the reform, it would change to 0.60 new dollars per euro immediately after the reform. In much the same way, a halving of the U.S. money supply would eventually lead the dollar to appreciate from an exchange rate of 1.20 dollars/euro to one of 0.60 dollars/euro. Since the dollar prices of all U.S. goods and services would also decrease by half, this 50 percent appreciation of the dollar leaves the relative prices of all U.S. and foreign goods and services unchanged.

拓展资源 12.1

We conclude that, all else equal, a permanent increase in a

country's money supply causes a proportional long-run depreciation of its currency against foreign currencies. Similarly, a permanent decrease in a country's money supply causes a proportional long-run appreciation of its currency against foreign currencies.

12.4.5 Inflation and Exchange Rate Dynamics

12.4.5 通货膨胀和动态汇率

In this section we tie together our short-run and long-run findings about the effects of monetary changes by examining the process through which the price level adjusts to its long-run position. An economy experiences inflation when its price level is rising and deflation when its price level is falling. Our examination of inflation will give us a deeper understanding of how the exchange rate adjusts to monetary disturbances in the economy.

12.4.6 Short-run Price Rigidity versus Long-run Price Flexibility

12.4.6 短期价格刚性和长期价格弹性

Our analysis of the short-run effects of monetary changes assumed that a country's price level, unlike its exchange rate, does not jump immediately. This assumption cannot be exactly correct, because many commodities, such as agricultural products, are traded in markets where prices adjust sharply every day as supply or demand conditions shift. In addition, exchange rate changes themselves may affect the prices of some tradable goods and services that enter the commodity basket defining the price level.

Many prices in the economy, however, are written into long-term contracts and cannot be changed immediately when changes in the money supply occur. The most important prices of this type are workers' wages, which are negotiated only periodically in many industries. Wages do not enter indices of the price level directly, but they make up a large fraction of the cost of producing goods and services. Since output prices depend heavily on production costs, the behavior of the overall price level is influenced by the sluggishness of wage movements. The short-run "stickiness" of price levels is illustrated by Figure 12.11, which compares data on month-to-month percentage changes in the dollar/yen exchange rate $E_{\$/¥}$, with data on month-to-month percentage changes in the ratio of money price levels in the United States and Japan P_{US}/P_J. As you can see, the exchange rate is much more variable than relative price levels, a fact consistent with the view that price levels are relatively rigid in the short run. The pattern shown in the figure applies to all of the main industrial countries in recent decades. In light of this and other evidence, we will therefore continue to assume that the price level is given in the short run and does not make significant jumps in response to policy changes.

This assumption would not be reasonable, however, for all countries at all times. In extremely inflationary conditions, such as those seen in the 1980s in some Latin American countries, long-term contracts specifying domestic money payments may go out of use. Automatic price level indexation of wage payments may also be widespread under highly inflationary conditions. Such developments make the price level much less rigid than it would be under moderate inflation, and large price level jumps become possible. Some price rigidity can remain, however, even in the face of inflation rates that would be high by everyday industrial-country standards. For example, Turkey's 30 percent inflation rate for 2002 seems high until it is compared with the 114 percent depreciation of the Turkish lira against the U.S. dollar over the same year.

拓展资源 12.2

Our analysis assuming short-run price rigidity is nonetheless most applicable to countries with histories of comparative price level stability, such as the United States. Even in the cases of low-inflation countries, there is a lively academic debate over the possibility that seemingly sticky wages and prices are in reality quite flexible. Although the price levels appear to display short-run stickiness in many countries, a change in the money supply creates immediate demand and cost pressures that eventually lead to future increases in the price level. These pressures come from three main sources.

1. Excess demand for output and labor. An increase in the money supply has an expansionary effect on the economy, raising the total demand for goods and services. To meet this demand, producers of goods and services must employ workers overtime and make new hires. Even if wages are given in the short run, the additional demand for labor allows workers to ask for higher wages in the next round of wage negotiations. Producers are willing to pay these higher wages, for they know that in a booming economy, it

will not be hard to pass higher wage costs on to consumers through higher product prices.

2. Inflationary expectations. If everyone expects the price level to rise in the future, their expectation will increase the pace of inflation today. Workers bargaining over wage contracts will insist on higher money wages to counteract the effect on their real wages of the anticipated general increase in prices. Producers, once again, will give in to these wage demands if they expect product prices to rise and cover the additional wage costs.

3. Raw materials prices. Many raw materials used in the production of final goods, for example, petroleum products and metals, are sold in markets where prices adjust sharply even in the short run. By causing the prices of such materials to jump upward, a money supply increase raises production costs in materials-using industries. Eventually, producers in those industries will raise product prices to cover their higher costs.

☞ Summary

☞ 本章小结

1. Money is held because of its liquidity. When considered in real terms, aggregate money demand is not a demand for a certain number of currency units but is instead a demand for a certain amount of purchasing power. Aggregate real money demand depends negatively on the opportunity cost of holding money (measured by the domestic interest rate) and positively on the volume of transactions in the economy (measured by real GNP).

2. The money market is in equilibrium when the real money supply equals aggregate real money demand. With the price level and real output given, a rise in the money supply lowers the interest rate and a fall in the money supply raises the interest rate. A rise in real output raises the interest rate, given the price level, while a fall in real output has the opposite effect.

3. By lowering the domestic interest rate, an increase in the money supply causes the domestic currency to depreciate in the foreign exchange market (even when expectations of future exchange rates do not change). Similarly, a fall in the domestic money supply causes the domestic currency to appreciate against

foreign currencies.

4. The assumption that the price level is given in the short run is a good approximation to reality in countries with moderate inflation, but it is a misleading assumption over the long run. Permanent changes in the money supply push the long-run equilibrium price level proportionally in the same direction but do not influence the long-run values of output, the interest rate, or any relative prices. One important money price whose long-run equilibrium level rises in proportion to a permanent money supply increase is the exchange rate, the domestic currency price of foreign currency.

☞ Key Terms

☞ 关键术语

aggregate money demand, deflation, exchange rate overshooting, inflation, long run, long-run equilibrium, money supply, price level, short run

总和货币需求、通货紧缩、汇率超调、通货膨胀、长期操作、长期均衡、货币供应量、物价水平、短期运转

☞ Questions

☞ 本章习题

1. Suppose there is a reduction in aggregate real money demand, that is, a negative shift in the aggregate real money demand function. Trace the short-run and long-run effects on the exchange rate, interest rate, and price level.

2. How would you expect a fall in a country's population to alter its aggregate money demand function? Would it matter if the fall in population were due to a fall in the number of households or to a fall in the size of the average household?

3. What is the short-run effect on the exchange rate of an increase in domestic real GNP, given expectations about future exchange rates?

4. Does our discussion of money's usefulness as a medium of exchange and unit of account suggest reasons why some currencies become vehicle currencies for foreign exchange transactions?

5. Imagine that the central bank of an economy with unemployment doubles its money supply. In the long run, full employment is restored and output returns to its full-employment

level. On the (admittedly unlikely) assumption that the interest rate before the money supply increase equals the long-run interest rate, is the long-run increase in the price level more than proportional or less than proportional to the money supply change? What if (as is more likely) the interest rate is initially below its long-run level?

Chapter 13

Financial Globalization: Opportunity and Crisis

第十三章

金融全球化：机遇与挑战

If a financier named Rip van Winkle had gone to sleep in the 1960s and awakened after 50 years, he would have been shocked by changes in both the nature and the scale of international financial activity. In the early 1960s, for example, most banking business was purely domestic, involving the currency and customers of the bank's home country. Five decades later, many banks were deriving a large share of their profits from international activities. To his surprise, Rip would have found that he could locate branches of Citibank in São Paulo, Brazil, and branches of Britain's National Westminster Bank in New York. He would also have discovered that it had long since become routine for a branch of an American bank located in London to accept a deposit denominated in Japanese yen from a Swedish corporation, or to lend Swiss francs to a Dutch manufacturer. Finally, he would have noticed much greater participation by non-bank financial institutions in international markets, and a huge expansion in the volume of international transactions.

The market in which residents of different countries trade assets is called the international capital market. The international capital market is not really a single market; it is instead a group of closely interconnected markets in which asset exchanges with some international dimension take place. International currency trades take place in the foreign exchange market, which is an important part of the international capital market. The main actors in the international capital market are the same as those in the foreign exchange market: commercial banks, large corporations, non-bank financial institutions, central banks, and other government agencies. And, like the foreign exchange market, the international capital market's activities take place in a network of world financial centers linked by sophisticated communications systems. The assets traded in the international capital market, however, include different countries' stocks and bonds in addition to bank deposits denominated in their currencies.

This chapter discusses four main questions about the international capital market. First, how has this well-oiled global financial network enhanced countries' gains from international trade? Second, what has caused the rapid growth in international financial activity since the early 1960s? Third, what dangers are posed by an integrated world capital market straddling national borders? And fourth, how can policy makers minimize problems raised by the global capital market without sharply reducing the benefits it provides?

13.1 The International Capital Market and the Gains from Trade

13.1 国际资本市场和贸易收益

In earlier chapters, the discussion of gains from international trade concentrated on exchanges involving goods and services. By providing a worldwide payments system that lowers transaction costs, banks active in the international capital market enlarge the trade gains that result from such exchanges. But most deals that take place in the international capital market are exchanges of assets between residents of different countries, for example, the exchange of a share of IBM stock for some British government bonds. Although such asset trades are sometimes derided as unproductive "speculation," they do, in fact, lead to gains from trade that can make consumers everywhere better off.

13.1.1 Three Types of Gain from Trade

13.1.1 贸易收益的三种类型

All transactions between the residents of different countries fall into one of three categories: trades of goods or services for goods or services, trades of goods or services for assets, and trades of assets for assets. At any moment, a country is generally carrying out trades in each of these categories. Figure 13.1 (which assumes that there are two countries, Home and Foreign) illustrates the three types of international transaction, each of which involves a different set of possible gains from trade.

So far in this book we have discussed two types of trade gain. Countries can gain by concentrating on the production activities in which they are most efficient and using some of their output to pay for imports of other products from abroad. This type of trade gain involves the exchange of goods or services for other goods or services. The top horizontal arrow in Figure 13.1 shows exchanges of goods and services between Home and Foreign.

A second set of trade gains results from intertemporal trade, which is the exchange of goods and services for claims to future goods and services, that is, for assets. When a developing country borrows abroad (that is, sells a bond to foreigners) so that it can import materials for a domestic investment project, it is engaging in intertemporal trade. The diagonal arrows in Figure 13.1 indicate trades of goods and services for assets. If Home has a current account deficit with Foreign, for example, it is a net exporter of assets to Foreign and a net importer of goods and services from Foreign.

The bottom horizontal arrow in Figure 13.1 represents the last category of international transaction, trades of assets for assets, such as the exchange of real estate located in France for U.S. Treasury bonds.

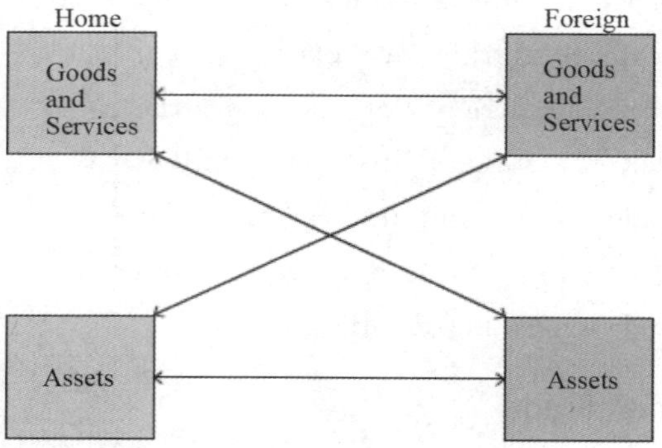

Figure 13.1 The Three Types of International Transaction

Residents of different countries can trade goods and services for other goods and services, goods and services for assets (that is, for future goods and services), and assets for other assets. All three types of exchange lead to gains from trade.

13.1.2 Risk Aversion

13.1.2 风险规避

When individuals select assets, an important factor in their decisions is the riskiness of each asset's return. Other things equal, people dislike risk. Economists call this property of people's preferences risk aversion. It showed that risk-averse investors in foreign currency assets base their demand for a particular asset on its riskiness (as measured by a risk premium) in addition to its expected return.

An example will make the meaning of risk aversion clearer. Suppose you are offered a gamble in which you win \$1,000 half the time but lose \$1,000 half the time. Since you are as likely to win as to lose the gamble, the average payoff on this gamble—its expected value—is $\left(\frac{1}{2}\right)\times(\$1,000)+\left(\frac{1}{2}\right)\times(-\$1,000)=0$. If you are risk averse, you will not take the gamble because, for you, the loss of losing \$1,000 outweighs the gain that you will get when you win, even though both outcomes are equally likely. Although some people (called risk lovers) enjoy taking risks and would take the gamble, there is much evidence that risk-averse behavior is the norm. For example, risk aversion helps explain the profitability of insurance companies, which sell policies that allow people to protect themselves or their families from the financial risks of theft, illness, and other mishaps.

If people are risk averse, they value a collection (or portfolio) of assets not only on the basis of its expected return but also on the basis of the riskiness of that return. Under risk aversion, for example, people may be willing to hold bonds denominated in several different currencies, even if the interest rates they offer are not linked by the interest parity condition, if the resulting portfolio of assets offers a desirable combination of return and risk. In general, a portfolio whose return fluctuates wildly from year to year is less desirable than one that offers the same average return with only mild year-to-year fluctuations. This observation is basic to understanding why countries exchange assets.

13.1.3 Portfolio Diversification as a Motive for International Asset Trade

13.1.3 作为国际资产交易动机的投资组合

International trade in assets can make both parties to the trade better off by allowing them to reduce the riskiness of the return on their wealth. Trade accomplishes this reduction in risk by allowing both parties to diversify their portfolios—to divide their wealth among a wide spectrum of assets and thus reduce the amount of money they have riding on each individual asset. The late economist James Tobin of Yale University, an originator of the theory of portfolio choice with risk aversion, once described the idea of portfolio diversification as "Don't put all your eggs in one basket." When an economy is opened to the international capital market, it can reduce the riskiness of its wealth by placing some of its "eggs" in additional foreign "baskets." This reduction in risk is the basic motive for asset trade.

A simple two-country example illustrates how countries are made better off by trade in assets. Imagine that there are two countries, Home and Foreign, and that residents of each own only one asset, domestic land yielding an annual harvest of kiwi fruit.

The yield of the land is uncertain, however. Half of the time, Home's land yields a harvest of 100 tons of kiwi fruit at the same time as Foreign's land yields a harvest of 50 tons. The other half of the time, the outcomes are reversed: The Foreign harvest is 100 tons, but the Home harvest is only 50. On average, then, each country has a harvest of $\left(\frac{1}{2}\right)\times(100)+\left(\frac{1}{2}\right)\times(50)=75$ tons of kiwi fruit, but its inhabitants never know whether the next year will bring feast or famine.

Now suppose the two countries can trade shares in the ownership of their respective assets. A Home owner of a 10 percent share in Foreign land, for example, receives 10 percent of the annual Foreign kiwi fruit harvest, and a Foreign owner of a 10 percent share in Home land is similarly entitled to 10 percent of the Home harvest. What happens if international trade in these two assets is allowed? Home residents will buy a 50 percent share of Foreign land, and they will pay for it by giving Foreign residents a

50 percent share in Home land.

To understand why this is the outcome, think about the returns to the Home and Foreign portfolios when both are equally divided between titles to Home and Foreign land. When times are good in Home (and therefore bad in Foreign), each country earns the same return on its portfolio: half of the Home harvest (100 tons of kiwi fruit) plus half of the Foreign harvest (50 tons of kiwi fruit), or 75 tons of fruit. In the opposite case—bad times in Home, good times in Foreign—each country still earns 75 tons of fruit. If the countries hold portfolios equally divided between the two assets, therefore, each country earns a certain return of 75 tons of fruit—the same as the average or expected harvest each faced before international asset trade was allowed.

Since the two available assets—Home and Foreign land—have the same return on average, any portfolio consisting of those assets yields an expected (or average) return of 75 tons of fruit. People everywhere are risk averse, however, so all prefer to hold the fifty-fifty portfolio described above, which gives a sure return of 75 tons of fruit every year. After trade is opened, therefore, residents of the two counties will swap titles to land until the fifty-fifty outcome is reached. Because this trade eliminates the risk faced by both countries without changing average returns, both countries are clearly better off as a result of asset trade.

The above example is oversimplified because countries can never really eliminate all risk through international asset trade. (Unlike the model's world, the real world is a risky place even in the aggregate!) The example does demonstrate that countries can nonetheless reduce the riskiness of their wealth by diversifying their asset portfolios internationally. A major function of the international capital market is to make this diversification possible.

13.1.4 The Menu of International Assets: Debt Versus Equity

13.1.4 国际资产菜单：债务与权益

International asset trades can be exchanges of many different types of assets. Among the many assets traded in the international capital market are bonds and deposits denominated in different currencies, shares of stock, and more complicated financial instruments such as stock or currency options. A purchase of foreign real estate and the direct acquisition of a factory in another country are other ways of diversifying abroad.

In thinking about asset trades, it is frequently useful to make a distinction between debt instruments and equity instruments. Bonds and bank deposits are debt instruments, since they specify that the issuer of the instrument must repay a fixed value (the sum of principal plus interest) regardless of economic circumstances. In contrast, a share of stock is an equity instrument: it is a claim to a firm's profits, rather than to a fixed payment, and its payoff will vary according to circumstances. Similarly, the kiwi fruit shares traded in our example are equity instruments. By choosing how to divide their portfolios between debt and equity instruments, individuals and nations can arrange to stay close to desired consumption and investment levels despite the different eventualities that could occur.

The dividing line between debt and equity is not a neat one in practice. Even if an instrument's money payout is the same in different states of the world, its real payout in a particular state will depend on national price levels and exchange rates. In addition, the payments that a given instrument promises to make may not occur in cases of bankruptcy, government seizure of foreign-owned assets, and so on. Assets like low-grade corporate bonds, which superficially appear to be debt, may in reality be like equity in offering payoffs that depend on the doubtful financial fortunes of the issuer. The same has turned out to be true for the debt of many developing countries.

13.2 International Banking and the International Capital Market

13.2 国际银行业务和国际资本市场

The Home-Foreign kiwi fruit example above portrayed an imaginary world with only two assets. Since the number of assets available in the real world is enormous, specialized institutions have sprung up to bring together buyers and sellers of assets located in different countries.

13.2.1 The Structure of the International Capital Market

13.2.1 国际资本市场的结构

As we noted above, the main actors in the international capital market include commercial banks, corporations, non-bank financial institutions (such as insurance companies, money market funds, hedge funds, and pension funds), central banks, and other government agencies.

1. Commercial banks. Commercial banks are at the center of the international capital market, not only because they run the international payments mechanism but also because of the broad range of financial activities they undertake. Bank liabilities consist chiefly of deposits of various maturities, as well as short-term borrowing from other financial institutions, while their assets consist largely of loans (to corporations and governments), deposits at other banks (interbank deposits), and bonds. Multinational banks are also heavily involved in other types of asset transaction. For example, banks may underwrite issues of corporate stocks and bonds by agreeing, for a fee, to find buyers for those securities at a guaranteed price. One of the key facts about international banking is that banks are often free to pursue activities abroad that they would not be allowed to pursue in their home countries. This type of regulatory asymmetry has spurred the growth of international banking over the past 50 years.

2. Corporations. Corporations—particularly those with multinational operations such as Coca-Cola, IBM, Toyota, and Nike—routinely finance their investments by drawing on foreign sources of funds. To obtain these funds, corporations may sell shares of stock, which give owners an equity claim to the corporation's assets, or they may use debt finance. Debt finance often takes the form of borrowing from and through international banks or other institutional lenders; when longer-term borrowing is desired, firms may sell corporate debt instruments in the international capital market. Corporations frequently denominate their bonds in the currency of the financial center in which the bonds are being offered for sale. Increasingly, however, corporations have been pursuing novel denomination strategies that make their bonds attractive to a wider spectrum of potential buyers.

3. Nonbank financial institutions. Nonbank financial institutions such as insurance companies, pension funds, mutual funds, and hedge funds have become important players in the international capital market as they have moved into foreign assets to diversify their portfolios. Of particular importance are investment banks such as the Lazard Group, which are not banks at all but specialize in underwriting sales of stocks and bonds by corporations and (in some cases) governments. In 1933, U.S. commercial banks were barred from investment banking activity within the United States (and from most other domestic transactions involving corporate stocks and bonds), although the U.S. government eased these barriers in 1999. But U.S. commercial banks have long been allowed to participate in investment banking activities overseas, and such banks as Citigroup and J.P. Morgan Chase have competed vigorously with the more specialized investment banks.

4. Central banks and other government agencies. Central banks are routinely involved in the international financial markets through foreign exchange intervention. In addition, other government agencies frequently borrow abroad. Developing country governments and state-owned enterprises have borrowed substantially from foreign commercial banks.

On any measure, the scale of transactions in the international capital market has grown much more quickly than world GDP since the early 1970s. One major factor in this development is that, starting with the industrial world, countries have progressively dismantled barriers to private capital flows across their borders.

An important reason for that development is related to exchange rate systems. According to the trilemma, the widespread adoption of flexible exchange rates since the early 1970s has allowed countries to reconcile open capital markets with domestic monetary autonomy. The individual member countries of the European economic and monetary union have followed a different route with respect to their mutual exchange rates. However, the euro floats against foreign currencies and the euro zone as a unit orients its monetary policy toward internal macroeconomic goals while permitting freedom of cross-border payments.

13.2.2 Offshore Banking and Offshore Currency Trading

13.2.2 离岸银行业务和离岸货币交易

One of the most pervasive features of today's commercial banking industry is that banking activities have become globalized as banks have branched out from their home countries into foreign financial centers. In 1960, only eight American banks had branches in foreign countries, but now hundreds have such branches. Similarly, the number of foreign bank offices in the United States has risen steadily. The term offshore banking is used to describe the business that banks' foreign offices conduct outside of their home countries. Banks may conduct foreign business through any of three types of institutions.

1. An agency office located abroad, which arranges loans and transfers funds but does not accept deposits.

2. A subsidiary bank located abroad. A subsidiary of a foreign bank differs from a local bank only in that a foreign bank is the controlling owner. Subsidiaries are subject to the same regulations as local banks but are not subject to the regulations of the parent bank's country.

3. A foreign branch, which is simply an office of the home bank in another country. Branches carry out the same business as local banks and are usually subject to local and home banking regulations. Often, however, branches can take advantage of cross-border regulatory differences.

The growth of offshore currency trading has gone hand in hand with that of offshore banking. An offshore deposit is simply a bank deposit denominated in a currency other than that of the country in which the bank resides—for example, yen deposits in a London bank or dollar deposits in Zurich. Many of the deposits traded in the foreign exchange market are offshore deposits. Offshore currency deposits are usually referred to as Eurocurrencies, which is something of a misnomer since much Eurocurrency trading occurs in such non-European centers as Singapore. Dollar deposits located outside the United States are called Eurodollars. Banks that accept deposits denominated in Eurocurrencies (including Eurodollars) are called Eurobanks. The advent of the new European currency, the euro, has made this terminology even more confusing!

One motivation for the rapid growth of offshore banking and currency trading has been the growth of international trade and the increasingly multinational nature of corporate activity. American firms engaged in international trade, for example, require overseas financial services, and American banks have naturally expanded their domestic business with these firms into foreign areas. By offering more rapid clearing of payments and the flexibility and trust established in previous dealings, American banks compete with the foreign banks that could also serve American customers. Eurocurrency trading is another natural outgrowth of expanding world trade in goods and services. British importers of American goods frequently need to hold dollar deposits, for example, and it is natural for banks based in London to woo these importers' business.

World trade growth alone, however, cannot explain the growth of international banking since the 1960s. Another factor is the banks' desire to escape domestic government regulations on financial activity (and sometimes taxes) by shifting some of their operations abroad and into foreign currencies. A further factor is in part political: the desire by some depositors to hold currencies outside the jurisdictions of the countries that issue them. In recent years, the tendency for countries to open their financial markets to foreigners has allowed international banks to compete globally for new business.

13.2.3 The Growth of Eurocurrency Trading

13.2.3 离岸货币交易的增长

The growth of Eurocurrency trading illustrates the importance of all these factors in the internationalization of banking. Eurodollars were born in the late 1950s, a response to the needs generated by a growing volume of international trade. European firms involved in trade frequently wished to hold dollar balances or to borrow dollars. In many cases, banks located in the United States could have served these needs, but Europeans often found it cheaper and more convenient to deal with local banks familiar with their circumstances. As currencies other than the dollar became increasingly convertible after the late 1950s, offshore markets for them sprang up also. While the convenience of dealing with local banks was a key factor inspiring the invention of Eurodollars, the growth of Eurodollar trading was encouraged at an early stage by two other factors we have mentioned: official regulations and political concerns.

In 1957, at the height of a balance of payments crisis, the British government prohibited British banks from lending pounds to finance non-British trade. This lending had been a highly profitable business, and to avoid losing it, British banks began financing the same trade by attracting dollar deposits and lending dollars instead of pounds. Because stringent financial regulations prevented the British banks' non-sterling transactions from affecting Britain's domestic asset markets, the government was willing to take a laissez-faire attitude toward foreign currency activities. As a result, London became—and has remained—the leading center of Eurocurrency trading. The political factor stimulating the Eurodollar market's early growth was a surprising one—the Cold War between the United States and the Soviet Union. The Soviets feared the United States might confiscate dollars placed in American banks if the Cold War were to heat up. So instead, Soviet dollars were placed in European banks, which had the advantage of residing outside America's jurisdiction.

The Eurodollar system mushroomed in the 1960s as a result of new U. S. restrictions on capital outflows and U. S. banking regulations. As America's balance of payments weakened in the 1960s, the Kennedy and Johnson administrations imposed a series of measures to discourage American lending abroad. All of these measures increased the demand for Eurodollar loans by making it harder for would-be dollar borrowers located abroad to obtain the funds they wanted in the United States.

Federal Reserve regulations on U.S. banks also encouraged the creation of Eurodollars—and new Eurobanks—in the 1960s. The Fed's Regulation Q (enacted in 1933 and phased out after 1980) placed a ceiling on the interest rates U.S. banks could pay on time deposits. When U.S. monetary policy was tightened at the end of the 1960s to combat rising inflationary pressures, market interest rates were driven above the Regulation Q ceiling and American banks found it impossible to attract time deposits for relending. The banks got around the problem by borrowing funds from their European branches, which faced no restriction on the interest they could pay on Eurodollar deposits and were able to attract deposits from investors who might have placed their funds with U.S. banks in the absence of Regulation Q. With the move to floating exchange rates in 1973, the United States and other countries began to dismantle controls on capital flows across their borders, removing an important impetus to the growth of Eurocurrency markets in earlier years. But at that point, the political factor once again came into play in a big way. Arab members of OPEC accumulated vast wealth as a result of the oil shocks of 1973—1974 and 1979—1980 but were reluctant to place most of their money in American banks for fear of possible confiscation. Instead, these countries placed funds with Eurobanks. (In 1979, Iranian assets in U.S. banks and their European branches were frozen by President Carter in response to the taking of hostages at the American embassy in Teheran. A similar fate befell Iraq's U.S. assets after that country invaded neighboring Kuwait in 1990, and the assets of suspected terrorist organizations after the September 11, 2001, attacks on New York's World Trade Center and the Pentagon.)

13.3 Regulating International Banking

13.3 国际银行业务监管

13.3.1 The Importance of Regulatory Asymmetries

13.3.1 监管不对称的重要性

The history of Eurocurrencies shows how the growth of world trade, financial regulations, and political considerations all helped form the present system. The major factor behind the continuing profitability of Eurocurrency trading is, however, regulatory: In formulating bank regulations, governments in the main Eurocurrency centers discriminate between deposits denominated in the home currency and those denominated in others and between transactions with domestic customers and those with foreign customers. Domestic currency deposits generally are more heavily regulated as a way of maintaining control over the domestic money supply, while banks are given more freedom in their dealings in foreign currencies.

Regulatory asymmetries explain why those financial centers whose governments historically imposed the fewest restrictions on foreign currency banking became the main Eurocurrency centers. London is the leader in this respect, but it has been followed by Luxembourg, Bahrain, and other countries that have competed for international banking business by lowering restrictions and taxes on foreign bank operations within their borders.

13.3.2 The Shadow Banking System

13.3.2 影子银行系统

In recent decades, a major regulatory asymmetry has arisen between banks and what is often referred to as the shadow banking system. Nowadays, numerous financial institutions provide payment and credit services similar to those that banks provide. U.S. money market mutual funds, for example, provide check-writing services to customers and also are major players in providing credit to firms (through commercial paper markets) and in lending dollars to banks outside the United States. Investment banks also have provided credit to other entities while offering payment services. The shadow banking system even has included investment conduits that are sponsored by banks but are supposedly independent of the banks' own balance sheets. However, shadow banks have usually been minimally regulated compared to banks.

Why has this been the case? Historically, monetary policy makers have viewed banks as the prime focus of concern because of their centrality to the payments system and to the implementation of monetary policy. But the shadow banking system has grown dramatically. Total shadow banking sector assets are difficult to measure precisely, but in the United States today, they are probably comparable to the assets of the traditional banking sector.

Moreover, shadow banks are closely intertwined with banks as both creditors and borrowers. As a result, the stability of the shadow banking network cannot easily be divorced from that of the banks: if a shadow bank gets into trouble, so may the banks that have loaned it money. This became painfully clear during the 2007-

2009 global financial crisis, as we shall see later in this chapter. We now turn to a discussion of banking regulation, but readers should be aware that banks are only one category of player in the international financial markets and that banks' fortunes are likely to depend on those of other players.

13.3.3 Regulating International Banking

13.3.3 国际银行业务监管

Many observers believe that the free-wheeling nature of global banking activity up until now left the world financial system vulnerable to bank failure on a massive scale. The financial crisis of 2007—2009, which we will discuss below, supports that belief. What measures had governments taken prior to 2007 to reduce banking risk?

The Problem of Bank Failure

A bank fails when it is unable to meet its obligations to its depositors and other creditors. Banks use borrowed funds to make loans and to purchase other assets, but some of a bank's borrowers may find themselves unable to repay their loans, or the bank's assets may decline in value for some other reason. When this happens, the bank might be unable to repay its short-term liabilities, including deposits, which are largely payable on demand.

A peculiar feature of banking is that a bank's financial health depends on depositors' confidence in the value of its assets. If depositors come to believe that many of the bank's assets have declined in value, each has an incentive to withdraw his or her funds and place them in a different bank. A bank faced with the wholesale loss of deposits is likely to close its doors, even if the asset side of its balance sheet is fundamentally sound. The reason is that many bank assets are illiquid and cannot be sold quickly to meet deposit obligations without substantial loss to the bank. If an atmosphere of financial panic develops, therefore, bank failure may not be limited to banks that have mismanaged their assets. It is in the interest of each depositor to withdraw his or her money from a bank if all other depositors are doing the same, even when the bank's assets are basically sound.

Bank failures obviously inflict serious financial harm on

individual depositors who lose their money. But beyond these individual losses, bank failure can harm the economy's macroeconomic stability. One bank's problems may easily spread to sounder banks if they are suspected of having lent to the bank that is in trouble. Such a general loss of confidence in banks undermines the credit and payments system on which the economy runs. A rash of bank failures can bring a drastic reduction in the banking system's ability to finance investment, consumer-durable expenditure, and home purchases, thus reducing aggregate demand and throwing the economy into a slump. There is strong evidence that the string of U.S. bank closings in the early 1930s helped start and worsen the Great Depression, and financial panic certainly worsened the severe worldwide recession that began in 2007.

Because the potential consequences of a banking collapse are so harmful, governments attempt to prevent bank failures through extensive regulation of their domestic banking systems. Well-managed banks themselves take precautions against failure even in the absence of regulation, but the costs of failure extend far beyond the bank's owners. Thus, some banks, taking into account their own self-interest but ignoring the costs of bank failure for society, might be led to shoulder a level of risk greater than what is socially optimal. In addition, even banks with cautious investment strategies may fail if rumors of financial trouble begin circulating. Many of the precautionary bank regulation measures taken by governments today are a direct result of their countries' experiences during the Great Depression.

In most countries, an extensive "safety net" has been set up to reduce the risk of bank failure. The main safeguards are:

1. Deposit insurance. One legacy of the Great Depression of the 1930s is deposit insurance. In the United States, the Federal Deposit Insurance Corporation (FDIC) insures bank depositors against losses of up to a current limit of $250,000. Banks are required to make contributions to the FDIC to cover the cost of this insurance. FDIC insurance discourages "runs" on banks because small depositors, knowing their losses will be made good by the government, no longer have an incentive to withdraw their money just because others are doing so. Since 1989, the FDIC has also

provided insurance for deposits with savings and loan (S&L) associations. The absence of government insurance is one reason for the comparatively light regulation of banks' offshore operations as well as of the shadow banking system.

2. Reserve requirements. Reserve requirements are one possible tool of monetary policy, influencing the relation between the monetary base and monetary aggregates. At the same time, reserve requirements force the bank to hold a portion of its assets in a liquid form that is easily mobilized to meet sudden deposit outflows. In the United States, banks tend to hold reserves in excess of required reserves, so reserve requirements are not important.

3. Capital requirements and asset restrictions. The difference between a bank's assets and its liabilities, equal to the bank's net worth, is also called its bank capital. Bank capital is the equity that the bank's shareholders acquire when they buy the bank's stock, and since it equals the portion of the bank's assets that is not owed to depositors or other creditors, it gives the bank an extra margin of safety in case some of its assets go bad. U.S. bank regulators set minimum required levels of bank capital to reduce the system's vulnerability to failure. Other rules prevent banks from holding assets that are "too risky," such as common stocks, whose prices tend to be volatile. Banks must also deal with rules against lending too large a fraction of their assets to a single private customer or to a single foreign government borrower.

4. Bank examination. Government supervisors have the right to examine a bank's books to ensure compliance with bank capital standards and other regulations. Banks may be forced to sell assets that the examiner deems too risky or to adjust their balance sheets by writing off loans the examiner thinks will not be repaid. In some countries the central bank is the main bank supervisor, while in others a separate financial supervision authority handles that job.

5. Lender of last resort facilities. Banks can borrow from the central bank's discount window or from other facilities the central bank may make available. While lending to banks is a tool of monetary management, the central bank can also use discounting to prevent bank panics. Since a central bank has the ability to create

currency, it can lend to banks facing massive deposit outflows as much as they need to satisfy their depositors' claims. When the central bank acts in this way, it is acting as a lender of last resort (LLR) to the bank. Indeed, the Federal Reserve was set up in 1913 precisely as a safeguard against financial panic. When depositors know the central bank is standing by as the LLR, they have more confidence in the bank's ability to withstand a panic and are therefore less likely to run if financial trouble looms. The administration of LLR facilities is complex, however. If banks think the central bank will always bail them out, they will take excessive risks. So the central bank must make access to its LLR services conditional on sound management. To decide when banks in trouble have not brought it on themselves through unwise risk taking, the LLR should ideally be closely involved in the bank examination process.

6. Government-organized bailouts. Should all else fail, the central bank or fiscal authorities may organize the purchase of a failing bank by healthier institutions, sometimes throwing their own money into the deal as a sweetener. In this case, bankruptcy is avoided thanks to the government's intervention as a crisis manager, but perhaps at the public's expense.

The U.S. commercial bank safety net worked reasonably well until the late 1980s, but as a result of deregulation, the 1990—1991 recession, and a sharp fall in commercial property values, bank closings rose dramatically and the FDIC insurance fund was depleted. Like the United States, other countries that deregulated domestic banking in the 1980s—including Japan, the Scandinavian countries, the United Kingdom, and Switzerland—faced serious problems a decade later. Many overhauled their systems of banking safeguards as a result, but as we shall see, those safeguards were not nearly sufficient to prevent the financial crisis of 2007—2009.

13.3.4 Difficulties in Regulating International Banking

13.3.4 国际银行业监管的难点

Banking regulations of the type used in the United States and other countries become even less effective in an international environment where banks can shift their business among different regulatory jurisdictions. A good way to see why an international banking system is harder to regulate than a national system is to look at how the effectiveness of the U.S. safeguards just described is reduced as a result of offshore banking activities.

1. Deposit insurance is essentially absent in international banking. National deposit insurance systems may protect domestic and foreign depositors alike, but the amount of insurance available is invariably too small to cover the size of the deposits that are usual in international banking. In particular, inter-bank deposits are unprotected.

2. The absence of overseas reserve requirements was historically a major factor in the growth of Eurocurrency trading. While Eurobanks derived a competitive advantage from escaping the required reserve tax, there was a social cost in terms of the reduced stability of the banking system. No country could solve the problem single-handedly by imposing reserve requirements on its own banks' overseas branches. Concerted international action was blocked, however, by the political and technical difficulty of agreeing on an internationally uniform set of regulations and by the reluctance of some countries to drive banking business away by tightening regulations. Nowadays, reserve requirements are less important in many countries. In part this is because governments simply realized the requirements' futility in a world of globalized banking.

3 & 4. Bank examination to enforce capital requirements and asset restrictions becomes more difficult in an international setting. National bank regulators usually monitor the balance sheets of domestic banks and their foreign branches on a consolidated basis. But they are less strict in keeping track of banks' foreign subsidiaries and affiliates, which are in theory more tenuously tied to the parent bank but whose financial fortunes may well affect the parent's solvency. Banks have often been able to take advantage of this laxity by shifting risky business that home regulators might question to regulatory jurisdictions where fewer questions are asked. Further, it is often unclear which group of regulators would ideally be responsible for monitoring a given bank's assets. Suppose the London subsidiary of an Italian bank deals primarily in Eurodollars. Should the subsidiary's assets be the concern of

British, Italian, or American regulators?

5. There is uncertainty over which central bank, if any, is responsible for providing LLR assistance in international banking. The problem is similar to the one that arises in allocating responsibility for bank supervision. Let's return to the example of the London subsidiary of an Italian bank. Should the Fed bear responsibility for saving the subsidiary from a sudden drain of dollar deposits? Should the Bank of England step in? Or should the European Central Bank bear the ultimate responsibility? When central banks provide LLR assistance, they increase their domestic money supplies and may compromise domestic macroeconomic objectives. In an international setting, acentral bank may also be providing resources to a bank located abroad whose behavior it is not equipped to monitor. Central banks are therefore reluctant to extend the coverage of their LLR responsibilities.

6. When a bank has assets and liabilities in many countries, several governments may have to share operational and financial responsibility for a rescue. The resulting uncertainties can slow down or even impede the rescue operation.

13.3.5 International Regulatory Cooperation

13.3.5 国际监管合作

The internationalization of banking has weakened national safeguards against banking collapse, but at the same time it has made the need for effective safeguards more urgent. Offshore banking involves a tremendous volume of interbank deposits—roughly 80 percent of all Eurocurrency deposits, for example, are owned by private banks. A high level of interbank depositing implies that problems affecting a single bank could be highly contagious and spread quickly to banks with which it is thought to do business. Through this ripple effect, a localized disturbance could, conceivably, set off a banking panic on a global scale. In the early 1970s, the new regime of floating exchange rates presented a new source of disturbance: a large, unexpected exchange rate change that might wipe out the capital of an exposed bank.

In response to this threat, central bank heads from 11 industrialized countries in 1974 set up a group called the Basel Committee, whose job is to achieve "a better coordination of the surveillance exercised by national authorities over the international banking system..." (The group got its name from Basel, Switzerland, the home of the central bankers' meeting place, the Bank for International Settlements.) The Basel Committee remains the major forum for cooperation among bank regulators from different countries.

In 1975, the Basel Committee reached an agreement, called the Concordat, which allocates responsibility for supervising multinational banking establishments between parent and host countries. In addition, the Concordat calls for the sharing of information about banks by parent and host regulators and for "the granting of permission for inspections by or on behalf of parent authorities on the territory of the host authority." In further work, the Basel Committee has located loopholes in the supervision of multinational banks and brought these to the attention of national authorities. The Basel Committee has recommended, for example, that regulatory agencies monitor the assets of banks' foreign subsidiaries as well as of their branches. In 1988, the Basel Committee suggested a minimally prudent level of bank capital (generally speaking, 8 percent of assets) and a system for measuring capital. These guidelines, widely adopted throughout the world, have become known as Basel Ⅰ. The committee revised the Basel I framework in 2004, issuing a new set of rules for bank capital known as Basel Ⅱ.

A major change in international financial relations has been the rapidly growing importance of new emerging markets as sources and destinations for private capital flows. Emerging markets are the capital markets of poorer, developing countries that have liberalized their financial systems to allow private asset trade with foreigners. Countries such as Brazil, Mexico, Indonesia, and Thailand were all major recipients of private capital inflows from the industrial world after 1990.

Emerging market financial institutions have, however, often proven to be weak. This vulnerability contributed to the emerging markets' severe financial crisis of 1997—1999. Among other problems, developing countries tend to lack experience in bank regulation, have looser prudential and accounting standards than developed countries, and have been more prone to offer domestic banks implicit guarantees that they will be bailed out if they get into trouble.

Thus, the need to extend internationally accepted "best practice" regulatory standards to emerging market countries became a priority for the Basel Committee. In September 1997, the Committee issued its Core Principles for Effective Banking Supervision, worked out in cooperation with representatives from many developing countries. That document sets out 25 principles deemed to describe the minimum necessary requirements for effective bank supervision, covering licensing of banks, supervision methods, reporting requirements for banks, and cross-border banking. The core principles were revised in 2006. The Basel Committee and the IMF were monitoring the international implementation of the revised Core Principles and Basel II when the global financial crisis erupted in August 2007. The crisis revealed weaknesses in Basel Ⅱ that led the Basel Committee to agree on a new framework, Basel Ⅲ, late in 2010. No doubt further sequels will follow.

The international activities of non-bank financial institutions are another potential trouble spot. The failure of a major actor in the shadow banking system, like the failure of a bank, could seriously disrupt national payments and credit networks. Increasing securitization (in which bank assets are repackaged in readily marketable forms and sold off) and trade in options and other derivative securities have made it harder for regulators to get an accurate picture of global financial flows by examining bank balance sheets alone. Indeed, as we shall see, securitization and derivatives were at the heart of the 2007—2009 crisis. As a result, the need for authorities to collect and pool data on internationally active non-banks has become acute. The near-collapse of the global hedge fund Long-Term Capital Management (LTCM) in September 1998 is an example of the nightmare that haunted global regulators' sleep before the most recent financial crisis. The Fed, acting as a crisis manager, was able to prevent a possibly devastating collapse of LTCM by pressuring its major creditors to continue lending. But the world economy was not so lucky a decade later.

13.4 How Well Have International Financial Markets Allocated Capital and Risk?

13.4 国际金融市场如何分配资本和风险？

The present structure of the international capital market involves risks of financial instability that can be reduced only through the close cooperation of bank and financial supervisors in many countries. But the same profit motive that leads multinational financial institutions to innovate their way around national regulations can also provide important gains for consumers. As we have seen, the international capital market allows residents of different countries to diversify their portfolios by trading risky assets. Further, by ensuring a rapid international flow of information about investment opportunities around the world, the market can help allocate the world's savings to their most productive uses. How well has the international capital market performed in these respects?

13.4.1 The Extent of International Portfolio Diversification

13.4.1 国际投资组合多元化的程度

Since accurate data on the overall portfolio positions of a country's residents are sometimes impossible to assemble, it can be difficult to gauge the extent of international portfolio diversification by direct observation. Nonetheless, some U.S. data can be used to get a rough idea of changes in international diversification in recent years.

In 1970, the foreign assets held by U.S. residents were equal in value to 6.2 percent of the U.S. capital stock. Foreign claims on the United States amounted to 4.0 percent of its capital stock (including residential housing). By 2008, U.S.-owned assets abroad equaled about 56 percent of U.S. capital, while foreign assets in the United States had risen to about 66 percent of U.S. capital.

These percentages are much larger than those in 1970 but still seem too small. With full international portfolio diversification, we would expect them to reflect the size of the U.S. economy relative to that of the rest of the world. Thus, in a fully diversified world economy, something like 80 percent of the U.S. capital stock would be owned by foreigners, while U.S. residents' claims on foreigners would equal around 80 percent of the value of the U. S. capital stock. Moreover, the numbers in the previous paragraph describe total foreign assets, stocks and bonds alike, not just stocks, which alone represent claims on capital. What makes the apparently incomplete extent of international equity portfolio diversification even more puzzling is the presumption most economists would make that the potential gains from diversification are large. An influential study by the French financial economist Bruno Solnik, for example, estimated that a U.S. investor holding only American stocks could more than halve the riskiness of her portfolio by further diversification into stocks from European countries.

The data do show, however, that international asset trade has increased substantially as a result of the growth of the international capital market. Further, international asset holdings are large in absolute terms. At the end of 2009, for example, U. S. claims on foreigners were equal to about 129 percent of the U.S. GNP in that year, while foreign claims on the United States were about 148 percent of U. S. GNP. Stock exchanges around the world have established closer communication links, and companies are showing an increasing readiness to sell shares on foreign exchanges. The seemingly incomplete extent of international equity diversification attained so far, however, is not necessarily a strong indictment of the world capital market. The market has certainly contributed to a stunning rise in asset trade in recent decades. Further, the U. S. experience is not necessarily typical.

13.4.2 The Efficiency of the Foreign Exchange Market

13.4.2 外汇市场的效率

The foreign exchange market is a central component of the international capital market, and the exchange rates it sets help determine the profitability of international transactions of all types. Exchange rates therefore communicate important economic signals to households and firms engaged in international trade and investment. If these signals do not reflect all available information about market opportunities, a misallocation of resources will result. Studies of the foreign exchange market's use of available information are therefore potentially important in judging whether the international capital market is sending the right signals to markets. We examine three types of tests: tests based on interest parity, tests based on modeling risk premiums, and tests for excessive exchange rate volatility.

13.4.3 Studies Based on Interest Parity

13.4.3 基于利益平价的研究

The interest parity condition that was the basis of the discussion of exchange rate determination has also been used to study whether market exchange rates incorporate all available information. Recall that interest parity holds when the interest difference between deposits denominated in two different currencies is the market's forecast of the percentage by which the exchange rate between those currencies will change. More formally, if R_t is the date t interest rate on home currency deposits, R_t^* is the interest rate on foreign currency deposits, E_t is the exchange rate (defined as the home currency price of foreign currency), and E_{t+1}^e is the exchange rate that market participants expect when the deposits paying interest R_t and R_t^* mature, the interest parity condition is

$$R_t - R_t^* = (E_{t+1}^e - E_t)/E_t \qquad (13.1)$$

This equation implies a simple way to test whether the foreign exchange market is doing a good job of using current information to forecast exchange rates. Since the interest difference, $R_t - R_t^*$ is the market's forecast, a comparison of this predicted exchange rate change with the actual exchange rate change that subsequently occurs indicates the market's skill in forecasting.

Statistical studies of the relationship between interest rate differences and later depreciation rates show that the interest difference has been a very bad predictor, in the sense that it has failed to catch any of the large swings in exchange rates. Even worse, as we noted there, the interest difference has, on average, failed to predict correctly the direction in which the spot exchange rate would change. If the interest rate difference were a poor but unbiased predictor, we could argue that the market is setting the exchange rate according to interest parity and doing the best job possible in a rapidly changing world where prediction is inherently difficult. The finding of bias, however, seems at odds with that interpretation of the data.

The interest parity condition also furnishes a test of a second implication of the hypothesis that the market uses all available information in setting exchange rates. Suppose that E_{t+1} is the actual future exchange rate people are trying to guess; then the forecast error they make in predicting future depreciation, u_{t+1} can be expressed as actual minus expected depreciation:

$$u_{t+1}=(E_{t+1}-E_t)/E_t-(E^e_{t+1}-E_t)/E_t \qquad (13.2)$$

If the market is making use of all available information, its forecast error, u_{t+1} should be statistically unrelated to data known to the market on date t, when expectations were formed. In other words, there should be no opportunity for the market to exploit known data to reduce its later forecast errors. Under interest parity, this hypothesis can be tested by writing u_{t+1} as actual currency depreciation less the international interest difference:

$$u_{t+1}=(E_{t+1}-E_t)/E_t-(R_t-R^*_t) \qquad (13.3)$$

Statistical methods can be used to examine whether u_{t+1} is predictable, on average, on the basis of past information. A number of researchers have found that forecast errors, when defined as above, can be predicted. For example, past forecast errors, which are widely known, are useful in predicting future errors.

13.4.4 The Role of Risk Premiums

13.4.4 风险溢价的作用

One explanation of the research results described above is that the foreign exchange market simply ignores easily available information in setting exchange rates. Such a finding would throw doubt on the international capital market's ability to communicate appropriate price signals. Before jumping to this conclusion, however, recall that when people are risk averse, the interest parity condition may not be a complete account of how exchange rates are determined. If, instead, bonds denominated in different currencies are imperfect substitutes for investors, the international interest rate difference equals expected currency depreciation plus a risk premium, ρ_t:

$$R_t-R^*_t=(E^e_{t+1}-E_t)/E_t+\rho_t \qquad (13.4)$$

In this case, the interest difference is not necessarily the market's forecast of future depreciation. Thus, under imperfect asset substitutability, the empirical results just discussed cannot be used to draw inferences about the foreign exchange market's efficiency in processing information.

Because people's expectations are inherently unobservable, there is no simple way to decide between the above equation and the interest parity condition, which is the special case that occurs when ρ_t is always zero. Several econometric studies have attempted to explain departures from interest parity on the basis of particular theories of the risk premium, but none has been entirely successful.

The mixed empirical record leaves the following two possibilities: Either risk premiums are important in exchange rate determination, or the foreign exchange market has been ignoring the opportunity to profit from easily available information. The second alternative seems unlikely in light of foreign exchange traders' powerful incentives to make profits. The first alternative, however, awaits solid statistical confirmation. It is certainly not supported by the evidence reviewed, which suggests that sterilized foreign exchange intervention has not been an effective tool for exchange rate management. More sophisticated theories show, however, that sterilized intervention may be powerless even under imperfect asset substitutability. Thus, a finding that sterilized intervention is ineffective does not necessarily imply that risk premiums are absent. Another possibility is one of expected large but infrequent reversals in currency trends that standard statistical techniques are ill-equipped to detect.

13.4.5 Tests for Excessive Volatility

13.4.5 过度波动的校验

One of the most worrisome findings is that statistical forecasting models of exchange rates based on standard "fundamental" variables like money supplies, government deficits, and output perform badly—even when actual (rather than predicted) values of future fundamentals are used to form exchange rate forecasts! Indeed, in a famous study, Richard A. Meese of Barclays Global Investors and Kenneth Rogoff of Harvard University showed that a naive, "random walk" model, which simply takes today's exchange rate as the best guess of tomorrow's, performs better. Some have viewed this finding as evidence that exchange rates have a life of their own, unrelated to the macroeconomic determinants we have emphasized in our models. More recent research has confirmed, however, that while the random walk outperforms more sophisticated models for forecasts up to a year away, the models seem to do better at horizons longer than a year and have explanatory power for long-run exchange rate movements.

An additional line of research on the foreign exchange market examines whether exchange rates have been excessively volatile, perhaps because the foreign exchange market "overreacts" to events. A finding of excessive volatility would prove that the foreign exchange market is sending confusing signals to traders and investors who base their decisions on exchange rates. But how volatile must an exchange rate be before its volatility becomes excessive? Exchange rates should be volatile, because to send the correct price signals, they must move swiftly in response to economic news. Exchange rates are generally less volatile than stock prices. It is still possible, though, that exchange rates are substantially more volatile than the underlying factors that move them—such as money supplies, national outputs, and fiscal variables. Attempts to compare exchange rates' volatility with those of their underlying determinants have, however, produced inconclusive results. A basic problem underlying tests for excessive volatility is the impossibility of quantifying exactly all the variables that convey relevant news about the economic future. For example, how does one attach a number to a political assassination attempt, a major bank failure, or a terrorist attack?

13.4.6 The Bottom Line

13.4.6 底线

The ambiguous evidence on the foreign exchange market's performance warrants an open-minded view. A judgment that the market is doing its job well would support a laissez-faire attitude by governments and a continuation of the present trend toward increased cross-border financial integration in the industrial world. A judgment of market failure, on the other hand, might imply a need for increased foreign exchange intervention by central banks and a reversal of the global trend toward external financial liberalization. The stakes are high, and more research and experience are needed before a firm conclusion can be reached.

☞ Summary

☞ 本章小结

1. When people are risk averse, countries can gain through the exchange of risky assets. The gains from trade take the form of a reduction in the riskiness of each country's consumption. International portfolio diversification can be carried out through the exchange of debt instruments or equity instruments.

2. The international capital market is the market in which residents of different countries trade assets. One of its important components is the foreign exchange market. Banks are at the center of the international capital market, and many operate offshore, that is, outside the countries where their head offices are based.

3. Regulatory and political factors have encouraged offshore banking. The same factors have encouraged offshore currency trading, that is, trade in bank deposits denominated in currencies of countries other than the one in which the bank is located. Such Eurocurrency trading received a major stimulus from the absence of reserve requirements on deposits in Eurobanks.

4. Creation of a Eurocurrency deposit does not occur because that currency leaves its country of origin; rather, all that is required is that a Eurobank accept a deposit liability denominated in the currency. Eurocurrencies therefore pose no threat to central banks' control over their domestic monetary bases, and fears that Eurodollars, for example, will some day come "flooding into" the United States are misplaced.

5. Offshore banking is largely unprotected by the safeguards that national governments have imposed to prevent domestic bank failures. In addition, the opportunity that banks have to shift operations offshore has undermined the effectiveness of national bank supervision.

6. The losses caused by financial crises must be evaluated against the gains that international capital markets potentially

offer. The international capital market has contributed to an increase in international portfolio diversification since 1970, but the extent of diversification still appears incomplete compared with what economic theory would predict.

7. The foreign exchange market's record in communicating appropriate price signals to international traders and investors is mixed.

☞ Key Terms

Basel Committee, debt instrument, emerging markets, equity instrument, Eurobank, Eurocurrencies, Eurodollar, international capital market, lender of last resort (LLR), moral hazard, offshore banking, offshore currency trading, portfolio diversification, risk aversion, securitization, shadow banking system

☞ 关键术语

巴塞尔委员会、债务工具、新兴市场、权益工具、欧洲银行、欧洲货币、欧元、国际资本市场、最后贷出人、道德风险、离岸银行业务、离岸货币交易、投资组合多样化、风险规避、资产证券化、影子银行体系

☞ Questions

☞ 本章习题

1. Which portfolio is better diversified, one that contains stock in a dental supply company and a candy company or one that contains stock in a dental supply company and a dairy product company?

2. Imagine a world of two countries in which the only causes of fluctuations in stock prices are unexpected shifts in monetary policies. Under which exchange rate regime would the gains from international asset trade be greater, fixed or floating?

3. The text points out that covered interest parity holds quite closely for deposits of differing currency denominations issued in a single financial center. Why might covered interest parity fail to hold when deposits issued in different financial centers are compared?

4. Why might growing securitization make it harder for bank supervisors to keep track of risks to the financial system?

5. Return to the example in the text of the two countries that produce random amounts of kiwi fruit and can trade claims on that fruit. Suppose the two countries also produce raspberries that spoil if shipped between countries and therefore are non-tradable. How

do you think this would affect the ratio of international asset trade to GNP for Home and Foreign?

6. Sometimes it is claimed that the international equality of real interest rates is the most accurate barometer of international financial integration. Do you agree? Why or why not?

References

保罗·R. 克鲁格曼,莫里斯·奥伯斯法尔德,马克·J. 梅利兹.国际经济学：理论与政策[M]. 9 版. 北京：清华大学出版社,2016.

多米尼克·萨尔瓦多. 国际经济学[M].9 版. 北京：清华大学出版社,2008.

罗伯特·J. 凯伯.国际经济学[M].13 版. 北京：中国人民大学出版社,2013.

史蒂芬·赫斯特德,迈克尔·梅尔文.国际经济学[M]. 8 版. 北京：机械工业出版社,2011.

史蒂文·赫斯特德,迈克尔·梅尔文.国际经济学[M]. 7 版. 姜文学,译注. 大连:东北财经大学出版社,2008.

托马斯·A. 普格尔,彼得· H. 林德特. 国际经济学[M]. 11 版. 北京：经济科学出版社,2001.

W. 查尔斯·索耶,理查德·L. 斯普林克. 国际经济学[M]. 2 版. 北京：中国人民大学出版社,2005.

CARBAUGH R. *International Economics* [M]. 15th ed. Stanford : Cengage Learning, 2016.

GERBER J. *International Economics* [M]. London: Pearson Education Limited,2017.

KREININ M., CLARK D. *International Economics: A Policy Approach*[M]. 2nd ed. London: Pearson Learning Solutions, 2013.

FEENSTRA R, TAYLOR A. *International Economics* [M]. 2nd ed. London: Pearson Learning Solutions, 2014.

图书在版编目(CIP)数据

国际经济学＝International Economics：汉英对照/谢孟军主编．—杭州：浙江大学出版社，2020.12

ISBN 978-7-308-18823-4

Ⅰ.①国… Ⅱ.①谢… Ⅲ.①国际经济学—汉、英 Ⅳ.①F11-0

中国版本图书馆 CIP 数据核字（2019）第 000735 号

国际经济学 International Economics(汉英对照)

谢孟军　主编

责任编辑　李　晨　朱　玲

责任校对　郑成业

封面设计　春天书装

出版发行　浙江大学出版社

（杭州市天目山路 148 号　邮政编码 310007）

（网址：http://www.zjupress.com）

排　　版　杭州林智广告有限公司

印　　刷　浙江省邮电印刷股份有限公司

开　　本　787mm×1092mm　1/16

印　　张　18.75

字　　数　548 千

版 印 次　2020 年 12 月第 1 版　2020 年 12 月第 1 次印刷

书　　号　ISBN 978-7-308-18823-4

定　　价　59.00 元
